Science and Behavior

Science and Behavior

An Introduction to Methods of Psychological Research

Fourth Edition

Robert M. Liebert
Lynn Langenbach Liebert

State University of New York at Stony Brook

PRENTICE HALL, Upper Saddle River, NJ 07458

Library of Congress Cataloging-in-Publication Data

Liebert, Robert M.
 Science and behavior : an introduction to methods of psychological
research / Robert M. Liebert and Lynn Langenbach Liebert. — 4th ed.
  p. cm.
 Rev. ed. of: Science and behavior / John M. Neale, Robert M.
Liebert. 3rd ed. c1986.
 Includes bibliographical references and index.
 ISBN 0-13-142721-0
 1. Psychology—Research—Methodology. I. Liebert, Lynn Langenbach.
II. Neale, John M. Science and behavior. III. Title.
BF76.5.L54 1994
150'.72—dc20   94-40698
                  CIP

Editor/Production Supervision: **Betsy Winship**
Executive Editor: **Pete Janzow**
Senior Editor: **Heidi Freund**
Editorial Assistant: **Jennifer Fader**
Cover Designer: **Suzanne Behnke**
Page Layout: **Lorraine Paul**
Manufacturing Buyer: **Tricia Kenny**

 © 1995, 1986, 1980, 1973 by Prentice-Hall, Inc.
A Simon & Schuster Company
Upper Saddle River, New Jersey 07458

Printed in the United States of America

10 9 8 7 6 5 4 3 2

ISBN 0-13-142721-0

Prentice-Hall International (UK) Limited, *London*
Prentice-Hall of Australia Pty, Limited, *Sydney*
Prentice-Hall Canada Inc., *Toronto*
Prentice-Hall Hispanoamericana, S.A., *Mexico*
Prentice-Hall of India Private Limited, *New Delhi*
Prentice-Hall of Japan, Inc., *Tokyo*
Simon & Schuster Asia Pte. Ltd., *Singapore*
Editora Prentice-Hall do Brasil, Ltda., *Rio de Janeiro*

CONTENTS

For Alexander

PREFACE

This book presents a general introduction to current methods of research in psychology. Despite increased education, even today few people are prepared to critically evaluate research claims. We believe that underlying valid psychological research is the core logic of the scientific method; mastery and application of this logic is what is principally needed to discriminate between trustworthy and invalid scientific claims. The primary aim of this book is to explain the logic of science as applied to questions about human thought, behavior, and experience.

We have assumed that readers do not have a priori knowledge of the technical matters in the text. Thus each concept is explained from scratch, every technical term is defined explicitly in the text itself and in an extensive Glossary at the end of the book, and a verbal "translation" is provided for the few simple mathematical expressions that are introduced.

Although this is the fourth edition of *Science and Behavior*, in many respects it is a new book. The entire organization has been revised, the text has been completely rewritten to make it accessible to the widest possible range of college students, numerous examples and illustrations have been added, and many of the very advanced concepts and techniques appearing in earlier editions have been eliminated completely.

Chapter 1 is entirely new and presents the history of scientific thinking from classical Greek philosophy to modern times, culminating in the birth of scientific psychology in the 19th century. Employing a pedagogical tool we have not used before, close-up "boxes" on topics of special interest or importance, the chapter introduces the critical issue of deductive and inductive reasoning and describes the most recent (post-positivist) trends in philosophy of science.

Chapter 2, also entirely new, is devoted to ethical issues in psychological research. The history of psychology's growing concern with ethics is traced from the 1930s, through the controversy raised by Stanley Milgram's famous obedience experiments. This chapter concludes with a comprehensive overview of the APA's 1992 Code of Ethics, with particular emphasis on those issues of concern to research psychologists.

Chapter 3 introduces the basic issues surrounding data collection, including a new section on naturalistic observational research. This chapter includes preliminary discussions of populations and samples, psychological instruments, quantification, scales of measurement, and making comparisons, all of which are built on later.

Chapter 4 addresses the question of detecting associations between variables and goes on to a basic discussion of correlation and regression. Readers are provided with a simple, dramatic demonstration of the power of multiple regression, and there is a box entitled, "What IQ heritability does *not* imply."

Chapter 5 focuses entirely on how to deal with the problem of cause and effect. Here we introduce classical and null hypothesis testing, explain why causal inferences can't be drawn from simple correlations, and give a nontechnical description of the nature and value of theoretical modeling. Chapter 6 picks up on these themes, with a description of the four faces of validity, including a discussion of the subtle interplay among them.

Chapter 7 introduces the true experiment, including its logic and a consideration of the practical issues of subject selection and assignment to groups, matching vs. free random assignment, the use and risks of pretests, as well as a practical list of factors that can increase the power of an experiment. As in the rest of the book, we try to prepare our readers not only to effectively *evaluate* research but also to *conduct* it.

Chapter 8 is devoted to the most common extensions of the basic experiment: factorial designs, block designs, and repeated measures (mixed) designs. Chapter 9 describes ways to approach causality when true between group experiments are not possible, specifically single-subject designs and quasi-experimental designs.

Chapter 10, also a completely new chapter, is entitled "Pitfalls for the Unwary," and provides examples and solutions to five recurrent issues in psychological research: volunteer bias, reactivity, demand characteristics, the placebo effect, and experimenter bias.

Chapter 11 is an entirely "hands-on" exposition, with a detailed description of how to use library and computer resources to perform a literature search and a step-by-step explanation of how to write an APA-style research report. A complete example of an APA style manuscript is included to illustrate all the details of its preparation and final presentation.

The text concludes with two new "hands-on" appendices. Appendix A deals with developing questionnaires and conducting surveys, and Appendix B is a brief statistics refresher. An extensive end Glossary defines all the key terms and concepts that are highlighted throughout the text. Key terms are also listed at the end of each chapter in which they appear.

Two pedagogical features have been retained from the previous edition. One is to provide a detailed outline of each chapter at the outset, preparing the reader for the concepts to be introduced. The other is to provide provocative review and discussion questions at the end of each chapter, enabling students to test their own understanding and retention of the material.

As to general philosophy, the book emphasizes systematic repetition and usage of basic terms and ideas throughout, so that each major concept appears under several different, complementary lights. To present critical issues in concrete form, examples and illustrations are drawn heavily from familiar or "real-life" situations. At the same time, several occasions are taken throughout to describe a piece of very basic research in the behavioral or even the physical sciences in order to illustrate a point or emphasize the logical continuity of the scientific approach, regardless of the domain to which it is applied.

In preparing this edition we were assisted by many people. Alex Liebert contributed his creative talents in the form of Cartoon 8-1. We owe particular thanks to Drew Velting, Carol A. Russell, and Charles Cain for their meticulous reviews and library work, and their many constructive suggestions. We are especially grateful for the patient support and assistance of Betsy Winship in the final preparation of the text. Heidi Freund, at Prentice Hall, was warm, supportive, and tolerant as we passed through the many drafts that turned this edition into the type of final product we all wished to achieve. We also thank the following reviewers for their thoughtful suggestions: Joel Freund, University of Arkansas; Doug Marshall, Georgia Southern University; William Addison, Eastern Illinois University.

Robert M. Liebert
Lynn Langenbach Liebert

Science and
Behavior

BACKGROUND

1

In *A Connecticut Yankee in King Arthur's Court*, Mark Twain tells the story of Hank Morgan, an enterprising 19th century time traveler who brings the scientific wonders of his age to sixth century Camelot. Morgan begins by passing off a solar eclipse he had read about in a book as his ability to darken and relight the heavens. This amazed King Arthur and his knights. Capitalizing on their impression, Morgan declares himself to be the greatest magician in the realm. Before long, he has hired an army of local workers and started up silver mines, machine shops, and factories; the miracles he introduces (running water and plumbing, explosives, a telegraph system, and so on) are a smashing success; by popular acclaim he is dubbed "The Boss." In time he becomes second only to King Arthur himself at the Round Table.

Then one day, in the height of his glory, "the Boss" is confronted by a rival magician. Morgan tells us this of the rival:

> His specialty was to tell you what any individual on the face of the globe was doing at the moment; and what he had done at any time in the past, and what he would do at any time in the future. He asked if any would like to know what the Emperor of the East was doing now?

People in the crowd shouted that they *did* want to know. So the rival mumbled incantations, drew mystical figures in the air and on the ground, and declared:

> "The high and mighty Emperor of the East doth at this very moment put money in the palm of a holy begging friar—ONE . . . TWO . . . THREE PIECES, AND THEY ALL BE OF *SILVER*!"
>
> A buzz of admiring exclamations broke out, all around: "It is marvelous!" "Wonderful!" "What study, what labor it must take to have acquired so amazing a power as this!"

The rival now had the crowd's full attention, as Morgan despairs:

> Would they like to know what the Supreme Lord of Inde was doing? Yes. He told them what the Supreme Lord of Inde was doing. Then he told them what the Sultan of Egypt was up to; and then what the King of the Remote Seas was occupied with right now. And so on and so on: and with each new marvel the crowd's astonishment at his accuracy rose higher and higher. They thought he must surely strike an uncertain place sometime; but no, he never had to hesitate, he always knew, and always with unerring precision. (Twain, 1889/1991).

In the story, the rival's claims are greeted by the local population as miraculous truths. But when I read the passage above to students in my classes and ask what they think of the rival's miraculous revelations, I get reactions like this:

> "The rival couldn't possibly know those things. It makes no sense!"
> "I'd like to see him prove that!"
> "The people in the crowd must be idiots."
> "What a crock!"

The contrast between the crowd and my students (or any other people brought up in modern times) stems from the way in which they treat the rival's claims.

The medieval crowd, simple folk who were impressed by the rival's exotic clothes (described by Twain as "the extreme of the fantastic") and his self-confident manner, take all that he says on faith. They do not ask *how* the rival can know the whereabouts of all the monarchs in the world, nor do they seem concerned about verifying any of his statements. In a word, they are accepting him uncritically as an authority. And it was from *authority* that the ordinary people of the sixth century took their knowledge.

Authority is relied on much less now than in King Arthur's day. Take for example the students in my class. They are skeptical of the claims of authority figures—not only the rival's, but mine as well. They want claims to make sense and to be backed by proof—preferably the kind they can see with their own eyes. In short, they reject authority as a source of knowledge and instead impose the general criteria of *science*!

WHAT IS SCIENCE?

If you look for the definition of science in a dictionary, you will find something like "a body of systematic knowledge, especially as regarding the physical or natural world." (The word derives from the Latin *scientia*, which means knowledge.) Looked at this way, there are distinct bodies of knowledge for the separate sciences, (e.g., physics and chemistry).

But science has another, quite different meaning. Namely, science can be defined as a process of inquiry, a method of formulating and answering questions. In this meaning, science is a way of generating knowledge, not knowledge itself. Thus, for our purposes, **science** can be defined as *a process of disciplined inquiry*. The goal of science is the prediction and control of natural phenomena.

In ancient times, natural phenomena were almost invariably explained in terms of supernatural agencies—usually, "the gods." These explanations were accepted uncritically by the populace, on the basis of authority and tradition. The modern idea of science as disciplined inquiry evolved gradually, over almost 3000 years. For most of this time, only an intellectual elite was familiar with either the methods or the content of science. "Science," as a term that everybody knows something about, is a 20th century phenomenon. But the *idea of scientific inquiry* has its origins in classical Greek philosophy.

CLASSICAL GREEK PHILOSOPHY

Doubting that authority and tradition were the best ways to garner useful knowledge, the early Greek philosophers began to ask how knowledge is acquired and secured, a philosophical specialty which they called *epistemology*. It was these early thinkers who first proposed to supplant authority and tradition with the two tools of epistemology: *rationalism* and *empiricism*.

Rationalism and Empiricism

Rationalism is *the practice of employing reason as a legitimate source of knowledge.* In *strict rationalism,* the "pure" form, reason is considered the *only* source of trustworthy or "certainly true" knowledge.

Empiricism is *the practice of employing direct observation as a legitimate source of knowledge.* It is difficult to imagine a form of pure empiricism, a world in which we have "the facts, and *just* the facts." Nonetheless, a degree of empiricism characterizes all the sciences. And modern scientific psychology was built on the belief that differences of opinion on theoretical questions can always be resolved empirically—by the observable facts.

The Socratic Method

Socrates (469–399 BC) introduced what we have come to call the "Socratic method." The method entailed leading others to arrive at sound conclusions based on a stepwise progression through basic questions. He demanded precise definitions, clear thinking, and careful analysis in approaching any question. But Socrates' primary interests, and the main concerns of his famous student Plato, were moral and political questions, such as "What is the meaning of virtue?" and "How shall the state be governed?"

Aristotle: Founder of Science

Aristotle (384 BC–323 BC) started out as a physician and later studied with Plato for 20 years. In his early forties, he was chosen by King Philip of Macedon to serve as teacher to Philip's son, later known as Alexander the Great. Aristotle started the world's first zoo, in which specimens of plants and animals from every part of Alexander's kingdom could be found. He also wrote at least 400 volumes of philosophy!

Of Aristotle's many publications, the most important for us are his works on logic and biology. (*Logic* can be defined as the method of correct thinking; it provides the *logy* of bio*logy*, anthropo*logy*, socio*logy*, psycho*logy*, and so on.)

Aristotle's logical works were subsequently collected together as the *Organon* (OR-guh-NAHN), that is, the organ or instrument of correct thinking. In the *Organon*, Aristotle asserted that the process of correct thinking can be expressed as a set of rules. Some of these rules had their origins with Socrates: *define* your terms; make a continuing effort to *refine* every concept and idea. Thus, the *Organon* expounded the **rational approach** to knowledge.

But in his biological work, Aristotle turned to direct observation, that is, to *empiricism.* He spent endless hours in his great zoo, carefully observing the spectacular range of living forms he had brought together. From his observations he noted small, step-by-step progressions from the simplest organisms to the most complex. This led him to a rudimentary version of the theory of evolution.

Aristotle was not only an astute observer, he was also an experimenter. For example, by breaking hens' eggs open at various stages of incubation, he provided a description of chicks' development that still arouses the envy of embryologists today.

EARLY EUROPEAN PHILOSOPHERS OF SCIENCE

The astonishing thing about the history of western science is that a period of almost 2000 years passed from Aristotle's writings until the next significant philosophical development.

Most historians of science view the 17th century as the beginning of a "scientific revolution" that led to our modern idea of science. Two philosophers of that century, Rene Descartes and Francis Bacon, became the architects of the modern scientific method.

Rene Descartes

Rene Descartes (1596–1650) was born into a family of minor French nobility and was educated by Jesuit priests. After receiving a broad education in philosophy, science, and mathematics, he took a degree in law. Then he set about traveling all over Europe, telling friends he was studying the "book of the world." During his travels, he dreamt that his destiny was to be a philosopher and scientist who would seek knowledge for the benefit of humanity. Shortly thereafter, at the age of 25, he announced that he had devised a universal method of reasoning, applicable to all the sciences.

Descartes began with four rules that he asserted must govern all philosophical and scientific reasoning. They were:

1. Accept nothing as true that is not self-evident.
2. Divide problems into their simplest parts.
3. Solve problems by proceeding from the simple to the complex.
4. Always recheck your reasoning and calculations.

Based on his first rule, Descartes said he would accept no claim unless he could formulate it in his mind so clearly and distinctly that there was no room for doubt. He said one should not believe authority, for it may be fallible; one should not believe the senses, for they can be deceived (for example, by illusions and mirages); one should not even trust most "logical" lines of reasoning, because a problem can always be insufficiently analyzed.

Then, in his most famous passage, Descartes wrote:

> I noticed that while I was trying to think everything false, it must needs be that I, who was thinking this, was something. And observing that this truth, *I am thinking, therefore I exist*, was so solid and secure that the most extravagant suppositions of the skeptics could not overthrow it, I judged that I could accept it as the first principle. . . . (Quoted in Williams, 1972, p. 347.)

This argument came to be called the *cogito*, because *Cogito, ergo sum* is Latin for "I think, therefore I am." From the *cogito*, Descartes reasoned there must be a sharp distinction between mind and body. This position is referred to as *Cartesian dualism*.

Descartes arrived at his dualism with reasoning that went like this: The "I" whose existence is proved in the *cogito* has as its only characteristic that it thinks. Thinking itself has no physical existence. So the "I" has no physical existence; it is "an immaterial substance, which has nothing corporeal about it." (Williams, 1972, p. 348).

What, though, of the body? Unlike the mind, the body exists in space and time and can be measured in terms of geometric dimensions—height, width, and depth. Thus, *mind and body are distinct*. Inasmuch as mind and body are distinct, the methods we use to study them should also be distinct.

Descartes asserted that material events—the movements and interactions of the body and all other physical objects we observe—result from "secondary causes" that are physical and mechanical. Secondary causes, said Descartes, can only be understood by observation and experimentation. Thus, he prescribed a strict rational approach for the study of the mind and spirit but an open empirical approach to the study of the body and all things worldly. The door to empirical science was now open.

Descartes is credited with many accomplishments. He described the circulation of blood through the body, made better lenses than Galileo, improved the design of the mechanical pump, and explored the idea that air has weight. The net effect was to establish a science of the physical world that was deterministic, mechanistic, and materialistic.

Francis Bacon

Francis Bacon (1561–1626) was the youngest son of an aristocratic family, and an English contemporary of Descartes. He (like Descartes) started out as a lawyer, and therefore his interest was in *gathering and weighing evidence*. By its nature, evidence is based on observation, especially observation that can be corroborated (confirmed) independently by more than one person. Bacon believed that this core process, the gathering and weighing of evidence, was at the heart of science as well as legal procedure. He also believed that human behavior should be considered a natural phenomenon and should be subjected to scrutiny in the same way as all natural phenomena. Thus, Bacon set himself the goal of systematizing an empirical approach to *all* knowledge. In doing so, he completed the groundwork begun by Descartes and extended science to the realm of the mind as well as the body.

Bacon's major scientific work, the *Novum Organum*, or *New Organon*, was published in 1620, after his legal career was over. It was intended to supplant Aristotle's *Organon* of 2000 years earlier, and did indeed become the new instrument through which science could be done.

First, the *New Organon* argues strongly for empiricism. Bacon tells us repeatedly that only through observation can we come to understand nature. Further, he is careful to point out that adequate observation often cannot be accomplished with the bare senses alone; Bacon encourages development and refinement of *instruments of observation* in all the sciences.

But Bacon's overriding purpose in the New Organon is to take Aristotle to task. Although Aristotle had used induction (especially in his biological studies), he had done almost nothing to explain how inductions should be performed. Aristotle, according to Bacon, provided an inadequate account of the inductive assent, flying from senses and particulars to the most general axioms. (See Box 1.1.)

BOX 1.1   *INDUCTION VERSUS DEDUCTION*

Aristotle distinguished two forms of reasoning, *deductive* and *inductive*. **Deductive reasoning** goes from general premises to a specific conclusion. If the premises are true and correctly arranged, a valid conclusion, or **deduction**, is logically implied. Aristotle's most important contribution to logic was his invention of the **syllogism**, a model of deductive reasoning.

A syllogism is a trio of propositions: 1) a major premise (or *maxim*), which makes a universal claim, 2) a minor premise, which makes a specific claim, and 3) a deductive implication, arising logically from the combination of the premises. If both premises of the syllogism are conceded to be true, the conclusion must be true. For example:

MAJOR PREMISE:	ALL HUMANS ARE MORTAL.
MINOR PREMISE:	I AM HUMAN.
DEDUCTIVE IMPLICATION:	I AM MORTAL.

Although the logical syllogism is a powerful tool, it cannot stand alone. This is because in the syllogism *the premises themselves are not proved; they are only assumed*. The syllogism thus is not a mechanism for the discovery of truth, it is only a means of clarifying thought. Here is a logically valid deduction; note that the conclusion is false because the major premise is false:

MAJOR PREMISE:	ALL BIRDS CAN FLY.
MINOR PREMISE:	PENGUINS ARE BIRDS.
DEDUCTIVE IMPLICATION:	PENGUINS CAN FLY.

Aristotle recognized that science does not start with general principles, but with specific observations or facts. The process of going from specific observations to a general premise Aristotle called **inductive reasoning**. For example:

AFFIRMING OBSERVATIONS:	DOZENS OF SPECIES OF MAMMALS HAVE BEEN FOUND THAT HAVE FACTOR W IN THEIR BLOOD.

NEGATING OBSERVATIONS: NO SPECIES OF MAMMALS HAVE BEEN
                           FOUND THAT DO NOT HAVE FACTOR W IN
                           THEIR BLOOD.
INDUCTIVE INFERENCE: ALL SPECIES OF MAMMALS HAVE FACTOR W
                           IN THEIR BLOOD.

Inductive generalizations are not *logically implied*; they are only *inferred*. Although Aristotle inferred a number of general principles from his specific observations, he did not provide an in-depth analysis of inductive reasoning (as he had for deductive reasoning). Such an analysis *was* provided by Francis Bacon in *The New Organon* (see text).

The heliocentric theory of the solar system advanced by Copernicus and Galileo was an inductive inference, as was Newton's theory of universal gravitation. The philosophers and scientists of the 17th century were totally committed to inductive reasoning. In the 18th century, however, David Hume demonstrated that, unlike deductions (logical implications), inductions (inferences) are never logically justifiable or certain. Immanuel Kant then offered a reconciliation of deduction and induction. Kant argued that the mind is "prewired" to reason deductively (as in a syllogism) and inductively (as when we construct generalizations and infer underlying principles).

Positivism, making its appearance in the 19th century, is the philosophy of science that has guided scientific psychology for most of its history. Logical positivists have concluded that inductive reasoning, from specific observations to general principles, is indispensable to the scientific enterprise.

It is somewhat misleading to think of deduction and induction as opposing processes. In science, induction and deduction complement each other, forming a dynamic system from which increased knowledge and greater understanding can emerge. That is, knowledge can be expanded when either 1) data (factual information) contributes to the development of theories (inductive reasoning) or 2) theory serves as a basis for deriving hypotheses that can be verified by observation (deductive reasoning).

Induction and deduction are analogous to the processes of evaporation and precipitation in the rain cycle. (See Figure 1-1.) The cycle begins when groundwater is absorbed into or becomes part of the atmosphere through the process of evaporation, which over time contributes to cloud formation. Clouds, in turn, return the water to the ground source through the process of precipitation (of which rain, snow, and sleet are obvious manifestations). Thus, evaporation involves the transformation of water from a liquid state to a gaseous state, whereas precipitation involves the transformation of water from a gaseous state to a liquid state.

Knowledge can be recycled and expanded through similar processes. Induction parallels evaporation, moving from concrete observables (the data pool) to the more abstract theoretical level of knowledge (cloud formation). Deduction, on the other hand, proceeds from the abstract, theoretical level toward the level of more specific conclusions. This parallels the precipitation (rain) process in our scheme. The overall result is that in both systems (weather patterns and accumulation of scientific knowledge), a reciprocal interchange produces growth over time. In each case, the two processes involved are both necessary and cannot work effectively in isolation.

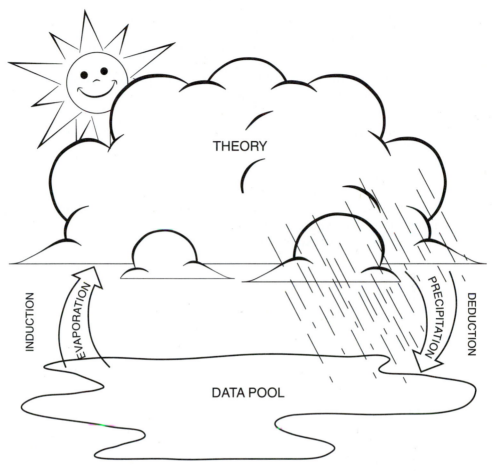

Figure 1-1   Induction and deduction are analagous to the processes of evaporation and precipitation in the rain cycle.

Bacon used a concrete example to illustrate how induction should proceed, namely, his own analysis of the nature of heat. His strategy was to gather together all the facts and then to arrange the facts so that underlying patterns and regularities would become visible. To understand heat, Bacon began by making two lists. One was a list of things or situations known to display heat (e.g., flames from a fire, sunshine, two sticks rubbed together vigorously), with the items arranged in terms of the amount of heat they displayed.

The second list contained things that are sometimes warm and sometimes cold. For example, a *living* body feels warm, whereas a *dead* body feels cold; rocks in the desert become quite hot in the afternoon sun, but at night they lose their heat completely.

Sitting down with his lists, Bacon created a series of tables. One table was designed to identify factors that were not associated with heat, i.e., those that occurred regardless of whether or not heat was present. (In this way, Bacon was able to conclude that the weight of an object had nothing to do with the heat it displayed.) This process of exclusion allowed him to eliminate many but not all of the possible causes of heat.

With a number of possible causes remaining, Bacon proceeded to take each of the common factors *and test the consequences of each idea against new data.* One after another, Bacon's list of possible causes dwindled. Eventually only one possible explanation of heat was left. Three hundred years ago Bacon induced the scientific principle that heat is a form of motion. It is a conclusion with which modern scientists agree!

So here we have Baconian induction. We begin with a wide base of empirical evidence that must be organized to the point where we may advance one or more conjectures or **hypotheses**. These hypotheses are then tested by experimentation. The hypothesis that passes all possible tests has, in essence, selected itself as the correct explanation.

THE NEW ASTRONOMY

Despite their enormous contributions to the history of science, Descartes and Bacon did not see themselves primarily as scientists, but as philosophers. The scientific revolution needed practicing scientists, and three astronomers came forward to revolutionize the way we see the universe.

Copernicus

Nicholas Copernicus (1473–1534) was a Polish astronomer who turned our view of the world inside out. Through the 15th century, the accepted view of the universe was *geocentric*, a system of sun, stars, and planets, with the Earth at its center. This view had been woven into an elaborate scheme for explaining planetary motion advanced by Ptolemy (120–160 AD) and had gone largely unchallenged for 1500 years.

To make his theory work (that is, to predict the positions of the planets and stars in the night sky), Ptolemy (TAH'lah mee) proposed an extremely cumbersome system of celestial orbits. For example, he claimed that small circular orbits, called "epicycles," occurred against the backdrop of much larger orbits, called "deferents," around which they moved.

If this sounds complicated to you, it also sounded complicated to Copernicus. He complained:

> It is as though an artist were to gather the hands, feet, head and other members for its images from diverse models, each part excellently drawn, but not related to a single body, and since they in no way match each other, the result would be a monster rather than a man. (Quoted in Kuhn, 1957, p. 138.)

So Copernicus suggested a simpler, *heliocentric* system, that is, one with the Sun, and not the Earth, at the center. The Earth, according to Copernicus, moved in a daily rotation around its own axis and a yearly revolution around the Sun. In this view the universe was infinite, with the stars scattered throughout space.

Galileo

Galileo (1564–1642) was an Italian astronomer attracted by the simplicity of Copernicus' theory. It was his genius that provided further empirical evidence for the Copernican view, through careful observation and experimentation.

As a student, Galileo had pondered a lamp swinging back and forth on its chain like a pendulum. On the basis of his careful observations he concluded (rightly) that the duration of the pendulum's swing is independent of the distance it travels. As the swing's distance decreases, its rate of movement also slows. Therefore the pendulum is a perfect device for keeping time!

Galileo had been impressed by watching his father, a master musical instrument maker, experiment with and tune instruments. He himself built a telescope of exceptional quality, permitting him to become the first to observe the moons of Jupiter.

At the culmination of his career, Galileo restated Copernicus' theory. He then listed and commented on all the evidence favoring the heliocentric view. His exposition made the Copernican view appear extremely plausible and fully consistent with all the observable facts. Galileo's argument for a heliocentric system, *supported both by reasoning and by evidence*, became the prevailing view of the Universe.

Sir Isaac Newton

Sir Isaac Newton (1642–1727) is considered to be the most significant figure of the 17th century scientific revolution. Newton was skilled at building clocks and windmills; he was also convinced by Descartes that physical nature is an intricate, impersonal, inert machine—in short, rather like a giant clock. Equally important to Newton were the theoretical writings of Galileo, who had argued that there is uniformity in nature and that the universe is constructed according to mathematical regularities.

Although the story of an apple falling on his nose is probably just a story, he was a keen observer and experimenter. From his observations and experiments, and some ideas he borrowed from Galileo (such as the concept of inertia), Newton induced three "laws of motion."

1. A body at rest remains at rest and requires the exertion of force to move it.
2. The change in motion produced by force is proportional to the amount of force applied.
3. For every action there is an equal and opposite reaction.

Perform any experiments you like, and you will find these principles hold perfectly. Newton's inductions were so reliable, they became the basis of engineering technology and of pre-Einsteinian physics.

Newton's greatest accomplishment came when he applied his laws of mechanics to the problems of astronomy. Although Copernicus' heliocentric model had long since supplanted the Ptolemaic scheme, Copernicus was actually quite wrong in his belief that the orbits of the planets were circular. (In fact, they are elliptical.) Here Newton enters, with the concept of gravity and the theory of universal gravitation.

It had seemed clear for awhile that the Earth pulled things toward it. (Aristotle had commented on this.) How, though, could the phenomenon of weight (*gravitas*) be explained? Newton conceptualized the orbits of the Earth and other planets as a product of a force: gravitation. By assuming *universal gravitation*, and summing over a very diverse set of terrestrial and astronomical observations, he produced the most famous induction in the history of science:

> Every particle of matter in the universe attracts every other particle in the universe with a force that is proportional to the product of their masses and inversely proportional to the square of the distance between their centers.

What was marvelous about this formulation was that it predicted planetary orbits, as observed in the night sky, almost perfectly. The Sun and all the planets were always pulling on each other in amounts that could be calculated by knowing their diameters and the distances among them at any starting point.

It is hard to exaggerate the enthusiasm with which this theory was received. It was mathematical. It was, in a sense, elegantly simple. And it worked!

Newton, like Descartes and Bacon provided *his* rules for doing science. Here is his list:

1. Admit no more causes of natural things than such as are both true and sufficient to explain their appearances.
2. To the same natural effects we must, insofar as possible, assign the same causes.
3. Qualities which are found to be true of all bodies within the reach of our experiments, are to be esteemed the universal qualities of all bodies whatsoever.
4. Look upon propositions inferred by general induction from phenomena as accurate or very nearly true until other, contradictory phenomena are observed.

Points 1 and 2 are merely alternate ways of calling for economy or *parsimony of explanation*. Points 3 and 4 also seem to boil down to a general principle: *Accept persuasive inductions as universally true*. But an unguarded acceptance of inductions seemed to 18th century philosophers too extreme.

EIGHTEENTH CENTURY TEMPORIZING

Induction appeared to work well in the hands of Bacon and Newton, but the success of these individuals doesn't prove the validity of their method. Cladding himself in the doubting pose that Descartes had struck six decades earlier, Hume attacked the logic of induction head-on.

David Hume

Scottish philosopher David Hume (1711–1776) began with the claim that there are two quite different kinds of scientific argument: those based on reason (logical relationships among ideas) and those based on empirical observation. Matters of reason deal with logical deduction, as do all mathematical systems (arithmetic, algebra, geometry). In matters of reason (rationalism), we can achieve certainty.

But not so in matters of observation (empiricism). Whereas strictly logical arguments are *conclusive*, arguments based on empirical data are logically *inconclusive*.

Hume asserted that any generalization from facts in hand, regardless of its current empirical support, can always be contradicted in the future. If you have been all over the world, and all the swans you've ever seen are white, the possibility still logically remains that you will see a black swan tomorrow.

"The supposition that the future resembles the past," Hume declared, "is not founded on arguments of any kind. This is because there can be no demonstrative arguments to prove that those instances of which we have had no prior experience shall resemble those of which we have had experience." In induction, the conclusion is simply wider than the premises. Therefore, science must settle for less than absolute certainty in its enterprises—or come up with a new way of looking at things. Here the German philosopher, Immanuel Kant, enters the picture.

Immanuel Kant

Immanuel Kant (1724–1804) is considered the most difficult and the most important philosopher of the 18th century. His great work, the *Critique of Pure Reason*, was written to dispel the doubts about science suggested in the writings of Hume.

Kant's critique makes a fundamental distinction between the actual things and events of the universe, which he called *noumena*, and the things and events as we perceive them, which he called *phenomena*. His central thesis is that the world as we know it is, and must be, composed *only* of phenomena.

Contrary to Newton, Kant denied that space, time, and cause are things that exist in the world; rather, space, time, and causality are built-in categories of the mind. The mind interprets experience by selectively attending to and grouping sensations, so as to fit its own innate structure. Therefore, induction is not only justifiable, it is inevitable. But we must also accept the fact that the realm of objects themselves (the "real world") is forever inaccessible to us.

Kant was impressed with the fact that the pure rationalists had been notoriously *un*successful in increasing the sum of human knowledge. Induction, then, is not only justifiable, it is inevitable. However, under it all, we must accept the fact that the realm of objects themselves (noumena) is always beyond our reach.

NINETEENTH CENTURY POSITIVIST MOVEMENT

There is something decidedly pessimistic about the Kantian approach. His analysis appeared to be not so much the salvation of science as the destruction of the goal of science—to learn the truth. A more positive approach was needed, and one emerged. Its roots could be found in the writings of a French philosopher, August Comte.

August Comte

August Comte (1788–1887) argued that we must take a positive approach to science. This begins, first of all, by ridding science of any entities that are beyond empirical investigation. *Hypotheses beyond the reach of empirical inquiry are meaningless.* It is pointless, then, to talk of Kantian noumena, about which we can know nothing. The purpose of science is to *predict and control phenomena.* The sciences are inherently unified, because they all share this common purpose.

Science begins by establishing explicit observational methods, so that the observations of any one scientist can be *replicated* by other scientists. These methods allow scientists to confirm or verify hypotheses through observation and experimentation. The positivist approach made it possible to ignore much of the philosophical debate of the past two centuries and get on with the business of science.

As much as anything, Comte's writings were a pep talk, a call to action, rather than a close analysis of methods. The latter task remained for the logical positivists of the 20th century.

TWENTIETH CENTURY LOGICAL POSITIVISM

Logical positivism, also called *logical empiricism*, is associated not with a single individual but with a circle of individuals, many of whom met together in Vienna in the early 20th century. Among these are Ludwig Wittgenstein (1889–1951), Hans Reichenbach (1891–1953), Rudolf Carnap (1891–1970), and Bertrand Russell (1872–1970).

The goal of logical positivism was to provide a union between logicians and empiricists. The logical positivists argued that science was logical *and* concerned itself with observable facts. Moreover, they were totally committed to the **verification principle**. Verification means empirical testing. With Comte, they assert that a proposition that cannot be verified is meaningless.

The guiding methodological principle of logical positivism was **operationalism**. To find the length of an object, we have to perform certain operations. It is these operations that define length. A theoretical term is not meaningful until we give it an **operational definition**.

When we use a theoretical term, we must develop a correspondence rule that links the term to the operations we use to measure it. Such a link is called a **reduction sentence**. For example, the theoretical term *temperature* may be defined by the height of a column of mercury as registered on a thermometer.

Verification vs. Falsification

Karl Popper (1902–1994) is the last of the logical positivists. Popper took issue with the principle of verification, complaining that it is often too easy to obtain verification for a theory. Confirmations are only good if they arise from *risky predictions*.

Suppose, for example, we have a theory that explains rainfall in terms of build-up of moisture in the soil. On the basis of the theory, we predict it will rain tomorrow—and it does. But inasmuch as it rains on many summer days, verification of this prediction (it *does* rain tomorrow) is not very impressive. We have predicted something that could well turn out to be true, even if our theory about soil moisture is all wet. In short, this is *not* a risky prediction.

But suppose instead our theory had predicted that the rainfall tomorrow will be 3.2 inches. This prediction has a much higher *empirical content* than merely predicting it will rain. The prediction seems quite likely to be wrong. It is this **potential for falsifiability** that makes the theory impressive (especially if tomorrow's rainfall is *exactly 3.2 inches*). Thus, the more likely a prediction is to be false, the higher its empirical content.

Popper believes that by introducing the idea of falsification, we can bypass the logical problems associated with induction. We can get closer and closer to a true image of the real world by systematically eliminating (falsifying) theories until we arrive at those that seemingly cannot be falsified. Recently, though, some philosophers have again doubted that science can reach "absolute truth." (See Box 1.2.)

Positivists believe that science is (or at least can be) truly objective. In the past few decades, this belief has come under increasing attack from philosophers of science. These *postpositivist* thinkers have made two important points.

There is No "Privileged Frame of Reference"

Albert Einstein (1879–1955) showed that Newton's principles of physics were flawed. At first, this may seem impossible because they work so well. The trouble is, this means "works here on Earth." Newton had taken the Earth to be a **privileged frame of reference** and made all his observations from the vantage point of where he happened to be standing. Einstein thought this was an error.

Einstein concluded that there is no privileged frame of reference, and thus that all observations are *relative*. Here is a simplification of his basic idea. Imagine two objects, moving at constant but different speeds. At some airports, for example, there are slowly moving platforms you can stand on and thus (slowly) get to where you are going without having to walk. If you are on one of these moving platforms for awhile, it begins to look as if the objects beyond the walkway are moving while you are standing still. Similarly, when two trains on parallel tracks pass each other, they relate to each other as "uniform but different rates of motion," and again, which entity is moving and how fast become confused.

Based partly on examples like this, Einstein concluded that, in general, *what we see, observe, and measure is always what is seen from our vantage point.* From a different vantage point, different relationships would be perceived. It is not possible just to say you are *moving*, only that you are *moving relative to something else.* Einstein concluded that scientific conclusions are always *relative*, and therefore are never true in an absolute sense. (Oldroyd, 1986).

Observation is "Theory–Laden"

In the years that followed the Einsteinian revolution, many philosophers of science, notably Thomas Kuhn (1922–), Imre Lakatos (1922–1974), and Paul Feyerabend (1924–) began to rethink the fundamental nature of the scientific enterprise. Against the traditional view that facts are "theory–neutral" and objectively true, these philosophers of science claim that all observation is "theory–laden."

The heart of this claim is that all perception, whether it be the ordinary perception of lay persons going about their daily lives, or the perception of physicists using specialized instruments and apparatus to track the behavior of a subatomic particle, is shaped by the preconceptions and purposes of the observer. In this view, our perceptions are always actively created rather than passively received.

Thomas Kuhn (1970), for example, argues that two groups of scientists taking different theoretical viewpoints (he calls them **paradigms**) "practice their trades in two different worlds" and therefore that "the two groups of scientists see different things when they look from the same point of view in the same direction" (1970, p. 150). A similar conclusion about all people and all perception has been reached by an experimental psychologist, Irwin Rock (1983), who claims that perception is a "thoughtlike process" in which prior knowledge and expectancies play a central role. In other words, for scientists (and ordinary lay people) *what we see depends upon what we "know" as well as what we are looking at.*

As Manicas and Secord (1983) point out, the significance of this new view of science is in showing that "scientific meanings could not be found in observations alone, as the logical empiricists had maintained. [Therefore] the idea that there could be unambiguous logical connections between theory and observation was overthrown" (p. 401).

A Comment on Science and Philosophy

Here we have taken a sharp turn in our discussion of the logical underpinnings of science. Ordinary psychological research is, however, quite able to proceed as usual without waiting for ancient philosophical debates to be resolved. Perhaps they never will be. As Manicas and Secord (1983) note:

> Philosophy of science has most commonly been the work of philosophers, not scientists. . . . A few philosophically oriented scientists may perhaps be partly influenced in their choice of criteria by philosophical writings, but more commonly, scientists contrast with philosophers in generating their own criteria out of their daily practices in scientific research (p. 412).

THE BIRTH OF SCIENTIFIC PSYCHOLOGY

Although modern science can be traced back to the 17th century, there was no science of psychology until the late 19th century. Before then, practicing scientists worked strictly in the material worlds of physics, chemistry, and biology. The history of scientific psychology begins with Johannes Mueller (1801–1858), who was a physiologist.

Johannes Mueller

In Mueller's time, the traditional belief was that a sensory nerve is like a hollow tube, transmitting stimulation exactly as it is received. For example, if someone is exposed to a firecracker going off, the related sights and sounds are transmitted through a nerve the way water flows through a garden hose. Mueller demonstrated that this analogy is false. According to his *Law of Specific Nerve Energies*, any particular sensory nerve produces only a single type of sensation, regardless of how it is stimulated. For example, (Fancher, 1990, p.109):

> If . . . you turn your eyes as far to the right as you can, close your eyes, and then press gently on the left side of your left eyeball, you will see a spot of colored light in the right-hand side of your visual field. You have here stimulated the retina and hence the optic nerve with tactile pressure rather than the normal light rays—but the effect is still visual sensation. You have literally seen the pressure on your eyeball, because the stimulated optic nerve can convey no other sensations than visual ones. The same sort of specificity characterizes the other sensory nerves.

Hermann von Helmholtz

A student of Mueller's, Hermann Helmholtz (1821–1894) adopted his theory that nerve impulses are electro-chemical waves and travel slowly enough to be measured. Helmholtz then set out to measure the actual speed of nervous transmission. He invented a device to measure the speed with which a nerve impulse traverses a frog's leg. Helmholtz' device caused a stopwatch to go *on* the instant he electrically stimulated the leg nerve and *off* the instant the frog's foot twitched.

Helmholtz's investigations then led him to *trichromatic theory of color vision*, showing that separate nerves in the retina transmit the sensation of the primary colors. Thus he demonstrated that the neurological processes underlying mental phenomena could be studied experimentally.

Wilhelm Wundt

An assistant of Helmholtz, Wilhelm Wundt (1832–1920) made a discovery that earned him the title "father of experimental psychology." He began with the commonsense assumption that if two different stimuli strike our senses at the

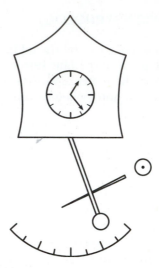

Figure 1-2   Wundt's "thought meter."

same time, we will become aware of them at the same time. To see if this is so, Wundt rigged a pendulum clock into what he called a "thought meter" to examine the temporal relationship between visual and auditory stimuli. Figure 1-2 depicts the apparatus. A knitting needle attached to the clock's pendulum struck a bell, and the processing time of the visual input (needle striking bell) and the auditory input (bell sounding) could be directly compared. Wundt found that he did not hear the bell until the pendulum was already beginning its descent. The intervening time (about 1/8 second) was apparently required for the sound to reach *conscious attention.*

Wundt had succeeded in creating an objective measure of a purely psychological process. He made this discovery the basis for a whole new field, experimental psychology. In 1879 Wundt opened an institute of experimental psychology at the University of Leipzig, where students could earn a Ph.D. in experimental psychology. The optimistic outlook of positivism (see pp. 14–16) made the time right for scientific psychology. By the end of the century, there were more than 100 psychological laboratories spread around the world.

FOR REVIEW AND DISCUSSION

Key Terms
SCIENCE
RATIONALISM
EMPIRICISM
DEDUCTION
INDUCTION
SYLLOGISM

LOGICAL POSITIVISM
REDUCTION SENTENCE
VERIFICATION PRINCIPLE
OPERATIONALISM
POTENTIAL FOR FALSIFIABILITY
PRIVILEGED FRAME OF REFERENCE
PARADIGMS
HYPOTHESES
OPERATIONAL DEFINITION
INDUCTIVE REASONING
DEDUCTIVE REASONING

Discussion Issues

1. Discuss the major characteristics of science. Bearing these characteristics
    in mind, describe some of the difficulties facing a science of human be-
    havior.
2. What benefits does empiricism offer over "pure" rationalism?
3. What logical problems plagued the work of:
    a) Aristotle
    b) Descartes
    c) Copernicus
4. What are the advantages of employing falsification as opposed to verifica-
    tion as a criterion in research?
5. What is meant by the phrase "privileged frame of reference?"
6. Hermann von Helmholtz is considered a physiologist, whereas Wilhelm
    Wundt is considered a psychologist. What is it that makes Wundt's research
    interest "psychological" as opposed to physiological?
7. Why is operationalism an important scientific concept?
8. What is meant by the claim that "all observation is theory-laden?"

2

ETHICAL ISSUES IN PSYCHOLOGICAL RESEARCH

❖ **BACKGROUND**
   The Milgram Experiment
   Inherent Conflict of Interest
   Institutional Review Boards
❖ **SUBJECTS' RIGHTS**
   Informed Consent
   Right to Privacy
   Freedom from Harm
   Right to Withdraw
❖ **RESEARCHERS' RESPONSIBILITIES**
   Debriefing
      Dehoaxing
      Desensitization
   Reparation of Harm/Reinstatement of Well-Being
   Maintaining Confidentiality
❖ **THE 1992 APA CODE OF ETHICS**
   BOX 2.1 GENERAL PRINCIPLES OF THE 1992 APA CODE
   OF ETHICS
   The Code of Conduct
   Summary and Comments
❖ **EFFECTS OF ETHICAL STANDARDS**
   Effects on Research Results
   Effects on Subjects' Ethical Concerns

Research psychologists are trained to formulate hypotheses and to design research projects suited to evaluating them. But what of the impact of the research on participants? Some research violates a subject's right to privacy, as happens when the subject's behavior is monitored by hidden observers. In more extreme cases, participating in research may involve actual risk to the subject's health or psychological well-being. These issues lead us to ask about the ethics of psychological research.

BACKGROUND

Until the 1960s, research psychologists were expected to establish their own personal ethical standards and safeguards for their subjects. However, over the past 30 years, professional organizations, government agencies, and research psychologists themselves have abandoned the belief that ethics of research should be determined by an individual researcher.

In place of an individualistic system, a number of formalized codes of research ethics have been developed. The responsibility for determining what is and is not "ethical" behavior has fallen to government and professional organizations. This change is in part due to the realization that the standards of some individuals may well be inadequate by the standards of others.

Reports of brutal experiments performed on prisoners in Nazi concentration camps were one important stimulus in the ethics movement in psychology. (The Nuremberg Code of Ethics was formulated after the Nazi war crime trials. It provides a basis for the ethical treatment of human research subjects.) But reports of gross scientific misconduct were not linked solely to the Third Reich.

Beecher (1966) found that in the United States, human subjects were often placed at considerable risk through their participation in medical research. For example, in one study described by Beecher, penicillin was compared with a placebo (a compound with no specific pharmacological effect) as a treatment to prevent rheumatic fever. Although it was already known that penicillin was an effective treatment for respiratory infections, which can sometimes lead to rheumatic fever, 109 servicemen with respiratory infections were given only the placebo. Psychologists, too, have performed experiments that raise ethical issues. Of these, the Milgram experiment is the most famous.

The Milgram Experiment

News of horrible experiments on human subjects by Nazi scientists, such as leaving naked human beings in freezers to see how long they lived, shocked many people. One of the common explanations of these atrocities was that those who carried them out were blind to moral issues that most people see clearly. Harvard social psychologist Stanley Milgram disagreed. Milgram thought a tendency to take orders from apparently responsible authority is a general characteristic of most people. Under certain conditions, ordinary people will probably carry out orders that will do serious physical harm to others.

To make his point, Milgram (1963) had a drab laboratory assistant order adult male subjects to administer increasingly more painful electric shocks to another person in the context of a learning experiment. (In reality, the "other person" was Milgram's confederate and did not really receive any shocks.) The shocks were delivered by a shock generator with 30 graded switches from *Slight Shock* to *Danger: Severe Shock.*

At some point the other person hollered from the next room that he was a heart patient and could take no more, but the assistant just repeated to the subject that he must administer the next level of shock. Nearly two-thirds of Milgram's subjects went all the way, giving the person in the other room a final shock plainly labeled dangerous. The basic finding was replicated many times (Milgram, 1977), and ultimately "changed our understanding of the nature of obedience." (Sieber & Stanley, 1988, p. 52).

If Milgram's confederates were not really hurt by what happened, the same did not seem to be true of his subjects. Milgram (1963) reported:

> In a large number of cases the degree of tension reached extremes that are rarely seen in sociopsychological laboratory studies. Subjects were observed to sweat, tremble, stutter, bite their lips, groan, and dig their fingernails into their flesh. These were characteristic rather than exceptional responses to the experiment (p. 375.)
>   I observed a mature and initially poised businessman enter the laboratory smiling and confident. Within 20 minutes he was reduced to a twitching, stuttering wreck, who was rapidly approaching a point of nervous collapse. He constantly pulled on his earlobe and twisted his hands. (At one point he pushed his fist into his forehead and muttered: "Oh, God, let's stop it.") And yet he continued to respond to every word of the experimenter, and obeyed to the end. (p. 377)

Milgram's 1963 report of his experiment, "Behavioral Study of Obedience," provoked strong negative reactions. Among the harshest critics of Milgram's work was Diana Baumrind (1964), who pointed out the extreme vulnerability of subjects who are expected to perceive the experimenter as a trustworthy authority figure. Baumrind also pointed out that in the absence of an appropriate "corrective experience" (involving full disclosure and the opportunity for subjects to express openly their feelings about their behavior in the experimental situation, as well as their feelings about having been so deceived) subjects are likely to experience diminished self-esteem, loss of trust for authority, and continuing anxiety.

Inherent Conflict of Interest

Though none was as attention-getting as Milgram's, by the mid–1960s hundreds of psychological experiments were reported in which college students, children, and bystanders were entangled in a web of deceit in order to test some hypothesis about human behavior. The consensus arose that research with human subjects needed to be governed by explicit principles and controlled institutionally rather than individually.

In 1967 a panel appointed by the President's Office of Science and Technology issued a report on privacy and behavioral research. The panel concluded that there exists *an inherent conflict of interest* between two strongly held values: society's right to know anything that may be known or discovered versus the individual's right to privacy.

This panel issued the following recommendations for future research:

Whenever possible, a subject's informed consent should be obtained.

It is sometimes not possible to obtain informed consent; this is the case whenever the validity of an experiment would be destroyed if the subject knows all the details of its conduct.

When individual privacy and the right to know are in conflict, there must be a thoughtful evaluation of each case.

A primary responsibility for preserving individual rights is borne by the institution which employs the investigator.

The researcher working with human subjects has an obligation to insure that no permanent physical or psychological harm will ensue from the research procedures, and that "temporary discomfort or loss of privacy will be remedied in an appropriate way during the course of the research or at its completion." (p. 349)

Institutional Review Boards

Although professional organizations often formulate their own ethical guidelines for practitioners within their profession, the safety of research participants is generally also protected by *human subjects committees*. These committees are usually composed of people from diverse disciplines (community citizens, clergy, lawyers), who are charged with evaluating research proposals on ethical grounds.

Human subjects committees are often called IRBs (for *I*nstitutional *R*eview *B*oards) or CORIHS (COR'-iss) committees, an acronym for *C*ommittee *o*n *R*esearch *I*nvolving *H*uman *S*ubjects. Local committees may require changes in or even turn down a proposal that might place subjects at undue risk. In the United States, government funding for a research project is no longer possible unless the work has been approved by an appropriate human subjects committee at the investigator's institution.

SUBJECTS' RIGHTS

It is generally understood today that subjects involved in research have rights and that researchers have responsibilities and obligations toward their subjects.

Most researchers agree that subjects have the right to privacy, confidentiality, information about the nature of the research in which they participate, and not to be harmed either physically or psychologically because of their participation. Subjects also have the right to withdraw from a research project at any point if they begin to experience discomfort (either physical or psychological) as a result of their participation.

Informed Consent

A primary right of all subjects is the right to be asked in advance whether they wish to be a research participant, and to feel free to decline. Subjects also have the right to be told, in advance, all the facts about the research they need to make an *informed* decision about participation. In essence, the subject must enter into a voluntary agreement with the researcher. This constitutes informed consent and, in principle, no person shall be made to participate in psychological research without his or her prior informed consent.

In an effort to ensure that participants are adequately informed about the important aspects of a research project before participating, it is required that they sign a *consent form*. Such a form provides the following information: the name and affiliation of the researcher in charge of the project; the name of one or more members of the review board that reviewed the project; the title and brief description of the project; a comprehensive list of potential risks to subjects; and a description of the liability and remedies offered by those responsible for the research.

In research involving any "sensitive" topic (aggression, honesty, altruism, effects of drugs), it is often impossible to inform subjects fully about a study until their participation is complete. For instance, suppose a psychologist is interested

Cartoon 2-1 THE FAR SIDE, copyright ©1993 FARWORKS, Inc., distributed by Universal Press Syndicate. Reprinted with permission. All rights reserved.

in studying people's willingness to lie. How is the researcher to insure that subjects have been adequately informed of the study's purpose and risks without affecting the outcome of the study?

If *any* deception is involved, each participant must be given a full *debriefing* at the conclusion of their participation. This is a prime example of the inherent conflict of interest we discussed earlier.

Right to Privacy

Research participants have the right to privacy. Subjects need not disclose or reveal any information about themselves to the researcher which they elect not to.

Freedom from Harm

Participants in research must be protected from harm (either physical or psychological) that might result from their participation. It is the responsibility of the researcher (as well as the institution which employs her/him) to ensure that subjects are adequately protected from harm. In addition, researchers must ensure that subjects are informed before participation of the risk of any harm that could result from participation.

Right to Withdraw

Subjects maintain the right to withdraw from participation in a study at any time during its course and for any reason whatsoever.

RESEARCHERS' RESPONSIBILITIES

The researcher incurs certain responsibilities in deciding to undertake a study employing living subjects. One of these is to protect the rights of participants (as listed above).

Psychologists are personally responsible for their own behavior as well as for the behavior of subordinates involved in the research effort. The researcher is also responsible for any harm inflicted and is required to make appropriate reparations at the conclusion of the research. Psychologists must also be particularly mindful of factors that might compel participation, and must ensure that subjects are adequately informed at the beginning and end of their involvement. Finally, psychologists must ensure that information about the subject is not shared in any way not described explicitly to the subject in advance of participation.

Debriefing

Debriefing refers generally to the explanations provided to subjects by researchers at the conclusion of their participation in a research project. This may include revealing any deception involved (**dehoaxing**) as well as describing the ultimate goal of the research. **Desensitization** procedures must also be included in the debriefing if subjects have been led to behave in ways that they themselves may find disturbing.

Dehoaxing.   Dehoaxing is a type of debriefing in which the experimenter tries "to convince the subjects that the fraudulent information they were given (e.g., that they are seriously maladjusted) was *in fact* fraudulent and thereby relieve any anxiety engendered by that information." (Holmes, 1976a, p. 859) Dehoaxing is required in any experimental situation in which deception of the subjects is involved.

Desensitization.   Desensitization refers "to the process of helping the subjects deal with new information about themselves acquired as a consequence of the behaviors they exhibited during the experiment (e.g., in an obedience-type experiment, inflicting possibly lethal shocks on another person simply because he was instructed to do so by an experimenter)." (Holmes, 1976b, p. 868) Desensitization can be viewed as one aspect of the responsibility of the researcher to alleviate any harmful effects of the procedures employed.

Reparation of Harm/Reinstatement of Well-Being

If harm should result from research participation, it is the responsibility of the researcher to make appropriate reparations and ensure that subjects are relieved of any damage or discomfort produced by their participation.

Maintaining Confidentiality

Information gathered by the researcher about a given individual may not be shared in any way that reveals the identity of the particular participant. Protecting the confidentiality of subjects is imperative because researchers often gather a great deal of data on their subjects, some of which may be sensitive in nature or potentially damaging to subjects if revealed openly.

THE 1992 APA CODE OF ETHICS

In the early 1970s, the American Psychological Association (APA) appointed a committee on ethical standards in psychological research to formulate a comprehensive code of ethics for psychologists. The committee first solicited information from members of the APA concerning research that posed ethical questions. Five thousand research descriptions were generated. After reviewing these, the committee wrote the first draft of a new set of ethical principles.

This first draft was distributed throughout the profession and was published in the *APA Monitor* (the official newspaper of the organization). Reactions to the draft were then considered, and in 1973 a set of 10 principles was adopted by the APA. The original set of 10 principles was revised in 1982, and again in December, 1992.

The APA's 1992 version of the ethical responsibilities of psychologists is a three-part document (APA, 1992). The first section is the *preamble*, which describes the basic responsibilities of all psychologists, regardless of their specific occupational activities. The second part consists of six broad, *general principles* regarding professional behavior. The third part consists of *specific ethical standards* as applicable to a variety of scientific and professional activities.

Box 2.1 contains the general principles in their entirety (APA, 1992, pp. 1599–1600). The discussion that follows begins with the code of conduct, and summarizes the specific standards that govern the practice and reporting of research.

BOX 2.1 *GENERAL PRINCIPLES OF THE 1992 APA CODE OF ETHICS*

Principle A: Competence

Psychologists strive to maintain high standards of competence in their work. They recognize the boundaries of their particular competencies and the limitations of their expertise. They provide only those services and use only those techniques for which they are qualified by education, training, or experience.

Psychologists are cognizant of the fact that the competencies required in service, teaching, and/or studying groups of people vary with the distinctive characteristics of those groups. In those areas in which recognized professional standards do not yet exist, psychologists exercise careful judgment and take appropriate precautions to protect the welfare of those with whom they work. They maintain knowledge of relevant scientific and professional information related to the services they render, and they recognize the need for ongoing education. Psychologists make appropriate use of scientific, professional, technical, and administrative resources.

Principle B: Integrity

Psychologists seek to promote integrity in the science, teaching, and practice of psychology. In these activities psychologists are honest, fair, and respectful of others. In describing or reporting their qualifications, services, products, fees, research, or teaching, they do not make statements that are false, misleading, or deceptive. Psychologists strive to be aware of their own belief systems, values, needs, and limitations, and the effect of these on their work. To the extent feasible, they attempt to clarify for relevant parties the roles they are performing and to function appropriately in accordance with those roles. Psychologists avoid improper and potentially harmful dual relationships.

Principle C: Professional and Scientific Responsibility

Psychologists uphold professional standards of conduct, clarify their professional roles and obligations, accept appropriate responsibility for their behavior, and adapt their methods to the needs of different populations. Psychologists consult with, refer to, or cooperate with other professionals and institutions to the extent needed to serve the best interests of their patients, clients, or other recipients of their services. Psychologists' moral standards and conduct are personal matters to the same degree as is true for any other person, except as psychologists' conduct may compromise their professional responsibilities or reduce the public's trust in psychology and psychologists. Psychologists are concerned about the ethical compliance of their colleagues' scientific and professional conduct. When appropriate, they consult with colleagues in order to prevent or avoid unethical conduct.

Principle D: Respect for People's Rights and Dignity

Psychologists accord appropriate respect to the fundamental rights, dignity, and worth of all people. They respect the rights of individuals to privacy, confidentiality, self-determination, and autonomy, mindful that legal and other obligations may lead to inconsistency and conflict with the exercise of these rights. Psychologists are aware of cultural, individual, and role differences, including those due to age, gender, race, ethnicity, national origin, religion, sexual orientation, disability, language, and socioeconomic status. Psychologists try to eliminate the effect on their work of biases based on those factors, and they do not knowingly participate in or condone unfair discriminatory practices.

Principle E: Concern for Others' Welfare

Psychologists seek to contribute to the welfare of those with whom they interact professionally. In their professional actions, psychologists weigh the welfare and rights of their patients or clients, students, supervisees, human research participants, and other affected persons, and the welfare of animal subjects of research. When conflicts occur among psychologists' obligations or concerns, they attempt to resolve these conflicts in a responsible fashion that avoids or minimizes harm. Psychologists are sensitive to real and ascribed differences in power between themselves and others, and they do not exploit or mislead other people during or after professional relationships.

Principle F: Social Responsibility

Psychologists are aware of their professional and scientific responsibility to the community and the society in which they work and live. They apply and make public their knowledge of psychology in order to contribute to human welfare. Psychologists are concerned about and work to mitigate the causes of human suffering. When undertaking research, they strive to advance human welfare and the science of psychology. Psychologists try to avoid misuse of their work. Psychologists comply with the law and encourage the development of law and social policy that serve the interests of their patients and clients and the public. They are encouraged to contribute a portion of their professional time for little or no personal advantage.

The Code of Conduct

The Code of Conduct has eight sections:
1. General Standards
2. Evaluation, Assessment, or Intervention
3. Advertising and Other Public Statements
4. Therapy
5. Privacy and Confidentiality
6. Teaching, Training and Supervision, Research, and Publication
7. Forensic Activities
8. Resolving Ethical Issues

Within each area a number of highly specific statements are made pertaining to standards of behavior for psychologists in these various contexts.

Our specific interest is with a portion of section 6, namely, those articles having to do with the conduct and reporting of psychological research. Below are the names and numbers of the specific articles governing the practice of research and a summary of the content of each.

6.06 Planning Research

This section makes four points:

1. Research must be designed and executed in accordance with recognized ethical and scientific standards.
2. The risk of misinterpretation of results must be minimized.
3. Ethical acceptability of research must be insured.
4. The rights and welfare of all participants, animal or human, must be adequately protected.

6.07 Responsibility

This section also makes four points:

1. Research should be conducted with competence and due concern for the dignity and welfare of participants.
2. Psychologists are solely responsible for their own ethical conduct as well as for those in their employ.
3. Researchers may perform only those tasks for which they are adequately trained and prepared.
4. Psychologists should consider the potential effects of their research on any special populations.

6.08 Compliance with Laws and Standards

Psychologists must comply with all federal and local laws, as well as ethical standards governing the conduct of all research.

6.09 Institutional Approval

Psychologists must obtain prior approval from host institutions before conducting any research.

6.10 Research Responsibilities

Before undertaking any research, psychologists must enter into a formal agreement with participants which clarifies the responsibilities of each.

6.11 Informed Consent to Research

This section makes five points:

1. In obtaining **informed consent**, psychologists must use understandable language.
2. Psychologists must provide their potential subjects the following information:
   i.   the nature of the research,
   ii. their prerogative to decline participation or withdraw at any time,
   iii. factors that might influence their willingness to participate (such as risk, discomfort, or the limitations of confidentiality)
   iv. answers to any of their questions
3. When conducting research with students or subordinates, special care is necessary to protect the prospective participants from any adverse consequences for declining or withdrawing.
4. When research participation is required or offered for extra credit in a course, the student must be given a choice of equitable alternative activities.
5. When potential participants are legally incapable of informed consent, they must nonetheless be given an appropriate explanation and asked for their assent to participate. Appropriate legal consent from an authorized person should be obtained.

6.12 Dispensing with Informed Consent

Although some research may appear not to require informed consent of participants (such as anonymous questionnaires, naturalistic observations, or certain kinds of archival research), the decision to dispense with this requirement should only be made in consultation with institutional review boards and colleagues.

6.13 Informed Consent in Research Filming or Recording

Persons should not be filmed or have their behavior recorded in any form without informed consent, except for naturalistic observation in public places where individuals cannot be personally identified or harmed.

6.14 Offering Inducements to Research Participants

This section makes two points:

1. When professional services are offered as an inducement to research participation, the nature of the services, as well as the risks, obligations, and limitations of using the service should be made clear.
2. Inducements to participate in research should not be excessive or inappropriate, particularly when such incentives might tend to coerce participation.

6.15 Deception in Research

This section makes three points:

1. Studies involving deception should not be conducted unless a) the use of deception is justified by the study's prospective scientific, educational, or applied value *and* b) equally effective alternative procedures are not feasible.
2. Participants should never be deceived about aspects of the research that would affect their willingness to participate (such as risks or physical and/or psychological discomfort).
3. Deception should be explained as early as feasible, and no later than the conclusion of the research.

6.16 Sharing and Utilizing Data

Potential participants must be informed of all anticipated sharing of research data, as well as the possibility of unanticipated future uses.

6.17 Minimizing Invasiveness

Research should not interfere with the participants or the milieu from which data are collected beyond what is a) warranted by the research design *and* b) consistent with the role of scientific investigator.

6.18 Providing Participants with Information About the Study

This section makes two points:

1. Participants should be given an opportunity to learn about the nature, results, and conclusions of the research in which they have participated.
2. If scientific or human values justify delaying or withholding information, reasonable measures should be taken to reduce the risk of harm.

6.19 Honoring Commitments

All commitments made to research participants should be honored.

6.20 Care and Use of Animals in Research

This section makes eight points:

1. Research animals must be treated humanely.
2. Research animals must be acquired, cared for, used, and disposed of in compliance with government regulations and professional standards.
3. Animal research must be supervised by psychologists trained in the care of laboratory animals.
4. All individuals using animals under the supervision of a psychologist must be trained in the care and handling of the species being used.
5. Reasonable efforts must be taken to minimize the discomfort, infection, illness, and pain of animal subjects.
6. Pain, stress, and privation may only be used when a) an alternative procedure is unavailable *and* b) the goal is justified by its prospective scientific, educational, or applied value.
7. Surgical procedures must be performed under anesthesia, and precautions should be taken to minimize pain and avoid infection.
8. When a research animal's life is to be terminated, it should be done rapidly and with an effort to minimize pain.

6.21 Reporting of Results

This section makes two points:

1. Psychologists must not fabricate data nor falsify results.
2. Significant errors in published data must be corrected by erratum, retraction, or other appropriate publication means.

6.22 Plagiarism

Psychologists must not present the work of others as their own.

6.23 Publication Credit

This section makes three points:

1. Psychologists take responsibility and credit only for work to which they have contributed.
2. Authorship must accurately reflect the scientific or professional contributions of the individuals involved. Mere possession of an institutional position (such as Department Chair) does not justify authorship credit. Minor contributions should be acknowledged in a footnote or introductory statement.
3. Students should be listed as principal author on any article based on the student's dissertation or thesis.

6.24 Duplicate Publication of Data

Data that have been previously published may not be published again as original data.

6.25 Sharing Data

Psychologists must not withhold data of published research from other competent professionals who seek to verify substantive claims through re-analysis.

6.26 Professional Reviewers

Psychologists reviewing raw material for publication or grant proposals must respect the confidentiality and proprietary rights of those who submitted it.

Summary and Comments

In essence, the principles governing the conduct of research require the psychologist to plan research projects carefully so as to maximize the value of the information obtained while minimizing the potential risk to subjects. Gergen (1973) summarized researchers' obligations in seven points:

1) gaining the informed consent of the subject
2) maintaining honesty rather than deception
3) allowing subjects to withdraw at any time
4) keeping all promises

5) disclosing fully the nature of the research

6) honoring the subject's right to privacy

7) protecting the subject from harm (p. 907)

However, there is a tricky part to all of this. If these practices were followed without exception, Gergen concludes:

> . . . the vast majority of research dealing with negative affective states, including the effects of frustration, loss, rejection, conflict, failure, and competition would be altogether prohibited. I doubt that the majority of the Ethics Committee wishes to prevent these endeavors, and in some cases the "fine print" underlying the principles removes the moral necessity imposed by the principles (1973, p. 911).

Now we will examine more closely some of the effects of the imposed ethical standards on the conduct and outcome of modern research.

EFFECTS OF ETHICAL STANDARDS

From the first draft of the APA's "Ethical Standards and Psychological Research," psychologists in some quarters raised concerns about how the imposition of ethical standards would affect research.

Effects on Research Results

To demonstrate that ethical standards can alter research results, Resnick and Schwartz (1973) conducted a verbal conditioning experiment under two conditions. Basically, a number of studies conducted in the 1960s had shown that if subjects are asked to produce free verbal output (for example, by making up sentences) and subtly rewarded for certain types of utterances (such as use of plural nouns), the frequency of occurrence of the rewarded type of utterance will increase. In these experiments, subjects did not know the true purpose of the experiment until it was over. Resnick and Schwartz wanted to know what would happen if the subjects *did* know the purpose of the study from the beginning.

Subjects in the "nonethical" group were told the purpose of the experiment was to study "the factors that govern the ways in which college students form sentences and express themselves in verbal communication." (p. 135) The subjects in the "ethical" group were given a full and detailed description of all aspects of the study, including:

> There are two groups of subjects being run. One group, the one we are asking you to participate in, will be informed totally about the nature of the experiment, including all the hypotheses being investigated.
>
> The hypothesis of this experiment is to determine what effect full disclosure of telling you the hypotheses will have on your behavior in the experiment, in contrast to

the other group, who have been told only that the experiment involves "sentence construction."

> You will be asked to come into a room where you will be given one hundred 3 × 5 inch cards, one at a time, on each of which is printed six pronouns: I, We, You, They, He, She, and a verb. [You will be asked] to compose a sentence using the verb that is printed on that particular card, and to begin the sentence with one of the six pronouns.

> If you begin your sentence with either the pronoun "I" or "We," the experimenter will say "good," or "mmm-hmmm," or "okay." Previous findings using this method have shown that subjects will increase the use of the reinforced pronouns over the 100 trials to a significant degree beyond the level that they were using these pronouns in the initial trials, when the verbal reinforcement was not given (p. 135).

Subjects in the "unethical" condition showed a clear conditioning effect, more than doubling their use of "I" and "we" over the trials. This result replicates earlier reports by other investigators. In contrast, subjects in the "ethical" condition did *not* show a conditioning effect. In fact, they showed a *decrease* in their use of "I" and "we" over trials.

This study clearly illustrates the potential influence of disclosure of hypotheses on the outcome of research. The informed subjects not only failed to demonstrate the previously "known" effect, they in fact demonstrated an effect opposite to what would otherwise have been expected. Thus, what we learn through research is heavily dependent on the methods used, and ethical constraints may seriously restrict the available methods!

Effects on Subjects' Ethical Concerns

Research has consistently suggested that researchers and review boards may be more concerned about ethical issues than are the subjects themselves. For example, it has become common practice to require a number of hours of research participation of undergraduate students in introductory psychology courses. Students may also be offered extra credit for participation. In these cases, the question arises as to whether or not research participation is truly voluntary. Leak (1981) surveyed several hundred students who had participated in research for extra course credit. Overwhelmingly, students found participation worthwhile and did not object to or feel particularly coerced by the fact that their participation was associated with course requirements.

Similarly, research suggests that (for student subjects at least) deception may not represent the problem it has been assumed to be. Collins et al. (1979) surveyed almost 800 students and found "that students responded with significantly less concern about traditional deception in experimentation than do psychologists." (p. 155). Likewise, a study of almost 500 students by Smith and Richardson (1983) found that students had enjoyed deception experiments *more* than those involving no deception. Moreover, Smith and Richardson's work revealed that almost every student who felt potentially harmed by a deception, also felt that the debriefing he/she received adequately eliminated any negative effects.

A similar conclusion was reached by Christensen (1988), who wrote:

Deception has been attacked repeatedly as ethically and morally reprehensible.
However, research has revealed that subjects who have participated in deception experiments versus nondeception experiments enjoyed the experience more, received
more educational benefit from it, and did not mind being deceived or having their privacy invaded. Such evidence suggests that deception, although unethical from a moral
point of view, is not to be considered aversive, undesirable, or an unacceptable methodology from the researcher's point of view (p. 664).

FOR REVIEW AND DISCUSSION

Key Terms
PLACEBO
IRB
CORIHS COMMITTEES
INFORMED CONSENT
DEBRIEFING
DEHOAXING
DESENSITIZATION
CONFIDENTIALITY
DECEPTION

Discussion Issues

1. It seems probable that the Milgram experiment would not be considered
   ethically acceptable by today's standards. Do you think this experiment
   should *never* have been done? Why or why not?
2. Discuss the role of ethics, including the idea of informed consent, in psychological research.
3. Under what circumstances is deception justifiable?
4. Why are Institutional Review Boards (CORIHS committees) now a universal feature of the research process?
5. Explain the difference between "dehoaxing" and "desensitization."
6. Researchers seem more concerned about ethical issues than subjects do.
   What are some of the reasons why this might be so?

3

OBSERVATION, DESCRIPTION, AND COMPARISON

As we explained in Chapter 1, empiricism is the foundation of the scientific method. The empirical approach involves three basic steps: observation, description, and comparison.

OBSERVATIONAL RESEARCH

All science begins with observation. Often, special situations are set up (for example, in a laboratory) in order to make the observations called for by our hypotheses. However, special set-ups and artificial circumstances are not always a part of scientific observation. As in many other sciences, some important advances have been made in psychology through careful observation alone. Psychologists have used two methods of purely observational research: naturalistic observation and case studies.

Naturalistic Observation

All animal species, including humans, have characteristic patterns of behaving in their natural environments. The goal of **naturalistic observation** is to identify these patterns.

Naturalistic observation of humans has been done mainly by European *ethologists*. These behavioral scientists have systematically observed animals and humans "in the wild" and offer a vivid description of the behavior of humankind (Eibl-Eibesfeldt, 1989).

The nature and development of **pecking orders** is an area in which ethological observation has contributed to our knowledge of animal and human behavior. The phrase "pecking order" first appeared in the early 20th century, when a European naturalist, T. Schjelderup-Ebbe, reported his observations of what happens when a group of chicken hens is brought together for the first time.

Initially the hens fight among themselves (by pecking at one another), but the fighting subsides fairly quickly as each hen appears to learn who is superior and who is inferior to herself. Then she steps aside (e.g., from the food dish) to avoid those who previously subdued her, but pushes aside those she has subdued. Once established, pecking orders appear to be quite stable.

Chickens are not the only species to establish pecking orders. A similar phenomenon has also been observed in primates, including humans. A group of chimpanzees, for example, will initially "display" for one another by making loud and threatening noises, after which a dominance hierarchy will appear in terms of who has priority at feeding sites and in mating.

The pecking order phenomenon is also found in humans. When people are put in groups for almost any purpose, a dominance hierarchy soon appears. For example, one investigator observed the development of rank order relationships among kindergarten children in a variety of different schools in many countries (Hold, 1977). All the groups studied showed clear dominance hierarchies, and the characteristics of high and low-ranking children were quite similar across groups.

High-ranking children were more likely than other children to initiate play and game activities, moved more freely around the play area, were more likely to mediate conflicts among others, and showed off more. Low-ranking children were observed to offer gifts and assistance to high ranking ones, and to attend to and seek out high rankers. In general, the behavior of "low rankers" was yielding and submissive.

Another investigation focused on young adolescents as they arrived at summer camp (Savin-Williams, 1979). In a typical cabin of 5–6 boys, distinct rank orders appear within an hour of their being brought together. The higher-ranking individuals were those who were most athletic and physically mature. Interestingly, rank orders form somewhat more slowly among groups of female adolescents; moreover, the highest ranking girls were not the most athletic but the most mature and maternal. For both genders, preferred sites (e.g., beds, dining room seats, and so on) almost invariably went to the "high ranking" individuals, just as they seem to with chickens and chimpanzees.

The pecking order example illustrates the potential of naturalistic observation to provide rich descriptions. It also illustrates a limitation of the method: Descriptions, even relatively complete ones, must still be explained. Eibl-Eibesfeldt and other ethologists fashion their interpretations against the backdrop of the Darwinian theory of evolution, assuming that species-wide behavior patterns must play an adaptive role in survival and/or reproduction. After reviewing the pecking order data, Eibl-Eibesfeldt (1989, p. 314) concluded:

> The human disposition to form rank orders is based on our primate heritage. . . . Obedience and the readiness to become subordinated are as innate in humans as the striving for rank, and both tendencies combine to form a functional system.

This is an interpretation of the observations, and not everyone will agree with it. Likewise, not everyone agrees with interpretations made of case studies.

Case Studies

A **case study** is a detailed examination of part or all of one person's life, undertaken with a specific purpose in mind. Biographical novels and movies, for example, are often designed to illustrate or highlight some aspect of human nature. Everyone is familiar with this method on some level.

Although case studies are often both unsystematic and uncontrolled, they have made some important contributions to scientific psychology.

We can distinguish two broad ways in which the case study has been used: 1) as a source of descriptive information, and 2) as evidence to support or invalidate specific theories.

Descriptive Uses.   As a method of description, the case study has been used in each of the following ways:

1. to illustrate some form of behavior
2. to demonstrate important methods or procedures

3. to provide a detailed account of a rare or unusual phenomenon
4. as a source of hypotheses

Let's begin with the famous case of a "multiple personality" reported by C. H. Thigpen and H. M. Cleckley in 1954, and dramatized in a 1957 movie, The Three Faces of Eve. Thigpen and Cleckley described a patient, "Eve White,"[1] who displayed at various times three very distinct personalities. Eve White had been seen in psychotherapy for several months because she had severe headaches accompanied by blackouts. Her therapist described her as a retiring and gently conventional figure. However, one day during an interview Eve seemed to undergo a surprising and abrupt change:

> As if seized by sudden pain, she put both hands to her head. After a tense moment of silence, both hands dropped. There was a quick, reckless smile, and, in a bright voice that sparkled, she said "Hi there, Doc!" The demure and constrained posture of Eve White had melted into buoyant repose. . . . This new and apparently carefree girl spoke casually of Eve White and her problems, always using she or her in every reference, always respecting the strict bounds of a separate identity. . . . When asked her name, she immediately replied, "Oh, I'm Eve Black." (1954, p. 137).

Following this rather startling observation, Eve saw her therapist over a period of 14 months in a series of interviews that totaled almost 100 hours. During this time still a third personality, "Jane," emerged.

At first Jane appeared to be merely a composite of the two Eves, but later she seemed to become a well-integrated person. Many years afterward, an autobiographical account appeared (Sizemore & Pittillo, 1977). This autobiography revealed that Jane was not the final incarnation of Eve White. In fact, before her problem was resolved, she had revealed another twenty personalities!

This case is considered a valuable classic in psychiatric literature because it is one of a very few detailed accounts of a rare phenomenon, a true multiple personality. In addition to illustrating the phenomenon itself, the investigators' original report provides valuable details on the interview procedures they used and many sidelights on how the problem developed.

The Case Study as Evidence.   You may recall our previous discussion of **verification** and **falsification** as possible ways of validating a theory (see Chapter 1). Case studies can only make a minor contribution to verifying a theory, because they involve no *risky predictions*. But the case study can be very powerful in *dis*confirming or falsifying a theory.

Consider the "motor theory" of speech perception. According to this theory, the ability to decode the speech signals of others depends on the listener's own ability to speak. An important prediction follows. If subjects are unable to speak, they will also be unable to perceive speech; that is, they won't have the capacity to understand what others are saying.

---

[1]As is the case in most such reports, the names used are pseudonyms.

In 1962, Eric Lenneberg presented a case study of a severely handicapped 8-year-old boy who lacked the motor skills necessary for speaking. He had never spoken, and never would. Despite this deficit, the boy *could* understand and respond to what others said to him. Motor skills were obviously not required for this boy to comprehend speech. The motor theory of speech perception had to be discarded because of the data provided by a single but extremely pointed case.

On the other hand, the confirmatory power of the case study is usually quite low. Suppose a psychiatrist reports a **clinical trial**, using a new anti-anxiety medication to treat a single patient with persistent anxiety. Suppose, too, that after 6 months on the medication, the patient's anxiety has markedly decreased. Such a result *may* be due to the treatment, but it may also be due to other factors. The patient's anxiety may have been caused by an increase in life stress, and this stress may have decreased over the 6 months. As we shall see later, this is one reason why a **control group** is employed in most formal research (e.g., in experiments).

But the major problem with case studies, even as simple descriptions, lies in how the subjects are chosen. Typically, cases are *selected* to illustrate a particular point, or to support a theory. Rarely is any information presented on the **representativeness** of the case. If the point being illustrated by the case is presumed to be a general one, it is necessary to establish that the results from the case presented can also be expected with other, similar cases.

How, then, can we decide who must be observed to permit general conclusions? To answer, we must make an important distinction, between **samples** and **populations**.

CHOOSING A SAMPLE

In the summer, fresh berries are sold all over Long Island. Most often they are packaged in paper containers, sealed across the top with clear cellophane. So, you don't actually get to pick your own berries. But you do get to choose your own package. We hunt for the package with the freshest looking berries on top.

When we get home and open the package, there are always several berries that are discolored, too ripe, or moldy. These inferior berries never seem to be at the top of the package (where we could see them). They are always in the middle or at the bottom of the container. In our experience, then, the sample of berries at the top is always *biased*; it is *not representative* of the entire package. A description of the top layer of berries would most certainly *not* be an accurate description of the berries in the total package. You may have had similar experiences.

The example of the berries illustrates the basic issue we will be discussing in this section, namely, the relationship between *samples* and the *populations* which they are assumed to represent.

The distinction is necessary because research psychologists rarely, if ever, actually study or observe all the people in whom they are interested. That is, psychological research typically undertakes to describe a segment of the world, a *population*, on the basis of observing a much smaller subset, a *sample*.

A **population** is *the total collection of people, things, or events of interest*; it is whatever group the researcher wishes to make **inferences** about. (Recall from Chapter 1 that scientific inferences are central to the research enterprise.)

In psychological research, populations are defined by **rules of membership**. These rules are chosen by the researcher. For example, if you were doing a study on how high school students plan for college, all the high school seniors in the United States today might be the population in which you are ultimately interested.

Because of the way populations are used in psychological research, a population need not actually exist at any particular time; the only requirement is that it be well-defined. In fact, many populations are defined in terms of *potential membership*. For example, all the males in the Unites States who might be given a new birth control pill constitute a population defined by potential membership.

A **sample** is *some subset of a population*. Samples can be any size and can be selected in a number of different ways. However, the alternatives are not all useful ones, and poor sampling procedures plague psychological research as much as any other methodological problem.

What constitutes an appropriate sample? To answer this question we must actually address two issues: *Which cases* should be sampled? and *How many* cases should be included in the sample? The answers lie in an understanding of two additional concepts, **representativeness** and **variability**.

The Goal of Representativeness

If observations of a sample will be used to draw inferences about a population, then the critical requirement for a sample is that it reflects the characteristics of the population fairly and accurately. A **representative sample** thus *tends to display variations among its members that are proportional to the variations that exist in the actual population of interest.* If 50% of all babies in the United States have spoken their first word by 1 year of age and the other 50% have not, we would obviously hope that a sample of babies used to study the "normal" rate of infant language development consists of 1-year-olds who have and have not spoken their first words in the same proportion, about 50–50.

Biased Samples.   A **biased sample** is one that is *not representative of the population to which the investigator wishes to generalize.* A biased sample invites inaccurate inferences. One of the major problems with case studies is that we cannot determine in what ways a single case is or is not representative of the population of interest. Here is a dramatized example of the problem:

> Suppose that a team of scientists from another planet landed on Earth and met one man. They observed him carefully and noted he 1) had two eyes, 2) had 10 fingers, 3) reported having one sister, and 4) could play the "Star-Spangled Banner" on a ukulele with his toes. *We* know (but our extraterrestrial guests would not) that this sample of one human almost fully represents the population (of all people) on some characteristics (e.g., having two eyes), represents a fairly sizable portion on others (e.g., having one sister), and is almost unique in yet other characteristics, such as his musical ability.

Without this knowledge, our imaginary research team might mistakenly guess that all humans can play the ukulele with their toes (Johnson & Liebert, 1977, p.11).

Random Samples.   The procedure most likely to yield a sample that is representative of the population is *random sampling.* A **random sample** is one in which *1) every member of the population has an equal chance of being selected for the sample, and 2) the selection of any one member of the population does not influence the chance of any other member being selected.*

There are a number of different ways of obtaining a random sample. One way is to put the names or code numbers of all the members of a population into a hat, shake them up, and draw enough names for your sample without looking. This is the way Bingo numbers and winning lottery tickets are usually selected. Another way of accomplishing the same thing more efficiently is to use a random numbers table. A portion of one such table appears in Table 3-1.

The numbers in Table 3-1 were generated by a computer program that assures that each digit is as likely to appear as any other digit in a particular location. If you wished to select a sample of ten cases from a population of 600, you would enter the table at any arbitrary point you wished and read three-digit numbers until you found 10 numbers between 001 and 600.

For example, using Table 3-1, suppose we begin in the upper left hand corner and read down the first column. Our first three numbers would be: 528, 078, and 188. Note that 528 is the last three digits of the upper left-hand entry (39528), and that we skipped 616 and 767 entirely because they are larger than 600 (our hypothetical population size). This procedure, used in conjunction with a table such as this one (but typically a good deal longer), insures that the sample drawn is random. Mathematically it can be shown that the random number selection procedure will tend to yield samples that mirror the population on all relevant characteristics; it yields a **representative sample.**

TABLE 3-1   PORTION OF A RANDOM NUMBER TABLE

39528	72784	82474	25593	48545	35247
81616	18711	53342	44276	75122	11724
56078	16120	82641	22820	92904	13141
90767	04235	13574	17200	69902	63742
40188	28193	29593	88627	94972	11598
34414	82157	86887	55087	19152	00023
63439	75363	44989	16827	36024	00867
67049	09070	93399	45547	94458	74284
79495	04146	52162	90286	54158	34243
91704	30552	04737	21031	75051	93029
94015	46874	32444	48277	59820	96163
74108	88222	88570	74015	25704	91035
62880	87873	95160	59221	22304	90314
11748	12102	80580	41887	17710	59621
17944	05600	60478	03343	25852	58905

Note, however, that we said *tend to* rather than *will*, because the mathematical proof is very much dependent on a large sample. Small samples, even when drawn randomly, may fail to mirror the populations they are intended to represent. This is an important fact, and we will return to it later.

The Problem of Variability

We have placed a good deal of emphasis on proper sampling in psychological research. Why? Because members of a population—almost any population—will differ or vary among themselves on many important characteristics.

Variability is the degree to which scores in a set are dispersed or scattered versus tightly packed. For any particular characteristic, the variability within the population may be small or large. When the variability is large, large samples are required to assure that the sample is reasonably representative of the population.

The converse principle also holds. When the variability of some characteristic is small within a population, a relatively small sample will tend to reflect the population average reasonably well.

Imagine two bushel barrels of oranges. In the first barrel (low variability), the oranges are all about 3 inches in diameter; the biggest one is 3.1 inches, and the smallest is 2.8 inches. In the second barrel (high variability) the oranges range in diameter from 2 inches to 5 inches. If you blindly picked three oranges from the first barrel, your sample would represent the diameters of all the oranges in the bushel fairly well. But if you blindly picked three oranges from the second barrel, your sample would probably not be representative of the barrel. By chance, your first three oranges might all be larger (or smaller) than the average for the barrel.

SCALES, INSTRUMENTS, AND TESTS

We have spoken of observations so far as if they are somehow just "there." This is not quite true. In science, observation often requires the use of tools. So we must now turn to the tools of psychological research.

Scales of Measurement

Most of the events or characteristics of interest to research psychologists vary in magnitude. In some cases, we may be interested only in whether an event or characteristic was present or not. For example: Does Robbie have temper tantrums? But more often we are interested in being able to assess *magnitude*, not just presence or absence. For example, we might want to be able to characterize the *frequency* or *intensity* of Robbie's tantrums.

Typically, then, we want to *quantify* the variation in events and characteristics. We do so by developing rules for assigning numbers to represent the different magnitudes of the events or characteristics in which we are interested. Thus, in psychological research, observations are usually converted into **scores**.

For example, Robbie's temper tantrum score might be the number of tantrums he has in a week's time.

Once we move to the realm of numbers, we must ask whether the observations and scores (numbers we've assigned to them) actually correspond. The real number system, for example, includes both the concepts of magnitude and additivity: 40 + 40 = 80. Do the events or characteristics to which we have assigned numbers also have this property of additivity?

In some cases the answer is yes. Two 1-foot rulers have a combined length of 2 feet, and two 100-ohm resistors placed in series have a resistance of 200 ohms. But in psychological research, the events to which we assign numbers often do not possess all the properties of the real number system.

Suppose we arranged for someone to listen to a 1000-Hz tone of 40 decibels and rate, by assigning a number, the loudness he or she experiences. Now suppose that we simultaneously play *two* 40-decibel, 1000-Hz tones. Is the experienced loudness the sum of the two tones? No. Although experienced loudness increases somewhat, the increase is not nearly as large as would be predicted by the additivity of the real number system. How, then, do the scores used by psychologists relate to the real number system? According to Stevens (1968) the answer lies in the concept of **scales of measurement**, of which there are four kinds.

The simplest type of scale is called the **nominal scale**. Here the numbers are really only labels—for example, we may assign females the number 1 and males 2. The magnitude of the numbers has no real significance. We could as easily label the males 1 and the females 2.

The next type of scale, the **ordinal scale** allows the rank ordering of a set of events or characteristics. The dryness of champagnes, for example, can be rank ordered (from sweet to dry): *doux, demi-sec, dry, extra-dry,* and *brut.*

The numbers 1, 2, 3, 4, and 5 could be used to designate these five types of champagne—but so could any set of five numbers that preserve the ranking (for example, 3, 8, 22, 23, 38). There is no implication that a *demi-sec* (number 2) is twice as dry as a *doux* (number 1) or that an *extra-dry* (number 4) is twice as dry as a *demi-sec* (number 2). Indeed, a *doux* champagne typically contains about 10% sugar, a *demi-sec* 8%, a *dry* 4%, an *extra-dry* 3%, and a *brut* 1 1/2%. Thus, when working with an ordinal scale, most common mathematical operations (addition, multiplication) should *not* be performed, for they would produce misleading results.

With the **interval scale**, the researcher's numbers begin to match the real number system more closely. Equal differences in the magnitude of events are now associated with equal intervals between the numbers they have been assigned. However, *the interval scale still has no **true zero point**.* Fahrenheit temperature is an example of an interval scale. The difference between 30°F and 40°F is the same as that between 50°F and 60°F or 80°F and 90°F; nonetheless, 0°F does not represent the true zero point in temperature.[2] Temperatures often dip below 0°F in all but the tropical regions of the world.

---

[2] On the Kelvin temperature scale, a true zero point does exist (corresponding to −273.12° C), indicating the complete absence of heat.

Finally, with the **ratio scale** we have equal intervals *and* a meaningful zero point. The Fahrenheit scale does not have this property, and thus it is not meaningful to say such things as 40°F is twice as warm as 20°F. (In the Celsius system, these two temperatures would be 4.4°C and −6.7°C.)

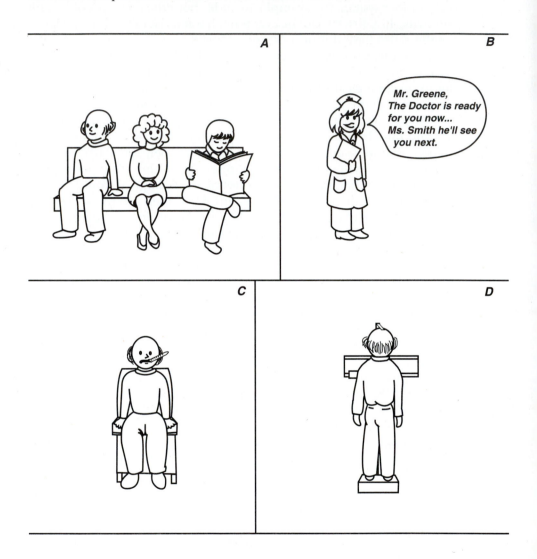

Cartoon 3-1 The four scales of measurement. In **A** the three patients waiting in the waiting room are only *named*, Mr. Greene, Ms. Smith, and Mr. Jones (*nominal scale*). In **B** the nurse announces the *order* in which the patients will be seen: first, second (and third). Thus, the patients are now ranked on an *ordinal scale*. In **C**, Mr. Greene has his temperature measured on a Farenheit thermometer (*interval scale*). And finally in **D**, Mr. Greene has his height and weight measured; both of these measurements are made on *ratio scales*.

When a true zero point exists, all ratios are meaningful; and we can properly speak of one measure as twice as much as another. Many scales of physical characteristics have a true zero point. For example, the length of a line or the weight of an object can be scaled with real numbers *so the "0" scores truly mean the absolute absence of the property being measured*; that is, a **true zero point**. Ten pounds of anything is twice as much as 5 pounds of the same substance, and 40 pounds of anything is 4 times as much as 10 pounds of it. This characteristic is what we have in mind when we speak of a **ratio scale**.

Being aware of the type of measurement scale being used is very important for a research psychologist. The type of scale has important implications for the way data are mathematically treated. Some statistical procedures are inappropriate for certain kinds of data. For example, two common procedures, the *t*-test and analysis of variance (ANOVA), may produce misleading results if they are applied to data that do not have *at least* interval properties.

The scores assigned to observations by a researcher must also reflect the phenomena of underlying theoretical interest. This requirement often limits the choice of a scale of measurement. Psychological constructs such as aggressiveness, intelligence, generosity, and stress, to name just a few, tend to refer to one's *relative* status, and cannot be readily conceptualized as having meaningful *absolute* zero points (at least, not in a living organism). Thus, measurement of complex behavioral phenomena is usually accomplished using interval, ordinal, or nominal scales.

The Role of "Instruments"

Look at Figure 3-1 below. Notice particularly the two horizontal line segments, labeled *P* and *Q* in the figure. Then decide which one of these statements best describes what you see.

a) *P* is shorter than *Q*
b) *Q* is shorter than *P*
c) *P* and *Q* are the same or very near the same length

Most people see *P* as shorter, and this is the answer given by about half of

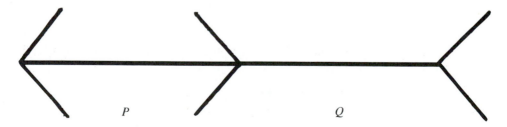

Figure 3-1

the college students to whom we have shown the figure. But not everyone reports what they see. The remaining students answer that *P* and *Q* are the same length. (Some of these confess that they think they've seen this illusion before.)

Now we are going to make a claim that may surprise you. *P* is actually *longer* than *Q*! Don't believe us? Suppose we use a ruler—*your* ruler—to see who's right. Go ahead and do the measurement now.

We have had a lot of fun with this figure, and we encourage you to show it to your friends and family. But it is being introduced to make a basic point: When people "just look with their eyes" and attempt to report what they see, there can be major differences—even contradictions—in their "raw" descriptions. Scientists are no less prone to this than anyone else.

In this case, we did come to agreement—by using the ruler. The ruler was used as our measuring instrument; with its aid we came to agree about line lengths. Not only that, we now have the feeling that we have found the "true" lengths of the line segments. A surprisingly large part of scientific training (in every area of science) involves learning how to use the tools of the trade. Fledgling scientists are immediately taught that their observations will be aided by certain instruments. Among the first things they learn is how to use the instruments, that is, how to "read" them (cf. Heelan, 1983).

So, too, in psychology. We almost invariably use instruments in our observational work. We use them to achieve agreement and accuracy, just as was done in the line segment example. But our instruments are more complicated than rulers. We use instruments not only to measure simple things like length, but also as tests, to measure various responses, characteristics, and attributes of people.

Tests and Test Scores

At the practical level, the purpose of using instruments is to scale or measure our observations in such a way that a number (or *score*) can be assigned to each observation. In a sense, then, each application of the instrument to our observations is a *test*, which yields a **test score**.

Whether using an instrument as simple as a ruler or as complex as the Scholastic Aptitude Test, we end up with a score (that is, a single number representing our observation). Thereafter it is the numbers, the scores, that we use to make further descriptions and to do statistical analyses.

DESCRIBING OBSERVATIONS QUANTITATIVELY

After observations have been made and scores assigned, we are left with a set of scores. The next step is to describe the set.

Central Tendency and Variability

Any set of observations can be characterized through the use of two descriptive statistics, one measuring central tendency and the other measuring variability.

Central Tendency.   By **central tendency** we mean *a number representing the most "typical" score in a set of scores.* Several different measures of central tendency are used in psychological research.

The **mean** is *the arithmetic average of the scores in the sample, obtained by summing the scores and dividing by the number of scores in the sample.* The mean is by far the most commonly used measure of central tendency, but it is not always the most appropriate.

The **mode** is *that score that occurs most frequently in a sample.*

The **median** is *that score above and below which 50 percent of the scores in the sample fall.*

The mode can be computed with any scale, including nominal; the median requires at least an ordinal scale; and the mean requires at least an interval scale to be meaningful.

Limitations of the Mean.   Most often the mean is used as the measure of central tendency in psychological research. The mean can be deceptive, however, even when a ratio scale is involved. This is especially true when the set of observations includes unusually extreme scores. Suppose we had the following set of eleven scores: 1, 2, 3, 4, 5, 6, 7, 7, 7, 11, 259. Although the mean of the set is 28.36, that number hardly reflects the typical score in the set. Here the mode (7) or the median (6) would be more representative.

Variability.   As mentioned earlier, the **variability** of a set of scores is *the typical degree of spread among the scores, or the degree to which they are scattered rather than tightly packed.* (Recall the example of the oranges.) In psychological research, the most commonly reported measures of variability are the *range* and the *variance* (or the square root of the variance, the *standard deviation*).

The **range** is simply *the difference between the largest and the smallest scores in a set, plus one.* The range alone is rarely an acceptable measure of variability because, like the mean, it is dramatically influenced by a single outlying score. For example, the range of the scores 3, 4, 1, 2, 1, 3, 1, 4, 40 is a whopping 40, hardly a good estimate of the typical variability, or scatter, among the nine scores in the set.

The **variance** is derived by measuring *the typical distance of the scores from the mean of the set in which they appear.* The variance is computed by subtracting each score from the mean to yield a so-called "deviation score," squaring each deviation score, summing these squares, and dividing by the number of scores in the set. The **standard deviation** of a set of scores is simply *the square root of the set's variance.*

"Variance Accounting".   Research psychologists will often speak of "accounting for the variance" in a set of scores. This is a difficult but important concept.

Imagine we picked a basket of peaches from a tree in the back yard and then weighed each one. Not all the weights will be the same; rather, the weights will vary. The concept "accounting for the variance" simply means identifying factors that explain why all the peach weights are not identical.

Typically, accounting for all the variance ("scatter") in a set of scores will involve several different factors. For example, one factor determining the weight of a peach is the amount of light it gets while growing; those receiving more light tend to grow larger. But if we somehow removed the effect of light differences, there would still be some variability left among the peaches.

A factor contributing to this remaining variability might be time on the tree. Although you picked the peaches at virtually the same time, not all of the peaches budded at exactly the same time. There might also be other factors, such as adequacy of the water supply to the limb feeding the peach, and so on. The point is that multiple factors may contribute to the variability in an obtained data set, and these factors can be examined separately.

There are statistical procedures to determine just how much variance is accounted for by each factor, as we will explain in Chapter 4. For the moment, however, you need to know that whenever there is variability in any set of scores, we use the variance statistic to 1) quantify the amount of variability and 2) measure the percentage of the total variability that is accounted for by each of the factors we think might cause variability in the first place.

RELIABILITY

The value of any scientific observation depends in part on its repeatability, or replicability. An observation that cannot be *replicated* is unreliable and should not be admitted as scientific evidence.

Reliability, as applied to psychological measurement, refers to *the degree to which a particular observation has yielded a replicable score*. A score is unreliable to the degree that it contains **random measurement error**, that is, *the extent to which it has been influenced by irrelevant or chance factors*.

Consider the following example. A student attending an introductory class in psychology knows that the class is scheduled to begin at 10:10 on Monday, Wednesday, and Friday mornings. A bell, controlled by a university-wide electronic clock system, signals the start of class. When it rings on Monday, the student looks at her watch, which reads 10:05.

The watch continues to run for the next two days but, when the bell rings on Wednesday, the student notices that her watch reads 10:20. Finally, on Friday, the watch reads 9:45 when the bell rings.

By this time the student has lost all confidence in her watch, despite the fact that it continues to run without stopping. She cannot trust, or *rely on*, the times given by the watch. Measured against the university clock and bell system (which she presumes is accurate) the watch does not provide stable information. The time reading changes *in an arbitrary or random fashion* against a criterion that remains constant. In sum, this watch, as an instrument to tell time, is *unreliable*.

An examination of two different methods for measuring a person's height provides a further illustration of these concepts. In a physician's office, height is

TABLE 3-2   HYPOTHETICAL DATA ILLUSTRATING THE RELATIONSHIP OF
SYSTEMATIC TO RANDOM VARIATION IN DETERMINING THE RELIABILITY OF A
MEASUREMENT PROCEDURE

Case I		Case II	
A	B	A	B
66.0	66.5	66.4	66.4
66.0	66.6	65.7	66.3
66.1	66.5	65.9	66.9
65.8	66.5	66.6	66.6
66.0	66.4	65.5	66.5

The difference *between* A and B is the systematic variation, whereas the differences among measurements *within* A or B is the random variation.

usually measured using a platform with an extendable precision ruler. The actual operations involve having the person stand barefoot straight up on the platform, while the ruler is extended until its height reaches the top of the person's head. If a person's height is measured on five occasions over the period of a week by five different individuals who all follow the same instructions, very likely the person's five height scores will be virtually identical. More important, if a second person's height were measured in the same way, and the second person were, in fact, .5 inch taller than the first, the measurements would probably allow us to discern this difference.

Now suppose that the heights of the same two people had each been measured five times by five different individuals *using a 6-inch plastic ruler instead of a physician's measuring platform.* In this second case, it is a good bet that the five height scores obtained for each person would be less consistent. This is because of the imprecision involved in using the plastic ruler. As a result, the systematic variation that actually exists in the height of two persons (one person is 1/2 inch taller than the other) may be masked by the random variation found in the less reliable method of measurement. Hypothetical data illustrating this point are shown in Table 3-2.

In this table, *Case I* measurements correspond with those taken in the doctor's office, and case II measurements were obtained by using a plastic ruler. The less precise procedure, *Case II*, yields random variation that masks the systematic variation (the true difference) in the heights of persons A and B. (In both cases the mean difference in height between A and B, the systematic variation, is equal.)

The need for determining the reliability of our measuring instruments and procedures is acute in psychological research. The great majority of people in North America will take some sort of personality, intelligence, or ability test in their lifetimes; many people's personal fates will depend on the outcome of these tests. Plainly, then, before using the information gathered from psychological tests to assign people to jobs, educational programs, or categories of any kind, we want to be sure that their scores provide a reliable index of what we wish to measure.

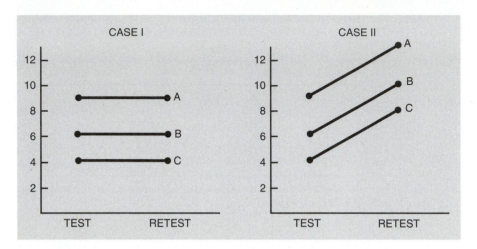

Figure 3-2 Hypothetical data for two possible sets of test-retest scores. In case I, persons A, B, and C each obtain the same score on the retest as on the original test. Yet because test-retest reliability measures only the degree to which a person's score is relatively (or positionally) stable across readministrations, the test-retest reliability is the same for case I and case II. In fact, in both cases the test-retest reliability would be "perfect."

So we need techniques that permit us to evaluate the degree to which a particular instrument, test, or evaluating procedure is free of measurement error. Several techniques for assessing reliability are available.

Retest Reliability

One way to evaluate the reliability of a test is to administer the test to a group of people on two separate occasions. Let us suppose that such a procedure is carried out. If an individual's relative position (to the other individuals who were tested) remained very nearly the same from test 1 to test 2, the instrument would be said to possess high **retest reliability**. What does this mean?

High retest reliability permits us to conclude *only* that the scores obtained with this instrument are *stable in their relative positions over time.* (Person A might remain high relative to person B, and low relative to person C, etc.)

However, a demonstration of high retest reliability *does not mean that a person's first and second test scores are interchangeable.* In fact, it is a serious error to view high retest reliability this way. High retest reliability implies *relative* stability but *not absolute* stability of test scores over administrations. In fact, a test in which scores always rise markedly from a first to a second administration may have perfect retest reliability, and thus not be discriminable on this measure from a test in which the scores are both relatively and absolutely stable. These points are illustrated in Figure 3-2.

Inter-item Reliability

A second measure of reliability, **inter-item reliability**, involves correlating scores on two subsets of items from a single test. This is often computed as **split-half reliability**. The items in the test are divided into halves, and the items in each half are correlated with those in the other. For example, individuals' scores on the first half of the items on a particular test can be correlated with scores on the second half of the items. Similarly, scores on the *even* items of a 30-item test can be correlated with scores on the *odd* items. Or we can go further and calculate the average of all possible split-half correlations. High inter-item reliability means that the items are *internally consistent.*

Inter-rater Reliability

Yet another form of reliability, **inter-rater reliability**, involves having the same individual rated or examined by two or more observers. The scores assigned to the individual by these observers are then compared. If the scores tend to be very similar, the investigator may conclude that the measurements obtained with the procedure are reasonably independent of who did the testing, examining, or measuring.

Item Sampling and Reliability

One of the most critical determinants of the reliability of any assessment procedure is the *number* of items that are taken from, or sampled from, the total population of items or events of interest. In an introductory history course, for example, it is likely that the students will be exposed to (or be asked to read) a very large number of facts during a term. The instructor must determine the degree to which the students have learned the assigned material. How can this be done?

Clearly, it will not be feasible to ask each and every possible question about all the material that has been covered during the semester. The full set of potential questions, not all of which can be asked, represents the **population** of items of interest in this instance. Since they all cannot be asked, the instructor must draw a **sample** from this population that will permit an inference about the degree to which the material has been learned. The question we must now answer is: How large shall that sample be?

To begin with the most extreme case, suppose the instructor gives a one item multiple-choice test. The single fact represented by this one question might be remembered by some students who were fortunate enough to have recalled this particular fact, even though they may have learned very little else from the course. At the same time, some otherwise good students might, by misfortune, *not* have been able to recall this particular fact, although they could recall an enormous number of *other* facts.

So, a one-item test is likely to be unreliable. Instructors should not feel confident that students who answer one item correctly would also have done well on a 200-item test. Knowing that Richmond Virginia was the original capital of the Confederacy does not necessarily indicate comprehensive knowledge of the

Civil War. Thus, although the entire population of potential items is clearly too large, a single-item test is too small. A compromise must be found.

In general it can be shown that a moderately large number of items will provide adequate reliability and that the addition of items thereafter will contribute little to reliability.

We have said that a one-item, multiple-choice test is unreliable. Such a test will not reliably predict performance on other sets of items drawn from the population of interest (all the materials presented in the course). It is likely, however, that performance on a one-item test would show high retest reliability. It would, in other words, serve as an excellent prediction of whether students who answered that particular question correctly once would be likely or unlikely to do so hours or days later (assuming none of the students had an opportunity to look up the answer).

Up to this point, we have been discussing reliability. There is another, equally important criterion by which psychological tests are judged, and that is their *validity*.

VALIDITY

Research psychologists are rarely interested merely in the observations and scores derived from their test procedures. Instead, they are interested in what the test scores presumably reflect. For example, most IQ tests require examinees to do such things as solve puzzles, dilemmas, or riddles put to them by the examiner, but obtaining a measure of puzzle-solving ability per se is not the aim of these tests. Rather, they are designed to measure an abstract, hypothetical characteristic of the examinee, namely, intelligence. This goal may or may not actually be accomplished by an IQ test.

Broadly speaking, two types of validity are discussed by research psychologists. One type has to do with the *validity of measuring instruments* and the other type has to do with the *validity of inferences* (for example, causal inferences) that the investigator draws from his or her research findings. Our discussion here is limited to the validity of tests and measurements. We will consider the problem of valid inference in detail in Chapter 6.

*A test enjoys **validity** to the degree that it measures what it purports to measure* (or what the investigator believes it to measure). All measures of validity involve determining the relationship between test scores and other independent observations about the subject's behavior. Three types of validity are recognized in psychological research: content validity, criterion validity, and construct validity. Here we will discuss content and criterion validity. We will take up the more complex idea of construct validity in Chapter 6.

Content Validity

Content validity is *the property of containing items directly sampled from the domain of interest.* A college examination possesses content validity to the extent that it samples fairly from reading assignments and lectures given during the course for which it is designed as an evaluation. In the same way, a behavioral test of depression possesses content validity to the degree that it actually samples the symptoms of depression (e.g., dysphoria, appetite disturbance, hopelessness).

Many tests could not substantiate their worth on the grounds of content validity alone. For example, IQ tests rely heavily on demonstrations of their criterion validity.

Criterion Validity

Criterion validity is *the degree to which test scores predict an individual's behavior in other situations involving the characteristic of interest.* Academic achievement is often used as a criterion (an external measure) for validating IQ tests. IQ tests should be predictors of how well people will do in school, because school performance is assumed to be heavily dependent on intelligence. Thus, school performance is a measure of criterion validity for IQ tests.

MAKING COMPARISONS

Once we have observed and described two or more samples, we are in a position to take the further step of making comparisons. Comparisons play a central role in psychological research.

Comparisons are made by use of **statistical tests**, which tell us the likelihood that a particular association or difference would have occurred by chance, that is, if there were no actual relationship for the populations involved. Comparisons can be made either "within-subjects" or "between-subjects."

Within- Versus Between-Subjects Comparisons

Within-subjects comparisons are those in which the comparison is made between *Y* scores obtained before some treatment or event (*X*) has occurred, and *Y* scores obtained for the *same subjects* after *X* has occurred. For example, an investigator might try to determine whether rewarding children for doing their homework improves homework performance. The investigator might compare the homework of a group of children before they were given reward for homework with the efforts of the same children after a reward-for-homework policy had been instituted. The comparison is made *within* the performance record of each subject (before vs. after); hence the term, "within-subjects comparison."

Between-subjects comparisons are those in which the comparison made is *between the Y scores of two separate groups* that differ in whether or not they have experienced X. For example, a research psychologist might try to determine whether rewarding children for doing their homework improves homework performance by comparing children who do and who do not receive reward for their homework efforts. The comparison is called "between-subjects" because it is made *between* the scores of one group of subjects and the scores of another distinct group.

Age-Related Comparisons

People change throughout their lives. There are age-related changes in cognitive abilities, motor skills, and most aspects of social behavior. Some of these changes (often called **developmental trends**) result from maturational processes within the body, while some result from learning and experience. (Most age-related changes of interest to research psychologists involve both maturational and experiential factors.)

The search for developmental trends can be made using either between- or within-subjects comparisons. Between-subjects age comparisons are referred to as **cross-sectional studies**; within-subjects age comparisons are called **longitudinal studies**.

Suppose, for example, that a team of developmental psychologists is interested in charting vocabulary growth during the preschool years. They might identify a sample of 2-year-olds, give each child a vocabulary test, wait a year, test each child's vocabulary again, wait another year, and then measure each child's vocabulary for the third time. This would be a longitudinal study, and the age comparisons would be made within-subjects. The study will yield mean vocabulary for the sample at ages 2, 3, and 4. Actual change will be measured directly. The study will also take 2 years to complete!

The alternative would be to test separate samples of 2-, 3-, and 4-year-olds at about the same time. This would be a cross-sectional study, and the age comparisons would be made between-subjects. By making cross-sectional comparisons, we save 2 years. Using between-subjects comparisons to infer developmental changes has a drawback, however. Namely, *the comparison groups must be identical on every dimension except age.* (See Box 3.1.)

BOX 3.1   *DEMONSTRATING DEVELOPMENTAL TRENDS*

Developmental trends are particularly difficult to study effectively because of the inherent problems of both longitudinal and cross-sectional comparisons.

In cross-sectional comparisons, *individuals of different ages are observed at the same calendar time.* For example, a study of age-related changes in vocabulary could sample 3, 7, 11, 15, and 19-year-olds and assess each group on a test of word knowledge. The average score of each group could be compared in a between-subjects fashion. At first it appears that the cross-sectional strategy has a clear economic benefit. A 16-year span of development (ages 3 to 19) has apparently been assessed with an outlay of only several weeks (rather than years) of work. But there is a rub. *The subjects in a cross-sectional study may differ on variables other than age.*

Let us examine our vocabulary example more closely. Suppose our observations revealed that the average vocabularies of each of the groups was as follows: 3-year-olds: 180 words; 7-year-olds: 2500 words; 11-year-olds: 10,000 words; 15-year-olds: 15,000 words; and 19-year-olds: 15,000 words. (The numbers are hypothetical and do not reflect the actual vocabularies of people of different ages.) From these data we might conclude that there is no vocabulary growth between ages 15 and 19.

But we must remember that we have assessed different people in each of these groups. The 15-year-olds whose mean score was 15,000 words in our study might show further growth in vocabulary over the next four years. At age 19 they might have much larger vocabularies than our present 19-year-old sample. Likewise, there is no reason to assume that our current sample of 19-year-olds didn't know fewer words at 15 than they know now. In either case, our inference that there is no change in vocabulary between age 15 and age 19 might be invalid.

Technically, the age groups in a between-subjects (or cross-sectional) comparison are referred to as **cohorts. Cohort differences** *always constitute a threat to the inference that an observed difference among groups reflects a true developmental trend.* For example, in our vocabulary study, the 15-year-old and 19-year-old cohorts may have differed in their educational backgrounds because of changes in public educational policy. (Perhaps vocabulary is emphasized more now than it used to be.)

A **longitudinal study** *involves within-subjects comparisons of measures taken repeatedly over time.* A longitudinal study of vocabulary development might start with a sample of 3-year-olds and periodically reassess them. Using the within-subjects longitudinal approach, we can measure developmental changes directly. Unfortunately, adequate longitudinal comparisons may be difficult to obtain.

Longitudinal comparisons are time-consuming and expensive. Furthermore, there is the risk of losing participants as the years pass. People may relocate or become unwilling to continue their participation. In both these cases the researcher may, at the end of the study, be left with a **biased sample**. Nonetheless, longitudinal data are indispensable for studying age-related changes and developmental processes.

Longitudinal data may be gathered either *retrospectively* or *prospectively*. **Retrospective accounts** involve asking subjects to "look back" and recall what was said or done at various earlier times. **Prospective accounts**, on the other hand, follow subjects forward in time, so that each important event or circumstance can be noted and recorded as it occurs.

Obviously, retrospective accounts are considerably less expensive to obtain than prospective accounts because they do not require a substantial time commitment. Unfortunately, however, retrospective accounts have been shown to be easily biased. Respondents often claim to have high confidence in what has turned out (from access to hard data such as archival records) to be quite wrong. *Thus, in general, retrospective data have dubious value and are no substitute for the more demanding but much more credible prospective approach.*

FOR REVIEW AND DISCUSSION

Key Terms
CASE STUDIES
VERIFICATION
FALSIFICATION
CLINICAL TRIAL
REPRESENTATIVENESS
POPULATION
RULES OF MEMBERSHIP

SAMPLE
REPRESENTATIVE SAMPLE
BIASED SAMPLE
RANDOM SAMPLE
SCALES OF MEASUREMENT
NOMINAL SCALE
ORDINAL SCALE
INTERVAL SCALE
TRUE ZERO POINT
RATIO SCALE
CENTRAL TENDENCY
MEAN
MODE
MEDIAN
VARIABILITY
RANGE
VARIANCE
STANDARD DEVIATION
TEST SCORE
RELIABILITY
RANDOM MEASUREMENT ERROR
RETEST RELIABILITY
SPLIT-HALF RELIABILITY
INTER-ITEM RELIABILITY
INTER-RATER RELIABILITY
VALIDITY
CONTENT VALIDITY
CRITERION VALIDITY
EMPIRICISM
NATURALISTIC OBSERVATION
PECKING ORDERS
CONTROL GROUP
INFERENCES
SCORES
STATISTICAL TESTS
WITHIN-SUBJECTS COMPARISONS
BETWEEN-SUBJECTS COMPARISONS
DEVELOPMENTAL TRENDS
CROSS-SECTIONAL STUDIES
LONGITUDINAL STUDIES
COHORTS
COHORT DIFFERENCES
RETROSPECTIVE ACCOUNTS
PROSPECTIVE ACCOUNTS

Discussion Issues

1. Of what value is the case study approach to theory testing?
2. What factors would you consider before making inferences about the population on the basis of a case study?
3. On one Friday morning, every fifth person who entered a certain grocery store in the suburbs was asked to take part in a poll assessing political candidates. Would you say that the result from this sample could be generalized to the relevant population? What is the relevant population?
4. Under what circumstances will the median, mode, and mean of a set of scores all tend to have the same value?
5. Under what circumstances would you expect retest reliability to be low even though interitem and interrater reliability are both high?
6. What is meant by the term scales of measurement? Explain the different properties of nominal, ordinal, interval, and ratio scales.
7. Explain the concept of variance.
8. In what ways do between- and within-subjects comparisons differ?
9. Explain the difference between a retrospective and a prospective account of changes over time.

ASSOCIATION, CORRELATION, AND REGRESSION

In the previous chapter, we explained how observations are described and converted into *scores*. Once we have sets of scores for two or more variables, we can begin to examine our data for connecting relationships or **associations.**

ASSOCIATION

It was by noticing the *association* between heat and motion that Francis Bacon made his way to the conclusion that heat *is* a form of motion (see Chapter 1). Likewise, Ivan Pavlov discovered the classical conditioning process by *noticing the association* between his dogs' increased salivation and the approach of their caretaker.

In our everyday lives, we often notice that two events are related or associated; when one is present, so is the other. Sometimes the relationship is an *invariant* one, as when we perceive that ice forms (one event) only on days when the temperature is below 32°F (the other event). Other times, though, the association is *variable*; it tends to rain on some, but not all, cloudy days. Here clouds and rain are associated, but the degree or strength of association is less than that between ice formation and temperature.

This chapter is about the ways in which associations are evaluated by research psychologists, beginning with simple correlations.

CORRELATION

Correlation, as the term suggests, refers to the co- or joint relationship between two variables. Correlations provide answers to such questions as, Do variable X and variable Y go together or *vary* together? In other words, are the two variables associated?

To see how we might use the concept of correlation in research, let's examine a concrete example. Imagine that a college professor typically gives 100 item True/False exams. Students may have up to one full hour to complete the exams; but almost no one stays that long. Exactly *how long* it takes to complete an exam varies greatly from student to student. A few students always hand in their answers within 25 minutes, and the average is just over 40 minutes. But there is always someone out there, sitting alone at the end, who takes the entire 60 minutes.

The professor began to wonder if there was an association between one variable, "time spent on exam," and another variable, "grade on exam." So, as each student turned in her/his exam, she wrote the number of minutes that had elapsed since the exam began. Once she had these data, the professor was in a position to examine the association between obtained grade and time spent on exam. Next she wished to determine the nature of the association between these two variables. We have constructed some hypothetical data, to illustrate how this is done.

Table 4-1 shows the hypothetical outcome of the study, in which 20 students took one of these 100-item exams. The students are "named" A through T. The "grade" is the student's grade on the exam (in percent correct), and "time" is the elapsed time recorded on each exam as it was handed in. The table also shows the

TABLE 4-1   HYPOTHETICAL OUTCOME OF A STUDY
CORRELATING "GRADE ON EXAM" AND "TIME ON EXAM"

Student	Grade on exam	Time on exam
A	88	60
B	96	53
C	72	22
D	78	44
E	65	34
F	80	47
G	77	38
H	83	50
I	79	51
J	68	35
K	84	46
L	76	36
M	92	48
N	80	43
O	67	40
P	78	32
Q	74	27
R	73	41
S	88	39
T	90	43
Mean	79.40	41.45
Range	65–96	22–60
Standard Deviation	8.48	9.09

basic descriptive statistics (mean, range, and standard deviation) for each variable. (Recall that we discussed the meaning and use of these statistics in Chapter 3.)

What, though, of the question of an *association* between the variables. Here the first step is to make a diagram of the relationship. This diagram is called a **scatter plot** (or *scatter diagram*). Scatter plots are made by creating a chart in which the range of one variable is displayed on the *x*-axis, and the range of the other variable is displayed on the *y*-axis. Then a point or other small mark is put in the graph to correspond to each subject's pair of scores.

For example, to plot student A's point on the graph (see Table 4-1), we find the intersect of 88 (his exam grade) and 60 (the number of minutes he took on the exam). For student B, we find the intersect of 96 and 53, and so on. When the process is completed, we have produced the scatter plot shown in Figure 4-1.

Note from the figure that the dots form a rough but detectable pattern. Grades are generally higher for those who take longer on the exam. If we tried to "fit" a straight line to the dots, it would extend from lower left to upper right of the diagram.

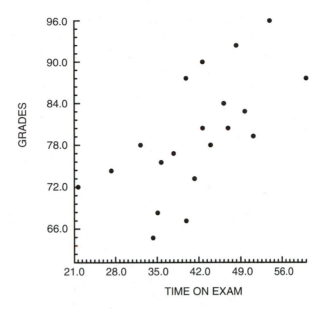

Figure 4-1   Scatter plots depicting a relationship between time on exam and grade from hypothetical study.

The scatter plot yields a picture of the relationship, which is graphic but difficult to describe quantitatively. So the next step is to express the relationship with a number, a *statistic*, to represent the particular relationship more precisely. We have such a statistic available. It is called the **correlation coefficient**.

The Correlation Coefficient

In the late 19th century, the great statistician Karl Pearson (1857–1936) devised a means of indexing the relationship between two variables. Referred to as the *Pearson product moment correlation coefficient*, it is often abbreviated *r*.[1]

r may take values between −1.00 and +1.00. Both the *magnitude* (size) and the *direction* (positive or negative) of a relationship are reflected in the correlation coefficient. The higher the *absolute value* of *r*, the larger or stronger is the relationship between the two variables. An *r* of either +1.00 or −1.00 designates a perfect linear relationship between two variables, whereas an *r* of .00 indicates that the variables are *un*related.

When we have a correlation of either +1.00 or −1.00 between two variables, we are able to predict one variable from the other perfectly. In contrast, with an *r* of .00, we can infer nothing about the value of one variable based on the observed value of the other. The variables are *not* associated.

---

[1]There are several correlation coefficients, of which *r* is only one. Our comments on correlation coefficients apply to the others as well. *r* is only meaningful when the underlying relationship between the variables is *linear*, that is, can be represented by a straight line. (Curvilinear relationships are discussed later in this chapter.)

Intermediate values of r (either plus or minus) indicate that the variables are associated to some extent. Because the relationship is less than perfect, attempts to predict one variable from the other will result in some degree of error. An example of such an intermediate correlation is the association between height and weight. In general, the taller people are, the more they weigh. But this relationship is not perfect. Some people are underweight and others overweight for their height. Thus, the relationship of height to weight *varies* from case to case. Whereas one person may be quite tall and quite heavy, it is not difficult to find another who is equally heavy, but of only average height.

If the sign of r is positive, the two variables are said to be *positively (or directly) related*. As scores on variable X increase, scores on variable Y also increase. Income, for example, is positively related to the purchase of luxury items. The more money people have, the more likely they are to indulge in luxuries. If the sign of r is negative, the variables are said to be *negatively (or inversely) related*: High scores on one variable are related to (or go with) low scores on the other. The frequency of schizophrenia, for example, is inversely related to socioeconomic status (SES). Higher SES is associated with lower incidence of schizophrenia.

Figure 4-2 presents diagrams of several of the possible forms of relationships. Note that in the figure each entry point corresponds to the two scores of a given subject (that is, the intersect of their score for variable X and their score for variable Y). In the case of perfect relationships (positive or negative, that is, $+1.00$ or -1.00), all the points fall on a single straight line. For these subjects, if we knew an individual's score on only one of the variables (and it would not matter which one), we could determine with certainty the score that he or she had on the other.

When there exists a perfect correlational relationship, regardless of direction, the corresponding graphic representation shows no "scatter" and forms a straight line.

Likewise, as Figure 4-2 shows, in the case of relatively large correlations, there is only a small degree of scatter about the line of perfect correlation. As the correlations become lower, the scores tend to scatter and become more dispersed. Finally, when the correlation equals .00, there is so much scatter that the scores tend to form a circular pattern.

With the technical information above in mind, we can go back to our earlier example and ask: What was the r between "grade on exam" and "time spent on exam?" For the data in the example, the answer is, $r = +.64$. The "+" tells us the relationship is positive, and the ".64" tells us that it was moderately high. But we are still left with the question "What does 'moderately high' mean?" It is here that the concept of **shared variance** enters the picture.

Shared Variance.   Just how strong is a correlation of $+.64$? Exactly how much stronger is an r of .60 than an r of .30? Questions like these come up often when dealing with correlational data.

The first point to note is that because of their mathematical derivation, r values form only an ordinal scale (see p. 45). Thus the r's of .10, .20, .30, and .40 do

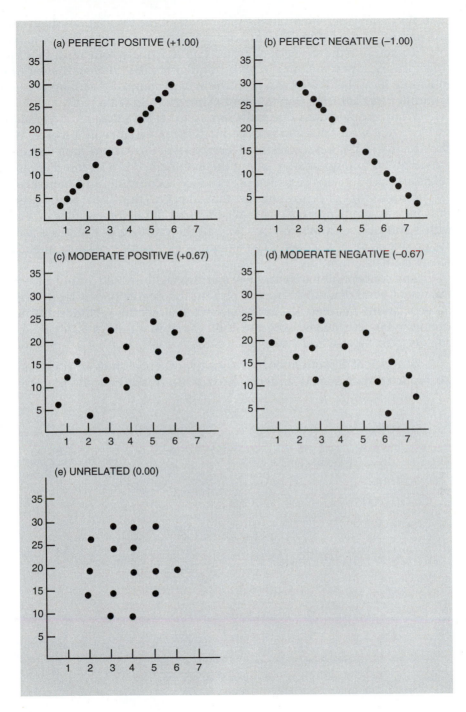

Figure 4-2 Scatter diagrams showing various degrees of relationships.

not reflect equal increments in the magnitude of the associations they represent, and an *r* of .80 does *not* represent twice the degree of relationship as an *r* of .40.

To describe the strength of a correlation properly, one must first square *r*, thus forming a new measure, r^2. r^2 is frequently called the **coefficient of determination**; it can be treated as a proportion, and compared with other r^2's. (This is another way of saying that values of r^2 form a **ratio scale**.)

What, though, does r^2 actually represent? It is a measure of the amount of variance in *Y* scores that can be accounted for by variance in *X* scores. When all the variance in *Y* scores is accounted for by variance in *X*, there is no unaccounted-for variability and no "scatter" about the line formed in a scatter diagram of the relationship. (See the discussion of "variance accounting" in Chapter 3.)

Another way of expressing the same idea is to think of r^2 as the proportion of *shared variance* between *X* and *Y*. When $r^2 = +1.00$, all the variance in *X* is shared with *Y* and vice versa. When $r^2 = +.50$, half the variance in *Y* scores is accounted for or shared with *X* scores. The remaining half of the variance in each set of scores is unaccounted for by the other.

The concept of shared variance can also be illustrated graphically, through the use of Venn diagrams. These represent the degree of overlap (the strength of association) between *X* and *Y*. Figure 4-3 shows the relationships that exist when *r* = .00, .20, .40, .60, .80, and 1.00. (Note that the corresponding r^2's are .00, .04, .16, .36, .64, and 1.00.)

Statistical Significance.   In our hypothetical study of grades and time, we reported data for 20 students. In fact, there are typically more than 100

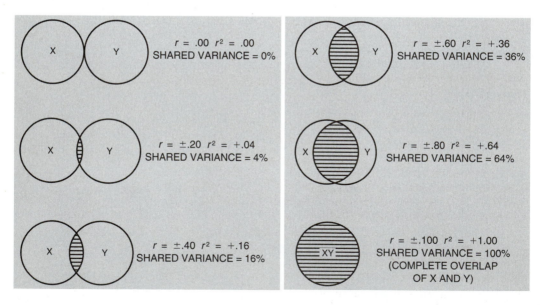

Figure 4-3   Correlation as shared variance.

students in undergraduate classes where we teach. Suppose the 20 in the study had been selected randomly from a class of 100. Now we can look at our study as one that has a **sample** (of 20 students), from which we want to draw an inference about the larger **population** of 100 students. (Recall that we encountered the issue of generalizing from samples to populations in Chapter 3.)

After obtaining a particular correlational relationship in a sample, we want to determine whether the relationship also holds in the population. Based on a sample r of +.64, we wish to determine whether a relationship exists between "time spent on exam" and "grade on exam" in the population of 100 students. Put another way, how likely are we to get a sample r of +.64 when no relationship exists in the population?

Statistical significance is a concept applied to evaluate this question. (Recall that we mentioned statistical tests in Chapter 3.) *A statistically significant result is one that has a low probability of occurring by chance alone.* Traditionally in psychological research, a result is considered statistically significant if the likelihood of obtaining a given outcome by chance alone is 5 in 100 or less. This level of significance is called the .05 level (commonly written "p < .05" and understood to mean "probability less than 5%").

Two factors influence the significance level of a sample r: the magnitude of r and the size of the sample employed.

The larger the value of r, the more likely it is to be statistically significant. For example, with a sample of 20 cases, an r of .40 or above will be significant at $p < .05$, whereas an r of .35 will not. (So, our obtained r of .64 with a sample size of 20 was significant at $p < .05$.)

With larger sample sizes, smaller correlation coefficients will achieve statistical significance. For example, with a sample of 100 cases, an r of only .20 is required to achieve significance at $p < .05$. Thus, *with a larger sample the test for statistical significance is more powerful, in the sense that smaller values of r will achieve statistical significance.* (The idea that research designs can differ in their power, or ability to detect relationships that are "really there," will come up again and again in later chapters.) Table 4-2 shows the relationship between sample size and statistical significance with 10, 20, 30, 40, and 100 cases.

With very large sample sizes, we encounter the problem that very small r's, although statistically significant, may have little *practical* importance. For example, a correlation of .19 between age at high school graduation and later performance in college will be statistically significant if the sample consisted of 200 cases. But such a small relationship would not be of much practical use for selecting successful students, because the magnitude of the relationship reflected by $r = .19$ is trivial, accounting for less than 4% of the overall variance (see Figure 4-3).

The important point to be noted is that *the size or magnitude of a relationship and the question of whether the relationship is statistically significant are independent features of any set of sample data.* This is true not only of studies involving classificatory variables (e.g., correlations) but also of statistical tests associated with manipulated variables (e.g., experiments), that will be discussed in later chapters.

TABLE 4-2   A PORTION OF A TABLE FOR
DETERMINING THE SIGNIFICANCE OF r

Number of cases*	Required r**	
	$p < .05$	$p < .01$
10	.53	.66
20	.40	.51
30	.35	.45
40	.30	.40
100	.20	.25

*Most tables use degrees of freedom (df) rather
than number of cases to index sample size. You
can convert from df to number of cases as follows:

$$df = \text{number of cases} - 2$$

**This is a so-called "two-tailed" test, inasmuch as
we did not specify the direction of the relationship
(positive or negative) in advance.

In sum, **statistical significance** *indicates the likelihood of error when inferring relationships in the population from sample statistics.* Obviously, though, inferences drawn from biased or nonrepresentative samples cannot be trusted regardless of the outcome of statistical tests. (See Chapter 3.)

For an accurate estimate of a population correlation, the sample must reflect as closely as possible the full range of scores that are found in the target population. This is another aspect of the concept of **representative samples**, which was introduced in Chapter 3. If an inadequate sample is used, we will be left with a restricted or **truncated range** of scores. Correlations based on a truncated range may be artificially depressed relative to the true correlation in the population. This point can be understood through a simple example using scatter plots.

Suppose we are interested in the relationship between the number of children in a classroom and the degree to which they engage in disruptive behavior. If the entire population of possibilities were represented, we might obtain a distribution or scatter plot between the scores (reflecting amount of disruptive behavior and number of children in the class) that would look something like the diagram presented in Figure 4-4a.

The relationship in Figure 4-4a is strong and positive, with a correlation coefficient of +.67. Now consider the restricted range of scores in the boxed area of Figure 4-4a. In Figure 4-4b, without changing any of the scores, the boxed area has been blown up to represent a scatter plot of its own.

In contrast to the strong positive relationship seen in Figure 4-4a, the data represented in Figure 4-4b depict a weak relationship. This appearance is confirmed by the obtained correlation for these data, which yields an r of only +.25. Likewise, you can demonstrate for yourself that by selecting a similarly restricted

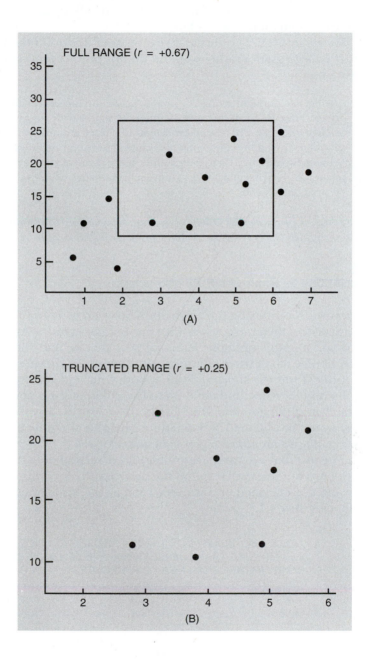

Figure 4-4   The magnitude of relationships can vary as a function of the range of scores employed. In this case, the truncated range lowers the obtained correlation.

sample from the low range of scores, or even a restricted sample from the middle range of scores, the obtained correlation will again be much less than exists in the population as a whole.

Weizmann (1971) offers as an example of this point the fact that IQ scores predict college grades rather well but do not predict graduate school grades at all. He observes:

> Intelligence quotient scores . . . predict academic success relatively well overall. They do not, however, predict success in graduate school with any great degree of accuracy, because graduate school applicants tend to cluster around the high end of the IQ distribution. Thus, although an obtained correlation accurately describes the relationships between two variables for a given sample, if the range of sample scores is truncated, that relationship will not generalize to more representative samples containing a wider range of variation (p. 589).

Thus, *a fundamental rule for selecting samples for correlational research is to represent adequately the true range of scores in the population of interest.*

Correlations as Rank-Order Relationships

The statistic for indexing the correlation between two variables primarily reflects the similarity of their rank orders. (See the discussion of retest reliability in Chapter 3). To take a simple example, let us suppose that we had obtained two measures of height on each of three children, with the results shown in Table 4-3.

Child 1 was the shortest child at both four and eight years of age: child 2 had the middle score; and child 3 was the tallest at each point in time. Because the *rank order* remains the same for both measures, a perfect correlation ($r = +1.00$) would be obtained between time 1 heights and time 2 heights, *even though the scores at age 8 are always higher than those at age 4.*

The fact that two variables are highly correlated does not necessarily mean that the two variables will respond the same way to environmental changes. This fact is often overlooked or misunderstood in the study of hereditary influences on IQ. (See Box 4.1.)

TABLE 4-3   HEIGHTS OF THREE CHILDREN AT AGES 4 AND 8 ILLUSTRATING THAT CORRELATIONS ARE SENSITIVE TO RANKS RATHER THAN MEAN DIFFERENCES

Child	Height at 4 (in inches)	Height at 8 (in inches)
1	37	48
2	40	51
3	42	53

BOX 4.1   *WHAT IQ HERITABILITY DOES NOT IMPLY*

Most studies of the inheritance of IQ have used a correlational approach to determine the degree to which the intelligence scores of identical or monozygotic (MZ) twins, or parents and their children, go together. Correlational evidence suggesting that heredity contributes to IQ has been supplied by several major studies involving identical twins who were separated early in life and reared in different homes. There is also a substantial correlation between the IQs of parents and their children, typically about .50. Correlations between adopted children's IQ scores and those of their adoptive parents are a good deal lower, ranging between 0 and .20 (Kail & Wicks-Nelson, 1993).

Because the effect of heredity seems so powerful, these data may suggest that IQ is fixed by heredity and cannot be increased by training programs or other environmental influences. Such an impression is erroneous! Whether IQ can be raised is simply a different question from whether IQ is heritable.

To illustrate this point concretely, consider the data in Table 4-4. On the left side of the table (column I), hypothetical data from seven identical male twin pairs are shown, along with the correlation coefficient (r) and the mean, or average, score. Note that r is quite high, that the overall means of the pairs of twins are quite similar, and that each twin has nearly the same IQ as his mate.

Let us assume that only one member of each pair is now given a special and intensive training program for increasing intellectual ability. If the program succeeded in raising IQ (and the IQ scores of the control twins remained unchanged), a comparison might reveal data like those shown in the right side of Table 4-4 (column II). Now the overall column means are quite different, and

TABLE 4-4   HYPOTHETICAL IQ SCORES OF A SET OF MZ TWIN BOYS BEFORE AND AFTER A SPECIAL TRAINING PROGRAM: AN ILLUSTRATION OF THE DIFFERENCE BETWEEN MEANS AND CORRELATIONS

			II (after)	
I (before)			[training]	[no training]
Twin A	Twin B		Twin A	Twin B
80	82		90	82
103	100		112	100
94	94		107	94
105	109		115	109
97	95		108	95
121	116		140	116
68	77		85	77
95.4	96.1	Means	108.0	96.1
$r = .98$		Correlations		$r = .96$

most twin pairs are not very similar in their scores. The environmental intervention has worked, and the group means reflect this effect.

But what about the correlation between twins *after* the environmental manipulation? In this example, it has remained virtually unchanged and still shows
an impressively high relationship. This is because the scores of the twins in each
pair still "go together" in the sense that if twin A in column II has a relatively high
score (compared to the other individuals in column II-A), his twin will have a relatively high score compared with the other individuals *in column II-B*. It is precisely this *ranking* that is tapped by the correlational approach, and *not necessarily*
the similarity between parent and child or twin and twin per se. To ask whether
the environmental intervention was effective, we must inspect group means rather
than correlations.

Curvilinear Relationships

Thus far we have focused on correlation as a measure of the degree of *linear* relationship between two variables. In such cases, a perfect relationship is indicated
when all the points of a scatter plot fall on a single straight line. For **curvilinear
relationships**, special correlational statistics sensitive to them must be employed.

As an example of a curvilinear relationship, consider the correlation between efficiency of performance and an individual's level of physiological arousal.
Many psychologists believe that performance will be best at moderate levels of
physiological arousal and that performance will be poorer when arousal levels
are either too high or too low. This hypothetical relationship, depicted in Figure
4-5, can be described as an *inverted U*.

If the usual correlational procedures (for example, Pearson's *r*) are applied
to these data, the obtained correlation coefficient will be extremely low. This is
because the existing relationship between the two variables in question is *not* linear, rather than because it is weak. The possibility of curvilinear relationships is
another important reason for inspecting scatter diagrams. In doing so, the researcher can determine whether special correlational procedures are required to
index the observed relationship accurately.

CORRELATION MATRICES

Often, a psychologist will want to examine more than two or three variables.
Suppose that we were interested in assessing the social adjustment of elementary
school children from the perspective of their peers. We might begin by constructing a large number of descriptive statements: "Is well liked," "Doesn't pay
attention to the teacher," "Is easily upset," and so on. After some pretesting, we
would construct a final version of an assessment instrument and then administer it to a large group of school children. The resulting data are often depicted
in a **correlation matrix**, in which the rows and columns list the variables, and the
entries provide the correlations between each possible pair of variables.

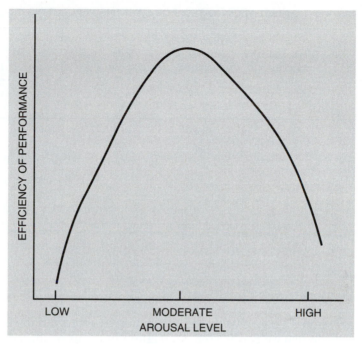

Figure 4-5 Hypothesized relationship between performance efficiency and level of arousal, illustrating a curvilinear relationship.

One purpose of generating a correlation matrix is to see how the variables relate to one another. Do the variables fall into groups or clusters? Let us first consider a simple case of a six-item assessment of classroom behavior.

A hypothetical correlation matrix is presented in Table 4-5. The items clearly form two clusters. Items 1, 2, and 3 are positively related to one another, but are either negatively (inversely) or minimally related to items 4, 5, and 6. Similarly, items 4, 5, and 6 are positively related to one another. From evidence such as this, an investigator could conclude that the six items seem to tap two dimensions of classroom behavior. The first dimension, reflected by items 1, 2, and 3, might be given a label such as "aggressive-disruptiveness." The second dimension, composed of items 4, 5, and 6, might be called "competence-popularity." The data suggest that these are two important dimensions of classroom behavior.

In actual research practice, many more than six variables would typically be included in a study of classroom behavior of this type. Instead of a six-variable correlation matrix, a researcher is often confronted with one based on 30, 40, 50, or more variables. When a correlation matrix reaches this size, it is no longer possible to comprehend it by visual inspection alone. However, a number of statistical techniques are available to systematically explore the interrelationships among a large set of variables. (A detailed discussion of this topic is beyond the scope of this book.)

TABLE 4-5   CORRELATION MATRIX FOR SIX ITEMS REFLECTING CLASSROOM BEHAVIOR

Item	Is mean and cruel to other children 1	Disturbs others when they are trying to work 2	Is disrespectful to the teacher 3	Is well liked 4	Does good work 5	Helps others 6
1	1.00	0.62	0.75	−0.40	0.06	−0.32
2		1.00	0.71	−0.19	0.14	−0.41
3			1.00	−0.11	−0.02	−0.14
4				1.00	0.63	0.79
5					1.00	0.63
6						1.00

REGRESSION

Regression is a way of using the association between variables as a method of prediction. When we considered correlation in terms of shared variance, it did not matter whether we began with X or Y. The correlation coefficient is a symmetrical measure of the relationship between two variables. In regression, however, one variable is specified as the **predictor variable** and the other as the **criterion variable** (the variable to be predicted).

Regression analysis begins with data just like those in the correlational examples used earlier. Suppose we have a sample of subjects and have collected two measures on each (for example, frequency of class attendance and grades). Using regression, our aim might be to predict grades from classroom attendance.

Imagine, first of all, that we simply tried to guess a student's grades. If we had no other information but the distribution of grades in the student's class, our best guess would be that the student's grades fall at the mean of that distribution.

Now suppose that we tried to improve our prediction by using information about classroom attendance as a predictor. To simplify, let us assume there are only six students in the class. Their scores on each of the two variables are shown in Table 4-6. In this classroom, attendance does *not* enhance our prediction. There is no relationship between attendance and grades. The average grade of people attending class for 40, 50, or 60 days is 2.0, regardless.

Now consider the data shown in Table 4-7. Here a knowledge of attendance *does* matter, because different grade point averages are associated with different attendance records. The mean grade point averages of students who attended 40, 50, or 60 days are 1.0, 2.0, and 3.0, respectively. Using attendance as a predictor variable, we can improve our prediction of the criterion measure: grades.

TABLE 4-6   HYPOTHETICAL DATA FOR
PREDICTING GRADES FROM CLASS ATTENDANCE

Days attended	Grade point average	Means
40	1.0	
40	3.0	2.0
50	1.0	
50	3.0	2.0
60	1.0	
60	3.0	2.0
Mean 50	2.0	

TABLE 4-7   HYPOTHETICAL DATA FOR
PREDICTING GRADES FROM CLASS
ATTENDANCE

Days attended	Grade point average	Means
40	0.0	
40	2.0	1.0
50	1.0	
50	3.0	2.0
60	2.0	
60	4.0	3.0
Mean 50	2.0	

The Linear Regression Equation

The formal regression technique seeks a linear relationship that will allow us to predict one variable from another. Such a relationship can be expressed as follows:

$$Y' = bX + a$$

where Y' is the predicted score on variable Y (grades), X is the score on variable X (attendance), and b and a are constants, derived from our data. The constants b and a are chosen to provide the best prediction of Y; b is called the **regression coefficient** for estimating Y from X, and a is the **regression constant**.

The linear regression equation is a prescription for drawing a line graph called a **regression line**. Figure 4-6 displays two regression lines for the data shown in Table 4-8. Note that the regression lines for predicting Y from X and X from Y are different. This is because each regression line is trying to minimize different sources of error. In predicting Y from X, we want to minimize the vertical distance between a data point and the regression line. In predicting X from Y, we are trying to minimize the horizontal distance from data points to the regression line.

TABLE 4-8   SAMPLE DATA FOR A REGRESSION
PROBLEM*

Subject	X Height (in.)	Y Weight
1	70	175
2	72	160
3	68	148
4	66	150
5	71	178
6	69	164
7	73	176
8	62	143
9	70	168
10	69	167

*After Welkowitz et al., 1974.

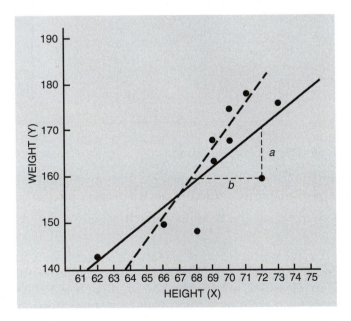

Figure 4-6   Regression line for data shown in Table 4-8. The solid line is for predicting *Y* from *X*; the broken line is for predicting *X* from *Y*. The distance *a* is an error in predicting *Y* from *X*; the distance *b* is an error in predicting *X* from *Y*.

Consider again the data presented in Table 4-1 (p. 62). A regression analysis performed on these data yields a regression coefficient of .60 and a regression constant of 54.6. Thus, in our example

$$\text{Predicted Grade } (Y') = .60 \text{ (Observed Time)} + 54.6$$

Applying the equation, we would have made the following prediction regarding Student "A"'s grade:

$$\text{Predicted Grade} = .60 \times 60 + 54.6 = 90.6$$

"A"'s actual grade was 88, so we didn't do too badly. With "B," though, we did less well. With rounding, we predicted she would get an 86 [$(.60 \times 53) + 54.6 = 86.4$], but she actually got a 96. Table 4-9 shows the predicted outcomes and the prediction error for each of the 20 students in our hypothetical example.

As was true of the correlation coefficient, regression coefficients are often evaluated for their statistical significance. The factors that affect the statistical significance of a correlation coefficient (for example, sample size and range) also apply to regression. Moreover, as with correlations, the assumption is that the underlying relationship between X and Y is linear, and thus predictions made using regression are accurate only to the extent that the variables are indeed linearly related.

TABLE 4-9 PREDICTED GRADES AND ERROR IN THE REGRESSION ANALYSIS OF OUR HYPOTHETICAL STUDY

Student	Time	Predicted grade	Actual grade	Error
A	60	91	88	3
B	53	96	86	10
C	22	68	72	4
D	44	81	78	3
E	34	75	65	10
F	47	83	80	3
G	38	77	77	0
H	50	85	83	2
I	51	85	79	6
J	35	76	68	8
K	46	82	84	2
L	36	76	76	0
M	48	83	92	9
N	43	80	80	0
O	40	79	67	12
P	32	74	78	4
Q	27	71	74	3
R	41	79	73	6
S	39	78	88	10
T	43	80	90	10

MULTIPLE REGRESSION

In attempting to predict psychological phenomena, more than one predictor variable can be helpful. When we have two or more predictors available, we can use a **multiple regression** analysis. With this form of analysis, the criterion is predicted in steps, by adding predictor variables one at a time. As a concrete illustration, we propose to guess your height. Of course, we don't know you; we can't even see you. But as we build up a set of facts about you, facts that will become **predictor variables**, our ability to guess your height will become increasingly accurate.

First, we are going to assume you have reached your adult height. (Most people do by the age of 17 or 18). Based on this assumption, and with nothing else to go by, *our first prediction is that your height is 5'7"*. This is about the average height of adult humans alive today.

Second, suppose we consider your gender as an additional predictor. Now our prediction becomes more refined. If you are male, we predict you are 5'10". If you are a female, we predict you are 5'4". These are the average adult heights, broken down by gender.

Third, suppose we learn the adult height of each of your biological parents. This can be valuable information for us, but it requires that the computations get a bit more complicated. Here is the idea: we want to add or subtract from the prediction we last made, according to the degree your parents deviated from the average heights of males (5'10") and females (5'4"). The whole scheme is displayed in Table 4-10. Please take a look at it now. (If you know the height of just one of your biological parents, a prediction can still be made. Just make the adjustment for the parent you know about.)

If you perform the relevant computations for yourself, you will probably find that our prediction came closer and closer to your actual height as we increased the number of predictors. But introducing additional predictors does not inevitably improve accuracy. In multiple regression, a new predictor will only improve prediction if it is *not* highly correlated with variables already included in the predictive equation.

You can see why this is so by examining Figure 4-7, a Venn diagram analysis of the effect of adding a second predictor, Z, to a prediction of Y from X. When X and Z are both perfectly correlated (case 1), Z adds nothing to our ability to account for variance in Y; all the variance in Z overlaps with the variance already explained (or "covered") by X. When X and Z are moderately correlated (case II), Z can account for that portion of the variance in Y that Z shares with Y, but not with X. Finally, when Z and X are uncorrelated ($r = .00$; case III), Z's *incremental contribution* is greatest.

In the multiple regression procedure we have just described, all variables are treated simultaneously and equally. This strategy is useful when the investigator is focusing simply on finding the best prediction rule and has no causal model in mind.

TABLE 4-10   PREDICTING YOUR HEIGHT FROM MULTIPLE PREDICTORS

If your mother is	Add(+) or subtract(−)	If your father is
5′0″ or less	−2.75″	5′6″ or less
5′1″	−2.50″	5′7″
5′2″	−2.00″	5′8″
5′3″	−1.00″	5′9″
5′4″	0.00″	5′10″
5′5″	+1.00″	5′11″
5′6″	+2.00″	6′0″
5′7″	+2.50″	6′1″
5′8″ or more	+2.75″	6′2″ or more
Average adult =		5′7″
Plus your gender adjustment [+3″ if male; −3″ if female]		_____
Plus your parent adjustment [father adjustment + mother adjustment]		_____
Your predicted height		_____

But there are other situations in which a **hierarchical regression** model is used. Here the researcher *specifies in advance* the order in which variables will be entered. The regression coefficient for the first variable to be entered is a simple regression coefficient. The regression coefficient for the second variable is a so-called **partial regression coefficient**; the influence of the first variable has been removed statistically. The regression coefficient for the third variable is also a partial coefficient; the influence of variables one and two has been removed.

As each variable is added to the equation, the investigator conducts a statistical test to determine whether the newly added variable significantly increases the predictability of *Y* beyond what has already been accomplished. Thus in the hierarchical model, the researcher evaluates not only the overall predictability of *Y*, but also the unique contribution to the prediction of each of a logically or theoretically ordered set of variables.

The process of ordering the variables is very important. The variance in *Y* accounted for by the last variable entered can only be the *Y* variance for which the previously entered variables have not already accounted. To the extent that this last-entered variable shares variance with other predictors, it is not as likely to increase the predictability of *Y* significantly. Only its *unique* contribution to predicting *Y* will be utilized at this point.

So far, we have emphasized how research psychologists identify associations in their data. In the next chapter we begin our discussion of what many psychologists consider the major purpose of their research, namely, demonstrating the existence of **causal relationships**.

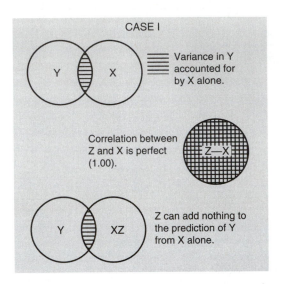

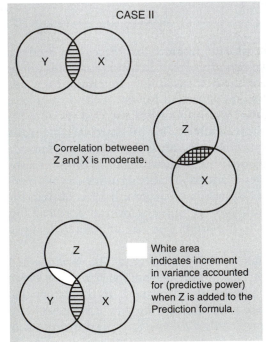

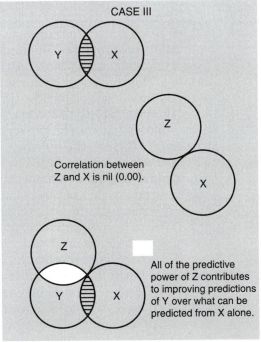

Figure 4-7 Increments in predictive power resulting from adding Z to the prediction of Y from X. Correlation between Z and X is perfect (case I), moderate (case II), and nil (case III). Note that lower correlations between Z and X result in higher contributions by Z.

FOR REVIEW AND DISCUSSION

Key Terms

ASSOCIATIONS
CORRELATION
SCATTER PLOT
CORRELATION COEFFICIENT
SHARED VARIANCE
COEFFICIENT OF DETERMINATION
SAMPLE
POPULATION
STATISTICAL SIGNIFICANCE
REPRESENTATIVE SAMPLE
TRUNCATED RANGE
CURVILINEAR RELATIONSHIPS
PREDICTOR VARIABLE
CRITERION VARIABLE
REGRESSION COEFFICIENT
REGRESSION CONSTANT
REGRESSION LINE
MULTIPLE REGRESSION
PARTIAL REGRESSION COEFFICIENTS
HIERARCHICAL REGRESSION MODEL
CORRELATION MATRIX
CAUSAL RELATIONSHIPS
RATIO SCALES
POWER
REGRESSION
REGRESSION ANALYSIS

Discussion Issues

1. State in words the hypothetical relationships between the following variables, as indexed by r. What is the amount of variance accounted for by each relationship?

   (a) $r = -.67$ between quality of prenatal nutrition and mental retardation.

   (b) $r = +.33$ between scores on a hyperactivity scale and an aggression scale.

   (c) $r = +.15$ between grades in college and number of dates.

2. Plot the following scores, which were obtained from 10 subjects on variables A and B. Does the resultant scatter plot indicate no correlation, a moderate correlation, or a high correlation? Is the correlation, if any, positive or negative?

(a)

Subject	A	B
1	3	2
2	4	9
3	5	8
4	6	1
5	7	3
6	5	5
7	8	7
8	2	8
9	9	7
10	2	4

(b)

Subject	A	B
1	4	5
2	3	5
3	2	3
4	6	5
5	7	9
6	3	3
7	8	8
8	1	1
9	5	7
10	9	10

3. Discuss the concept of statistical significance.

4. Discuss the factors that influence the magnitude of the correlation coefficient.

5. Why is it important sometimes to consider r^2 rather than r?

6. Suppose that the future status of the national economy is predicted by the amount of installment buying ($r = .65$). In this case you would be interested in improving your predictive powers, since you cannot account for approximately 60% of the variance. You also know that the price of stocks on the New York Stock Exchange correlates .50 with future economy. How would you improve your predictions using this additional data? What factors should you consider before implementing this procedure?

7. Discuss the concept of variance accounting.

5

CAUSE AND EFFECT

I used to have a 1951 Plymouth that gave me trouble starting when it was cold. On a chilly morning I would typically turn the key, hear the engine turn over a few times, and then "die."

On these mornings, I would usually try to "do something" to get the car started. My efforts typically began with pumping the gas pedal, turning the key, and holding the ignition on for several seconds. If this didn't work after a few tries (and it often didn't), I would conclude that I had "flooded the engine," wait 15 or 20 minutes, and try again. At this point the car would usually start. The car never failed to start in the long run. In an hour at most, the old Plymouth was going and I was off to the campus. After some time I concluded that I understood what was happening. The engine needed "priming" on cold mornings, and the colder the morning, the more priming was required.

My doubts began when a colleague, after listening to my priming explanation, asked: "Has it occurred to you that 'priming' may have nothing to do with it?" No, I hadn't thought of that. My priming idea fit my observations quite well, and I felt pretty satisfied with it.

My colleague had an entirely different idea. She said that what was involved was *not* priming, but was instead "warming up." Her explanation went like this:

First of all, she asked me at what time I usually left for the office. I said that I liked to be out by 7:00 AM. My colleague then pointed out that on cold mornings in Tennessee, the coldest part of the day was just before sunrise, and that the temperature rose quite rapidly during the first hour after the sun came up. Her idea was that all my priming really did was take up time. The temperature was rising rapidly during the period I was doing my priming routine; when the air (and thus the engine) got warm enough, the car would start. This, she said, would happen regardless of whether I spent the extra time priming or sleeping.

We agreed this hypothesis called for an empirical test. On the next few very cold mornings I simply did a little work at home and waited until 8:00 AM before even going out. Only then did I try to start the car. It started every time. So much for the priming explanation!

This example illustrates many of the core issues involved in answering a "why" question, that is, inferring a **causal relationship**.

As we emphasized in Chapter 1, the goal of science is almost always to go beyond description and into the realm of explanation. The scientist wants to know not only *that* a given percentage of the population is aggressive or conservative or obese; he or she also wants to know *why* these relationships occur. Answers to "Why?" questions involve bridging the gap between observed associations and correlations on the one hand, and inferences about cause and effect on the other. Such inferences must be made very carefully. There are many serious pitfalls for researchers who too readily infer the existence of a causal relationship.

In this chapter we will explain the limitations of simple correlations for determining causality. Then, we will discuss the various types of causal relationships possible. Finally, we will describe a logical means for identifying causal relationships without ambiguity.

WHY CAUSAL INFERENCES CANNOT BE DRAWN FROM SIMPLE CORRELATIONS

When a psychologist observes a naturally occurring correlation between two variables, X and Y, it is often tempting to assume that the relationship is causal in nature, that is, $X > Y$. This assumption is unsound. Often the observed relationship can be explained in other ways.

Plausible Rival Hypotheses

Causal inferences require research designs that can control for **plausible rival hypotheses**. (The colleague's hypothesis that air temperature rather than priming caused the old Plymouth to start is a clear example of a plausible rival hypothesis.) When X and Y are associated, there are two major rival hypotheses to the inference that $X > Y$:

(1) that instead $Y > X$
(2) that some third variable (arbitrarily called "Z") is the cause of both X and Y.

These rival hypotheses are referred to as the **directionality problem** and the **third variable problem**, respectively.

The Directionality Problem

A simple correlation between two variables tells us only that they are related, or tend to vary together. It does *not* tell us whether one is caused by the other. For example, there is a positive correlation between grades and attendance in class. One possible interpretation of this relationship is that greater attendance in class increases the amount learned and thus causes higher grades. A second and equally plausible hypothesis is that good grades lead students who obtain them to enjoy class and therefore to attend more often. Hence the oft-cited dictum: "Correlation does not imply causation."

But the directionality of the relationship is not always impossible to determine. Some relationships can be conceptualized only in one direction. For example, suppose a new car dealer finds a relationship between the income of car shoppers and the likelihood that they will actually buy a new car. Suppose, too, that the relationship is positive; the wealthier a potential customer is, the more likely he or she is to actually make a purchase. How can the dealer explain the relationship?

It is extremely unlikely that buying a new car will increase a person's income, but a greater income might enable a person to buy a new car. Here, the assumed causal relationship might lead the dealer to predict the circumstances (for example, a booming vs. a troubled economy) in which sales volume can be expected to increase or decrease.

Although simple "passive" correlations do not usually allow statements about causation, they may contribute to the *dis*confirmation of causal hypotheses. *Causation usually implies correlation.*

Consider the claim that cigarette smoking causes lung cancer. This claim implies that lung cancer and cigarette smoking will be positively related. If a correlation between smoking and lung cancer were *not* obtained, our confidence in the hypothesis should be reduced.[1] But the presence of a correlation between smoking and lung cancer still does not permit a causal inference, because the nature of the relationship has not been established. Specifically, the relationship could be due to a *third variable.*

The Third Variable Problem

The **third variable problem** refers to the possibility that neither of the two variables involved in a correlation produces the other. Rather, some unspecified third variable or process has produced the observed relationship. For example, there is a high positive correlation between the number of places of worship in a city and the number of crimes committed in that city. The more places of worship a city has, the more crimes are committed in it. Does this mean that religion fosters crime or that crime fosters religion? It means neither. The relationship is due to a third variable—population. The higher the population of a community, the greater are 1) the number of places of worship and 2) the frequency of criminal activities.

As a second example, consider the high positive correlation between the number of drownings on a particular day and the consumption of ice cream on that day. The drownings do not cause depressed people to comfort themselves by consuming large amounts of ice cream, nor does eating ice cream cause drowning. Instead, warm temperatures cause both. The warmer the weather, the more people are likely to be swimming (which is directly related to the frequency of drowning). And more ice cream is sold and eaten on warm days.

The fact that we cannot infer causation from simple passive correlations does not necessarily mean that a cause and effect relationship does not exist. It merely means that it is often impossible to obtain enough information to be sure of the specific nature and direction of this causal relationship.

The examples above are fairly obvious. It is easy 1) to see that a third variable may be causally responsible for the relationship and 2) to identify the third variable. Often, it is not possible to determine whether or not a third variable is operating, or what the specific variable is.

There remain some other special circumstances in which observed correlations can yield causal conclusions which, although not wholly justified by pure logic, are compelling enough to warrant at least tentative acceptance. An example appears in Box 5.1.

---

[1]There are certain exceptions to this general proposition. For example, smoking might adversely influence only a small segment of the population, so that its effects would not show up in a study that included all smokers. Likewise, smoking might cause cancer in some individuals and reduce its likelihood in others, thus "washing out" the overall effect to zero. But in most circumstances such cumbersome arguments are poor rivals for the proposition, "Causation implies correlation."

BOX 5.1   *CORRELATIONS WITHOUT CAUSAL ARROW AMBIGUITY: DIFFERENTIAL INCIDENCE*

In early 1985 a decision was made to put a warning on all aspirin packages indicating that children and adolescents with flu, chicken pox, or other viral infections should not be given aspirin. The warning reflected a recent discovery: Combined with these infections, aspirin may produce a **catalytic interaction** (two agents combining to produce an outcome which neither alone would yield) that results in Reye's syndrome. (Reye's syndrome occurs in some children after a viral infection. It is characterized by sudden onset of vomiting and severe headaches, which progress rapidly toward convulsions, delirium, and coma. Reye's is fatal in about one-quarter of all cases.)

The determination of a causal link between aspirin and Reye's was made in the absence of any experimental data, on the basis of a **differential incidence** of Reye's between children who had been given aspirin to relieve the symptoms of a viral infection and those who had not.

The underlying study, conducted by the Center for Disease Control, traced 29 cases of Reye's syndrome in which the victim had taken aspirin. Dr. Sidney Wolfe, of the Health Research Group, was quoted as saying that "the best statistical model indicated that aspirin raised the risk [of Reye's following a viral infection] by 25 times [and that] this extraordinarily high risk ratio was much higher than seen in any previous study [and was] one of the largest risk ratios found in any recent epidemiological study" (quoted by Boffey, 1985).

The evidence was considered strong despite its nonexperimental nature because the magnitude of the difference in incidence between the two groups was too large to readily admit any **plausible rival hypotheses**. Another, more pragmatic, consideration may have combined with this evidence to produce the warning. The potential benefits of adding the new warning clearly outweighed the risks, because other nonaspirin analgesics and fever-reducing agents were available at the time.

It is rare to find such a clear-cut and convincing pattern in psychological research, but the Reye's case does illustrate that differential incidence rates obtained without experimentation may, in principle, demonstrate a probable causal link. In this case, **temporal precedence** (the aspirin was administered *before* symptoms of Reye's syndrome developed) combined with the extreme difference in rate of occurrence of the disorder between the aspirin treated and nontreated groups to implicate aspirin in the process.

Thus, while correlation does not imply causation, it can be considered as a factor in determining a causal relationship, and the strength of the evidence depends very much on the specific circumstances involved. In this case, experimentation to demonstrate convincingly the causal role of aspirin in the development of Reye's syndrome would jeopardize the lives of the children involved and is not ethically justifiable. Therefore, the conclusion that aspirin probably contributes to the development of Reye's syndrome is legitimate in light of the limitations imposed by circumstances on further research.

TYPES OF CAUSAL RELATIONSHIPS

The search for causal relationships in nature is rarely straightforward. For one thing, there are a number of different types of causal relationships. Moreover, these different types can operate in various combinations to influence a given phenomenon.

Causal explanations vary in their specificity. What seems to be a single cause at one level of analysis may appear to leave an unresolved controversy between two or more possible causes at another level of analysis. For example, in his famous conformity experiments, Asch (1951) found that subjects were more likely to give incorrect judgments of the lengths of lines shown on a screen if the subjects were in a group in which *everyone else* gave an inaccurate judgment than they were if *one other person* in the group gave the correct judgment. Thus, at one level, we may say that exposure to a single person who judged accurately caused the subject to break from conformity and respond accurately as well.

But what caused the presence of one accurate judge to have this conformity-releasing effect? Perhaps the mere fact that the accurate judge disagreed with the majority was the critical ingredient. Or perhaps it was the fact that his judgment agreed with the as-yet-unstated private judgment of the subject. (The evidence seems to suggest that both elements play a role in the causal chain. An extreme dissenter makes some contribution to breaking the subject's conformity when the judgments are objective [for example, line length], but a colleague who actually agrees with the subject is required to cause a break in conformity when subjective opinions rather than objective judgments are involved; see Allen & Levine, 1969).

Regardless of the level of causal analysis involved, four broad types of causal relationships can be identified: necessary and sufficient relationships, necessary but not sufficient relationships, sufficient but not necessary relationships, and contributory relationships.

A **necessary and sufficient causal relationship** is one in which some factor or condition, *X*, is required to produce an effect, and will invariably do so. A specific genetic anomaly is necessary and sufficient to cause some hereditary diseases, such as Tay-Sachs disease. In psychology it is rare to find important causal relationships that are both necessary and sufficient.

The world is filled with causal relationships in which some specifiable factor, *X*, is **necessary but not sufficient** for *Y* to occur. For example, a writing instrument is necessary but not sufficient to compose a book; possession of a loaded gun is necessary but not sufficient for a shooting to occur.

Sufficient but not necessary causal relationships are those in which *X* is one of many causes that can independently produce *Y*. For most people, the sight of an angry bear is not a necessary condition to keep out of a mountain cave. A host of other factors will dissuade people from entering a dark cave, even if no bears are around to assert a territorial claim. Because most behavioral phenomena can be caused by many different factors and circumstances, all that can usually be done in psychological research is to identify sufficient but not necessary causes.

Cartoon 5-1 A bad day at the office may not have caused Fido to be kicked, but it certainly contributed to his master's aggression.

    Contributory causal relationships are those in which X is neither necessary nor sufficient to cause Y, but can nonetheless contribute to (that is, change the likelihood of) Y's occurrence. Annoying experiences during the day are often contributory causes to the arguments that couples have during the evening. A "bad day at the office" may not be sufficient or necessary to cause a domestic scuffle; but if a person has had a bad day, this factor may contribute (combine with other factors) to cause a fight at home in the evening.

    Several more complicated varieties of causal relationships have been discussed in recent years. Our previous example of a contributory causal relationship implied that X (a bad day at the office) $\rightarrow$ Y (an argument at home). But an argument at home in the evening, in turn, may contribute to having a bad day at the office the next day. So our causal model becomes complicated: $Y \leftrightarrows X$. X is still a cause of Y, but Y can now also be a cause of X. The mutual influence of X and Y on each other is an example of a **feedback loop**.

    Another recent idea is the **causal chain**: $X > Y > Z$. Here X causes Y and Y, in turn, causes Z. For example, poor social skills (X) may cause a person to receive little social reinforcement (Y), which then leads to depression (Z). In this case, poor social skills (X) would be regarded as an indirect cause of depression (Z).

Because many different patterns of causal relationships might underlie and explain any phenomenon, the unguided empirical search for causes can be a clumsy or even an impossible strategy.

For this reason, investigators in both the social and physical sciences typically begin with some **theoretical model**. This permits them to structure and conceptualize the phenomenon of interest and its possible causes. An illustration of the value of theoretical modeling is featured in Box 5.2.

BOX 5.2   *THEORETICAL MODELING*

Theoretical modeling can play an essential role not only in guiding and structuring research, but also in setting up compelling evidence for cause and effect relationships. Consider a technique that employs passive correlations in such a way as to make a reasonable case for causal inference, while minimizing the threats of the directionality and third variable problems. The technique is known as **causal analysis**. Theory and the measurement of a set of variables are the keystones of the approach.

In psychological research, it is rarely true that an explanation of some phenomenon postulates a single cause. More often, a theorist will propose that a phenomenon results from a sequence of events. In causal analysis, an explanatory model is proposed, several (or many) variables are measured, and the resulting network of associative relationships is then examined to determine whether the model has been supported.

Because we are now evaluating a network of relationships, the operation of a single third variable and the possible bidirectionality of relationships are less problematic.

Let us examine a rather informal example of the general logic of this approach. Chaffee and McLeod (1971) presented an analysis to examine the association between viewing of televised violence and aggressive behavior among children and young adolescents. The two major hypotheses for these findings are (H_1) that viewing violent TV leads to aggressive behavior, and (H_2) that aggressiveness leads to viewing violent TV.

Each of these hypotheses is based on a "subhypothesis" about the causal relationship underlying the effect. (See Table 5-1 for the specific subhypotheses involved, and note that each one clearly posits a different causal direction between aggressiveness and violent TV viewing habits.)

Note, in the table, that H_{1a} or the "learning hypothesis" is one of the intervening processes said to underlie H_1. Thus, support for H_1 can be obtained by showing that youngsters learn aggressive behaviors from watching TV, and that they recognize the possibility of later using this knowledge.

To determine whether such a process is operating, Chaffee and McLeod asked

TABLE 5-1   TWO HYPOTHESES ABOUT VIOLENCE VIEWING AND
ADOLESCENT AGGRESSIVENESS, SHOWING SUBHYPOTHESIS INVOLVED IN A
CAUSAL ANALYSIS

H_1:   Viewing television violence increases the likelihood of an adolescent behaving ag-
gressively.

   H_{1a}:   By viewing television violence, an adolescent learns aggressive forms of behavior; this increases the probability that he or she will behave in this fashion in subsequent social interaction.

H_2:   Aggressiveness causes adolescents to watch violent television programs.

   H_{2a}:   Aggressiveness leads to a preference for violent programs, which in turn
causes the aggressive adolescent to watch them.

Adapted from Chaffee and McLeod (1971).

youngsters (for whom they also had independent information on violence viewing and aggressive behavior) whether it was "like them" to respond to television
in the following ways:

> These programs show me how to get back at people who make me angry.
> Sometimes I copy the things I see people doing on these shows.
> Some programs give me ideas on how to get away with something without
> being caught.

As Chaffee and McLeod note, these questions were designed to probe a learning process that "can be thought of as an hypothetical path through which viewing violence might lead to aggressive interpersonal behavior" (1971, p. 12).

But what of the alternative? As Chaffee and McLeod indicate: "We would not
want to infer that aggressiveness causes violence viewing unless evidence indicates that this viewing is intentional and selective." (In other words, children
might be exposed to a great deal of violent fare simply because that is what is offered during the times when they are free to view television, or because that is
the preference of someone else in their household. These possible reasons would
not represent legitimate grounds for inferring a relationship between aggressiveness and choice of programming.)

This subhypothesis, H_{2a}, is tested in a manner analogous to H_{1a}, but the measure involved is the youngster's list of his or her four "favorite" programs. The
H_{2a} path requires that the violence preference measure be related to both prior
level of aggressiveness and later viewing of violent programs.

Given the foregoing information, H_{1a} and H_{2a} can be compared. One comparison, based on the data reported by Chaffee and McLeod, is shown in Figure
5-1. The learning hypothesis receives fairly clear support, whereas the violence
preference hypothesis does not hold up very well. The better account is thus provided by H_1, and the causal inference with which it is associated therefore becomes more convincing.

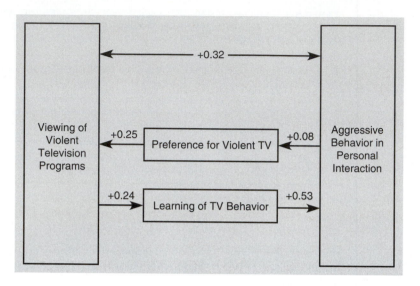

Figure 5-1   Correlations of violence viewing, aggressiveness, and two intervening processes. Entries indicate correlations between the two variables connected by each line (N = 473). Arrows indicate hypothesized time order. The overall relationship is clearly accounted for more adequately by the learning path (H_{1a}) than by the preference path (H_{2a}). (Source: Adapted from Chaffee and McLeod, 1971).

This is a relatively simple example of causal analysis. More formal approaches exist, employing far more complicated causal models and mathematics that are beyond the scope of the present discussion. The most important point to be understood is that in certain controlled situations, **theoretical models** combined with correlations can shed light on causality, if falling somewhat short of demonstrating clear proof.

X AS A SUFFICIENT CAUSE OF Y: MILL'S CRITERIA

We have seen that a passively observed simple correlation alone is not grounds to claim that X is the cause of Y. Under what circumstances, then, can one logically conclude that X is a sufficient cause of Y? The answer to this question can be found in the writings of John Stuart Mill (1806–1873).

Mill proposed that if X is a **sufficient cause** of Y, then when X occurs, Y should also occur. He called the procedure of demonstrating the conditional relationship, *if X, then Y*, the **method of agreement**. But, as Mill realized, the method of agreement alone does not prove that X causes Y. Y may have occurred even if X had not. Because the method of agreement is not sensitive to this possibility, Mill also proposed a second method, the **method of differences**.

The method of differences, like the method of agreement, states a conditional relationship between events: *Everything else being equal, if not X, then not Y.* Mill concluded that *on an abstract, logical level, sufficient causality can be inferred if it can be shown that 1) with everything else equal, Y occurs when X occurs, and 2) Y does not occur when X does not occur.*

At first glance this formulation may seem to imply that *X* is necessary (and not merely sufficient) for *Y* to occur. Such an impression is wrong, because other possible sufficient causes have not been logically excluded by the model. To see that this is so, consider a set of observations made about an electric light switch on the wall.

An observer first notes that the light in the adjacent hall is on (*Y*) when the light switch is "on" (*X*). Later, the observer notes that the light is not on when the switch is "off." Finally, a practical experimental test shows that throwing the switch "on" turns the light on, whereas throwing the switch "off" turns the light off. Mill's criteria are amply satisfied. When all other things are equal, throwing the switch "on" (*X*) has been shown to be a sufficient cause of turning the light on (*Y*).

But the "on" switch may not be *necessary* to turn the light on, and in fact other sufficient causes can readily be imagined. (Suppose, for example, that the switch is "three-way" wired so that another switch at the other end of the hall can also turn the light on and off.) Likewise, *X* may fail to cause *Y* when some other set of conditions prevails, as would be the case when the bulb itself is burned out. For these reasons, the Millian model (and most psychological research) is limited to showing empirically that *X* can be *a* cause of *Y*, not that *X* is *the* cause of *Y*.

The central aim of most psychological research is therefore to provide data that allow a comparison between effects (*Y*) that have and have not been preceded by a hypothesized cause (*X*). The problem for research psychologists is to translate the requirements of Mill's proposition into concrete terms. This includes the difficult burden of being sure that everything else but the critical element in a comparison has been kept as equal as possible. The Latin phrase *ceteris paribus* (SET-uhr-iss PEHR-ib-uss; "other things being equal") is often used in science, philosophy, and the law to refer to this same idea.

Much of the rest of this book is devoted to evaluating the strengths and weaknesses of various research designs for achieving a demonstration of causality that satisfies Mill's abstract requirements. Before introducing the research methods devised to achieve these goals, some discussion of the logic underlying them is necessary. A concept central to most scientific research is hypothesis testing.

HYPOTHESIS TESTING

The suggestion or possibility that changes in one variable (*X*) cause changes in another variable (*Y*) may be considered an **hypothesis**. Hypotheses may be derived from many sources, including formal theories, informal observation, or even hunches. It is useful to think of the search for causal relationships as **hypothesis testing**.

Hypothesis testing involves formulating an explicit claim about the relationship between two (or more) variables, choosing a design or plan for making relevant observations or gathering relevant data, and then analyzing the data to see if they support or fail to support the hypothesis. The goal of the researcher is always to reach a valid ("true" or "correct") conclusion from the data. The problem, therefore, is to avoid erroneous or unjustified conclusions. Our attention now turns to the multitude of issues involved in avoiding such errors. We begin with a central idea in the logic of research design and interpretation: **null hypothesis testing**.

Null Hypothesis Testing

Concerned with the problem of logical causal inference, Sir Ronald Fisher (1890–1962) developed the procedure called **null hypothesis testing**. Suppose, for example, that we have the average performance scores of two groups, only one of which received a particular treatment. The null hypothesis, set up artificially for logical purposes, would be that the means of the two groups do *not* differ significantly (and thus, that they were drawn from the same population of scores).

If the sample means differ enough from each other, the null hypothesis can be rejected. Logically, this is equivalent to the conclusion that the *population* means (for example, of potential treated and untreated groups) also differ, and thus that the observed experimental effect did not occur by chance. (See Figure 5-2.) Within Fisher's model, one has only two choices: 1) to reject the null hypothesis, and 2) to draw no conclusion; that is, to neither reject nor accept the null hypothesis (often stated as failure to reject the null hypothesis).

The question of how much the means must differ for the null hypothesis to be rejected involves the question of variability, and thus leads to further consideration of the concept of **statistical significance**. As noted previously, we are dealing only with samples, but wish to make inferences about populations (see Chapter 3). We want to be confident that observed sample differences, if obtained, actually reflect real differences in the populations of interest.

The critical need here is to determine the likelihood that a given result will occur by chance if the null hypothesis is true. In other words, given the null hypothesis that the two population means are equal, and given that a discrepancy between the two sample means was in fact observed, we ask: What is the probability of obtaining such a difference by chance alone? (Recall that results that occur rarely or with a low probability by chance are likely to result from real treatment effects. This is what we mean by a **statistically significant difference**.)

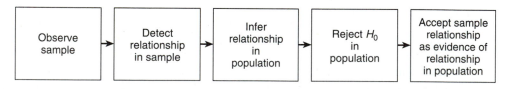

Figure 5-2 Hypothesis (H_1): relationship exists in population. Null hypothesis (H_0): no relationship exists in population.

The reasoning underlying null hypothesis testing can be understood through a concrete nonexperimental example. Suppose we knew the distribution of mean daily temperatures in Jacksonville, Florida, on January 1 of every year for 100 years (1850–1949) and plotted these data as in Figure 5-3. We now have a distribution that closely approximates the theoretical population of mean daily temperatures that have occurred (or will occur) on this day in Jacksonville. The mean of the distribution is equal to 50°F.

Of greater importance is the bell-shaped (or "normal" curve) form of the distribution, so that some of the means (those with values below 30 or above 70) have had a relatively low frequency of occurrence; we would therefore expect that, in the future, they will only rarely be found for this city on January 1. Thus, if we were given ten mean temperatures from January 1 for the years 1960 to 1969, and these samples had a mean of 18°, we could be virtually certain that the new readings were *not* taken from the theoretical population (that is, temperature readings in Jacksonville) shown in Figure 5-3.

The statistical inference problem is that most often only one sample, rather than 10 or more, is drawn. Further, on the basis of that single sample, we must decide whether the observed mean departs enough from the expected value in order to claim statistical significance. As may be seen from Figure 5-3, only these relatively unlikely results on the tails of the curve would be sufficient evidence to lead to the rejection of the null hypothesis. Such results occur by chance alone with very low frequency. Therefore, the likelihood of incorrectly rejecting the null hypothesis is minimal if these very unlikely values are obtained.

Type I Errors.   The experimenter must decide upon the particular probability of *incorrectly rejecting the null hypothesis* (concluding that there is a difference, when in fact there is not) that he or she is willing to tolerate. In practice,

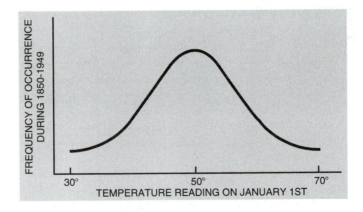

Figure 5-3 A hypothetical distribution of sample temperature means on January 1, in Jacksonville, Florida. The figure illustrates the problem of inferring that a sample has not been drawn from a given population. It is easy to see why a temperature reading of 18° probably was not taken in this city in any January between 1960 and 1969.

researchers often set their critical probabilities at a value of 0.01 or 0.05. (In statistics these critical values are called *alpha levels.*)

The probability of incorrectly rejecting the null hypothesis is therefore 1) under the experimenter's control and 2) set at a low value, either one in 100 or five in 100. The sample result must be sufficiently rare in the population to have a likelihood of occurrence of only five or fewer in 100 times if the null hypothesis were in fact true.

Thus the only consideration involved in setting up statistical hypotheses is the minimization of the possibility of incorrectly rejecting the null hypothesis, that is, concluding that a difference exists between two populations when in fact they are *not* different. Such errors are commonly referred to as **type I errors**.

Type II Errors.   An investigator also runs the risk of *failing* to reject the null hypothesis when it is, in fact, false. This involves failing to detect a true difference between the populations of interest. Such an error is called a **type II error**. The distinction between type I and type II errors is shown in Figure 5-4. Two hypotheses are considered: H_1 that cigarette smoking is dangerous to health, and its obverse, the null hypothesis (H_0), that cigarette smoking is not harmful. The question is whether H_1 is true in the population at large. On the basis of the observed data from a single experiment, the researcher must decide to reject or not reject H_0. (To reject H_0 is to implicitly accept H_1.)

Thus, there are two circumstances in which no error is made. First, H_0 may be correctly rejected; that is, if H_1 (cigarette smoking causes lung cancer) is true for the population, and we correctly *reject* the hypothesis (H_0) that it is not harmful. Second, we may fail to reject H_0 when H_0 is in fact true for the population.

There are also two circumstances in which an error *is* made. The error with which Fisher was most concerned is indicated in the upper left quadrant of Figure 5-4 (a type I error), the error of rejecting H_0 when it is in fact true in the population. The probability of a type I error is under the direct control of the investigator, through

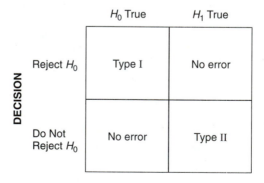

Figure 5-4   Four "states of the world" when testing the null hypothesis. Two states result in no error; one state yields a type I error; another yields a type II error. H_0: cigarette smoking is not harmful to health; H_1: cigarette smoking is harmful to health.

the selection of a level of significance (or alpha level). The error of failing to reject H_0 (the null hypothesis) when it is in fact false in the population (the type II error) is shown in the lower right quadrant of the table. How is a type II error to be avoided?

Type II errors have a determinable relationship to certain properties of the research. First, they decrease in probability as the number of subjects in an investigation is increased.

Second, the probability of a type II error is related to the level of statistical significance chosen by the investigator. The more stringent the level of statistical significance (for example, .01 instead of .05), the greater the probability of a type II error.

The Problem of Accepting the Null Hypothesis.   We have seen that, logically, rejecting the null hypothesis (H_0) allows us to accept the experimental hypothesis (H_1). However, the obverse does *not* hold: Failing to reject H_0 does not allow us to accept H_0.

The problem is that there are a host of reasons for failing to obtain a significant effect in any given experiment, other than just the possibility that the null hypothesis is true.

To illustrate, consider the 9-year-old boy who has lost his homework and searches his room for it. If he finds the homework there, we know that (at least this time) it was there all along.

But if a first inspection does not turn up the missing work, that does not necessarily prove that the homework is not in his room. Weighing against this null hypothesis (that the homework is really not there) is the possibility that the youngster may have looked too quickly, looked in the wrong places, and so on. Only after repeated searches (or, of course, if the papers turn up elsewhere) would it be justified to conclude that the homework is not in the child's room. Thus, it is the potential existence of numerous alternate explanations (rival hypotheses) that logically precludes the acceptance of the null hypothesis.

In order not to reject the null hypothesis, one need only design an experiment that is insensitive. For example, an experiment employing very few subjects or a very weak manipulation may easily fail to detect "real" effects. Such experiments are said to have **low statistical power**.

Because acceptance of the null hypothesis violates strict logic, the possible reasons for accepting it should be mentioned.

Imagine a new drug that is known to have many positive effects. The drug might also have negative side effects (as yet undiscovered) that should prevent it from being marketed. In such a situation, the null hypothesis states that the drug has no such ill effects and is pitted against the experimental hypothesis that such effects are present. If continuous comparisons of patients who have and have not been given the drug are made, and no ill effects are observed, it is not logically valid to accept the null hypothesis. But it will be informally accepted, and that is often a reasonable practical decision.

If powerfully designed experiments with a wide range of subjects repeatedly fail to display a particular effect, it may be prudent to violate stringent logic and tentatively accept the null hypothesis from experimental data (Greenwald, 1975). Nonetheless, acceptance of the null hypothesis should never be considered more than a provisional decision. Further, even provisional acceptance should not be considered until the corresponding experimental hypothesis has been tested fully and fairly (Cook et al., 1978).

Choice of Sample Size for Hypothesis Testing

Because one way of increasing the sensitivity (**statistical power**) of an investigation is to increase sample size, very large samples may lead to rejection of the null hypothesis based on quite small group differences. With a sufficiently large number of subjects, virtually any difference (even a trivial difference from a practical or theoretical viewpoint) could be detected as statistically significant. This fact is essentially a corollary of the effects of increasing sample size on reducing error variance, which was discussed in Chapter 3. Recall that very small samples may fail to reach significance even when there is a fairly substantial "true" relationship in the population.

How, then, should sample size be chosen? Research psychologists are not in full agreement on this issue. However, most psychological research is done with a **moderate-sized sample**, to avoid the opposing pitfalls of samples that are too large or too small.

The next chapter will introduce various issues concerning validity, in preparation for the introduction to the true experiment. Most of the rest of this book will be devoted to examination of the various methods of demonstrating causality through research, and the pitfalls of each.

FOR REVIEW AND DISCUSSION

Key Terms
NECESSARY AND SUFFICIENT CAUSAL RELATIONSHIP
NECESSARY BUT NOT SUFFICIENT CAUSAL RELATIONSHIP
SUFFICIENT BUT NOT NECESSARY CAUSAL RELATIONSHIP
CONTRIBUTORY CAUSAL RELATIONSHIP
FEEDBACK LOOP
CAUSAL CHAIN
PLAUSIBLE RIVAL HYPOTHESES
DIRECTIONALITY PROBLEM
THIRD VARIABLE PROBLEM
METHOD OF AGREEMENT
METHOD OF DIFFERENCES
HYPOTHESIS
HYPOTHESIS TESTING
NULL HYPOTHESIS TESTING
STATISTICAL SIGNIFICANCE
STATISTICALLY SIGNIFICANT DIFFERENCE
TYPE I ERRORS

TYPE II ERRORS
LOW STATISTICAL POWER
CAUSAL RELATIONSHIP
THEORETICAL MODEL
SUFFICIENT CAUSE
ACCEPTING THE NULL HYPOTHESIS
MODERATE-SIZED SAMPLE
CATALYTIC INTERACTION
DIFFERENTIAL INCIDENCE
TEMPORAL PRECEDENCE
THEORETICAL MODELING
CAUSAL ANALYSIS

Discussion Issues

1. What types of causal relationships are logically possible?
2. Give an example of a necessary but not sufficient causal relationship.
3. Explain how Mill's "method of agreement" and "method of differences" can show that X is a sufficient cause of Y.
4. Discuss the third variable problem as it relates to sample selection and equivalence of groups in correlational research.
5. If there is a high negative correlation between grades in high school and number of dates, can we conclude that people who make good grades are socially unattractive? What is a rival hypothesis?
6. In the text it is pointed out that almost any differences between groups can reach significance when the sample size is large enough. What value can there be, then, in placing so much emphasis on the "significance level" if the results may be trivial? In other words, why use statistical tests at all?
7. An investigator compares the number of cavities of children who have been advised to use either toothpaste A or toothpaste B for 1 year. At the end of the year, she finds group A has significantly fewer cavities (at the .05 level) than group B.
   a) State H_0 and H_1
   b) What would be the type I and type II errors?
   c) What is the probability of a type I error?
   d) If the experimenter had used .01 as her required significance level, would the probability of a type II error have changed? In what way?
8. A drug manufacturer wishes to test a drug she feels can cure cancer. She must consider the following before producing the drug for the public: a) its high expense, b) its side effects, and c) its effectiveness. Discuss the sizes of type I and type II errors you would be willing to accept before allowing production of the drug.

6

THE FOUR FACES OF VALIDITY

In Chapter 3 we briefly discussed **test validity**, saying that a test is valid to the extent that it measures what it purports to measure. In this chapter we will use the term *validity* in a broader way, as in the **validity of scientific inferences**.

According to the dictionary, *validity* means "well-grounded" or "sound." This is similar to its meaning in the law. A contract is said to be valid when it is correctly executed and binding upon the parties; otherwise, it is *in*valid. When we speak of the **validity of scientific inferences**, the term conveys much the same idea as it does in common and legal usage.

A scientific inference—a conclusion about a "true" relationship in the world—must always be examined for its soundness. A valid scientific inference is one that is rationally and empirically locked to the observations on which it is based. Inferences form the heart of any science; therefore, an examination of the conditions required for achieving valid scientific inferences is crucial at this point.

A scientific inference does not have to be wrong to be invalid. *A scientific inference is not valid until all plausible rival hypotheses have been ruled out.* This is the key factor that makes scientific inferences more persuasive than inferences or conclusions reached through other means.

When a scientist draws an inference from her/his data, we can ask four questions about its validity:

1. If the inference is partly statistical (most are), is the conclusion justifiable from the tests and comparisons used? This is the question of **statistical conclusion validity**.

2. If the inference is about cause and effect, have Mill's criteria been satisfied? This is the question of **internal validity**.

3. If the inference involves a generalization from a sample to one or more populations, did the sample properly represent the population(s) to which the generalization is drawn? This is the question of **external validity**.

4. If inferences are cast in theoretical terms, did the observables and the theoretical constructs they represented "fit" one another? This raises the most difficult of the four validity questions, namely, **theoretical (or construct) validity**.

STATISTICAL CONCLUSION VALIDITY

Most psychologists employ **statistical tests** in evaluating the outcome of their research. These tests are used to determine whether an observed relationship in a sample is statistically significant (and can therefore be taken to reflect a real relationship in the population). In deciding whether a relationship exists in the population, we risk committing either type I or type II errors (see Chapter 5), depending on the size of our sample and the tests, measures, and procedures used in our investigation. All of these issues fall under the heading of **statistical conclusion validity**. This type of validity faces six distinct threats.

Low Statistical Power

The possibility of committing a type II error (i.e., failing to identify associations that are, in fact, present) arises whenever **statistical power** is low. Small samples limit the power of statistical tests. Thus when using very small samples, even a large population effect may not be identified as statistically significant.

Violated Assumptions of Statistical Tests

Statistical tests employ mathematically derived estimates of chance occurrence (i.e., "p values") by making a set of **mathematical assumptions** about populations of numbers. For example, many commonly used statistical tests assume that the variances of the sets of scores being related or compared are roughly equivalent (i.e., "homogeneity of variance"). Violation of this or other assumptions in an actual set of data may invalidate the statistical conclusions reached, thus increasing the likelihood of either a **type I error or** a **type II error**. (The specific assumptions underlying each statistical test are identified and explained in virtually all advanced statistics texts.)

"Fishing"

Many investigations are designed so that a number of different statistical comparisons among various groups or conditions can be performed. For example, if we examined 100 r's (e.g., in a **correlation matrix**), five of them would be statistically significant by chance alone at $p < .05$.

Thus, *whenever an investigator "fishes" through all possible comparisons, some are almost certain to be statistically significant merely by chance.* Fishing is an inappropriate use of inferential statistics. Investigators who "fish around" for anything significant greatly increase their chances of making *type I errors* (see p. 95).

Unreliable Measures

In Chapter 3 we explained the importance of employing reliable measures (i.e., measures containing as little **random measurement error** as possible). Unreliable measures reduce the power of statistical tests. This increases the likelihood of *type II errors* (see p. 96).

Unreliable Treatment Implementation

In studies involving comparisons between **treatments**, it is essential that the treatment given to the participants within each group be as nearly identical as possible. If either the treatment implementation or the setting in which the treatment is delivered is poorly controlled (that is, varies from participant to participant within the same group), the result will be an undesirable *increase* in the error component of the response measures. This increased error variability will reduce the likelihood of detecting true group differences, thus increasing the likelihood of *type II errors*.

Heterogeneity of Subjects

If participants differ widely from one another on personal characteristics (such as age, experience, or abilities), these factors may also produce uncontrolled (error) variance. In turn, this uncontrolled variance reduces our ability to identify true effects. This, too, increases the likelihood of *type II errors*.

INTERNAL VALIDITY

A businessman wished to determine whether taking two aspirin on returning home from the office would relax him during the evening. To test this hypothesis, he took aspirin on some evenings but not on others. In this way, he hoped to assess the differential effects of the treatment (aspirin) and control (no aspirin) situations. Now it happens that this man always "washed down" the aspirin with a glass of beer, but rarely drank beer on control days. Thus, an important rival hypothesis for the conclusion that aspirin enhanced relaxation would be that the beer was responsible for any observed difference.

This example highlights the issue of internal validity. *Causal inferences are internally valid only when the observed change or difference can be attributed confidently to a specific variable that has been isolated by the investigator.* Internal *in*validity results when two comparison groups differ on variables *other than* the variable of primary interest. This was the flaw in our businessman's aspirin and beer experiment.

In order to establish internal validity for a causal inference, one must (among other things) demonstrate that the groups or conditions being compared were equivalent *except for* the treatment or event of interest. If the critical treatment cannot be isolated, no clear demonstration of causality can be made. Thus, the research *lacks* internal validity.

Plausible Rival Hypotheses

The central point underlying the concept of internal validity is that a causal inference is valid only if the research design has effectively eliminated all **plausible rival hypotheses**, so that the inference $X > Y$ is sound. *The burden of proof is on the investigator to demonstrate that the effect is indeed due to the claimed cause.*

It is important to emphasize the word *plausible*. In practice, almost any comparison that can be made in psychological research will be open to some remotely conceivable rival hypothesis. For example, in comparing groups of men who do and do not have high cholesterol diets, it would be almost impossible to be sure that the groups were exactly identical in height. Thus, technically, height differences might rival cholesterol intake as an explanation for an observed difference in the subjects' serum cholesterol levels. But generally, height would not be considered a *plausible* rival hypothesis in this comparison. Thus the presence of group differences in height would not greatly threaten the inference that high cholesterol foods increase blood cholesterol. (Of course, depending on the details of the study, some other factors might operate as plausible rival hypotheses and threaten the internal validity of the causal inference.)

Social science methodologists (e.g., Campbell & Stanley, 1966) have suggested 11 distinct threats to internal validity. Different threats are involved depending upon whether inferences are based on within- or between-subjects comparisons (see Chapter 3).

Threats to the Validity of Within-Subjects Comparisons

There are five general threats to the internal validity of any **within-subjects comparison:** maturation, testing, instrument change, statistical regression, and history (Campbell & Stanley, 1966). All of these may be considered potential third variables, giving rise to plausible rival hypotheses that can invalidate inferences of the type $X > Y$ drawn from within-subjects comparisons.

Maturation. The term **maturation** *refers to those processes within the person that produce changes in a subject over time that are* not *related to the variable of interest.* This definition of maturation is more general than the usual dictionary definition, inasmuch as it includes phenomena such as growing tired, growing hungry, and the like. Thus, *maturation refers to any or all systematic changes in an organism's biological or psychological condition over time.*

Consider the following study of the effects of tutoring on poor readers. At the beginning of the term all the children in a classroom are given a reading test, and a special tutoring program is initiated for everyone. At the end of the program (six months later) all subjects are retested, and it is found that their reading scores have risen markedly.

Although it is tempting to conclude that the tutoring program produced this effect, the improved reading scores could be due to maturation: in this case, changes produced by experience and the passage of time. For these reasons, the children might have shown an equally impressive gain if they had simply remained in their regular classrooms. This latter explanation is not necessarily the correct one, of course. Rather, maturation competes with the suggestion that the tutorial program caused the effect. The problem is that in this study there is no satisfactory way to discriminate between these two hypotheses.

Repeated Testing. **Repeated testing** as a source of causal ambiguity *refers to the possible effects on test scores of having already taken a similar test.* In general, it is known that taking a test in itself affects subsequent performance on the same test or a similar (parallel form) test. For example, on IQ tests there is typically an increase in IQ from the first to the second testing (Anastasi, 1968). On personality measures, an individual typically appears to be better adjusted when taking the test a second time. Clearly, people are unlikely to actually become either brighter or better adjusted as a function of taking a test. It is merely that their performance on these instruments is affected by repeated administrations.

In the case of children tutored in reading, we presumed that the children were given an initial test and then *retested* after the special program had been completed. If so, it is possible that the improvement in reading scores was at least partly attributable to repeated testing.

Instrument Change. **Instrument change** *refers to changes in the characteristics of a measurement instrument over time.* Simple physical measurements usually involve no more than minimal problems in instrumentation.

For instance, a ruler will typically show only trivial changes under ordinary conditions. The situation is quite different when we consider measurement in psychological research. An interviewer (who is, in the special sense in which we are using the term here, an "instrument") may easily become more skilled over time. Thus, with practice, interviewers may elicit more complete information from interviewees.

It can be difficult to distinguish between instrument change and subject change. Consider the 45-year-old man who begins an exercise program using an inexpensive rubber stretch cable to develop arm and chest muscles. To determine the effect of exercising, he measures the maximum length to which he could extend the cable each day. He finds that his ability to stretch the cable is steadily increasing. Can he conclude that this is an effect of increasing strength?

No. The cable might become easier to stretch either because the man is getting stronger through exercise *or* because the rubber is deteriorating and hence becoming more elastic. In this case, the possibility of instrument change is easy to see and, as in our previous examples, it stands as a clear **rival hypothesis** to the claim that exercise has caused a real increase in the man's strength.

Statistical Regression.   **Statistical regression** *refers to the fact that extreme scores within a distribution will tend to move (that is, "regress") toward the mean of the distribution upon repeated testing.* Statistical regression is different from maturation or the simple effects of repeated testing. It is caused by the imperfect relationship between the first and the second tests, that is, by **random measurement error** (see Chapter 3).

Because measurement error is randomly distributed, extremely high scores will decrease somewhat and extremely low scores will increase somewhat simply as a function of changes in the distribution of the error component of scores on retesting. (Similarly, other subjects' scores, which were *not* notably extreme at time 1, may be extreme at time 2.) Statistical regression contaminated the results of an evaluation of *Sesame Street's* effectiveness. (See Box 6.1.)

History.   **History** *refers to those environmental events other than the treatment or experience of interest that occur between a first and second testing.* Note the difference between this definition and the definition of *maturation.* Maturation refers to changes within the person, whereas *history* refers to events in the environment.

Imagine that a manufacturer of hurricane shutters in Florida is unhappy with its recent sales. An advertising agency is hired and a massive ad campaign is undertaken. Shortly thereafter, Florida is hit by the worst hurricane of the century. During the next few months, hurricane shutter sales reach an all-time high. Should the manufacturer conclude that the jump in sales was caused by the advertising campaign?

Certainly not. The hurricane, rather than the advertising campaign, may have been what suddenly convinced so many Floridians they needed hurricane shutters. In this case an event of *history*—the hurricane—is a plausible explanation for the explosion in shutter sales.

History need not be a result of natural causes like the weather. Changes in the political, social, or economic climate can all yield historical events or circumstances that will change a population between a first and second testing. And

BOX 6.1   *DOUBTS ABOUT THE EFFECTS OF SESAME STREET*

> An example of how statistical regression can become a significant rival hypothesis to a causal inference can be found in a study of the effects of the television series, *Sesame Street*. Bogatz and Ball (1972) found that among viewers of the show, children with the lowest initial scores on a variety of preschool academic skills (such as recognizing letters of the alphabet) gained *more* than other children over a season of viewing. That is, there was a negative correlation between the child's initial scores and the amount he or she seemed to gain from viewing *Sesame Street*.
>
> Does this mean that the more disadvantaged a child is, the more the child will gain from *Sesame Street?* Presumably, this is what the creators of the series had hoped. But the evidence is ambiguous because of the possibility that mere statistical regression accounts for the unusually large gains of the children with the lowest initial scores.
>
> That is, both the children's initial scores and their final scores contain (1) a **true score** and (2) **measurement error**. Measurement error, caused by transient random factors (such as having had an unusually tiring day before taking the test), is almost certainly one reason why some of the initial low scorers did as poorly as they did on the first test. These same chance factors will probably *not* befall these same youngsters again when they take the test at the end of the television season. Thus, the scores of this group will tend to regress upward regardless of the true effects of *Sesame Street* (Cook et al., 1975; Liebert, 1976).

history, like maturation, becomes an increasingly plausible rival hypothesis as longer intervals of time (with correspondingly greater opportunity for maturation or historical events to occur) elapse between the first and the second testing.

Threats to the Validity of Between-Subjects Comparisons

There are six major threats to the internal validity of **between-subjects comparisons:** selection bias, differential attrition, diffusion, compensatory equalization, compensatory rivalry, and resentful demoralization.

Selection Bias.   **Selection bias** *refers to any systematic difference that exists between the comparison groups before the administration of the treatment.*

Suppose, for example, that ten high school mathematics teachers are told about a new method of teaching math. Five members of this group volunteer to try the new program. The progress of their students is then compared to the progress of a group of comparable students who are taught mathematics in the traditional way, *by the five teachers who did not volunteer for the new program.*

Inasmuch as the volunteers may be more enthusiastic than the nonvolunteers, differences in the progress made by their students could result from differences in teaching style, rather than any differences in the teaching methods per se. Thus, the new instructional technique might in fact be no better than the old one, even though the students exposed to it seemed to do better than those studying the established curriculum.

In other cases, selection bias is introduced when subjects have been formed into groups for reasons other than participation in a research study. In psychiatric hospitals, for example, patients are often grouped in wards according to the severity of their conditions.

Suppose a researcher in one of these hospitals tries to determine the effects of supportive therapy by comparing patients from a ward receiving supportive therapy with patients from a ward where supportive therapy is not offered. Suppose, too, that the patients on the supportive therapy ward were found to care for themselves much better than those on the no-therapy ward. Is this a convincing demonstration of the effectiveness of supportive therapy?

No. **A plausible rival hypothesis** is that the patients on the no-therapy ward had been assigned there precisely because they were judged to be too mentally disturbed to care for themselves.

Differential Attrition.   Attrition refers to the loss of subjects from one or more groups of a study. **Differential attrition** *refers to differences in the number of subjects that are lost as a function of treatment group.*

Suppose that an investigator wishes to explore the influence of a treatment for reducing smoking. The investigator forms two groups, equated for the number of cigarettes per day that they smoke; one of the groups is given treatment, the other (control) group is not.

During the study, many subjects drop out of the treatment group, but few drop out of the control group. Thus, when the second measurement of the frequency of smoking is obtained, the comparison groups may now differ *because of the different dropout rates.* Perhaps, the heaviest smokers in the treatment group dropped out of the study because it was too difficult for them to reduce their smoking. The mean number of cigarettes smoked for the treated group would now be lower than that of the control group—but *not* as a result of successful treatment.

Diffusion.   **Diffusion** *refers to the spread of treatment effects from treated to untreated groups.* Diffusion is an important problem when the treatment involves providing information to some individuals or groups but not to others. For example, if some college students in a memory experiment are told that they will be tested again a week later, but other students are not told of the subsequent test, the investigator must insure that knowledge of the later test does not spread to all participants (e.g., by discussion of the experiment among friends or classmates before all the participants have completed the testing). Diffusion can mask or wipe out the true effects of a treatment.

Compensatory Equalization.   **Compensatory equalization** *refers to the situation in which untreated individuals or groups learn of the treatment received by others and demand the same treatment or something "equally good" for themselves.* For example, in comparing the effects of violent and nonviolent television on boys in a residential facility, one team of investigators faced the problem that boys in the nonviolent TV group learned that those in the other group were allowed to watch the series *Batman*. (*Batman* had just made its television premiere.) The boys in the nonviolent TV group demanded the right to watch *Batman* too. Thus, the primary intended group difference no longer existed, and the study failed to yield the predicted results.

A similar problem has arisen in evaluating many large-scale educational enrichment programs. Parents, teachers, and school administrators in areas not receiving the enrichment may hear of the special program and demand that their children receive something of equal value. As with diffusion, compensatory equalization can obscure real treatment effects that might otherwise be demonstrated.

Compensatory Rivalry. **Compensatory rivalry** *occurs when an untreated group learns of the treatment received by others and works extra hard to see to it that the expected superiority of the treatment group is not demonstrated.* Compensatory rivalry has been called the **"John Henry Effect,"** after the famous steel driver who learned that his performance was being compared to a steam drill. John Henry drove himself to outperform his inanimate competitor—only to die of overexertion as a result.

Resentful Demoralization. **Resentful demoralization** is the flip side of compensatory rivalry. It *occurs when individuals in an untreated or control group learn that others are receiving special treatment, and become less productive, less efficient, or less motivated than they would have been because of feelings of resentment.* Resentful demoralization may occur even when the special treatment given to the other group is in fact of no benefit. In such cases, resentful demoralization can create the false appearance of an advantage for the treated group (a type I error) when the treatment itself actually has no beneficial effect.

EXTERNAL VALIDITY

After internal validity is examined, there remains the question of *external validity*, or the *generalization* of results. Broadly speaking, there are two types of external validity in psychological research: **population validity and ecological validity**.

Population Validity

Population validity *refers to the question of whether the responses or behavior of subjects in the actual research sample can be generalized to the target population*, that is, the population of ultimate interest.

Recall from Chapter 3 that generalizations from a sample to a population are logically justified only when it can be shown that a **representative sample** has been used. One way to insure a representative sample is to select subjects randomly from the population of interest.

The problem in psychological research is often that the population of interest cannot be specified clearly, or that a truly random (or representative) sample cannot be drawn. Rather, accidental samples or **samples of convenience** are often used. For this reason, generalization in psychological research typically involves two steps.

First, the investigator generalizes from the sample employed to the **accessible population** from which it was drawn. And second, the investigator generalizes from the accessible population to the target population of ultimate interest. This leads us to the distinction between *random selection* and *random assignment*.

Random Selection versus Random Assignment. **Random selection** involves *the selection of individuals who will participate as subjects* from the target population (that is, the **population of ultimate interest**). **Random assignment** involves assigning subjects to groups such that each subject has an equal chance of being assigned to any of the groups (see Chapter 3). The distinction is an important one to keep in mind for two reasons. For one, whereas random assignment is fairly common in psychological research (especially in laboratory experiments), *random selection is extremely rare*. And second, whereas the absence of random assignment is principally a threat to internal validity, *the absence of random selection is principally a threat to external validity*.

Most researchers have a very wide population of ultimate interest in mind, but are compelled by cost considerations to draw their subjects from only a narrow segment of it. This is called **cost-restricted sampling**. For example, a team of investigators in San Francisco may be interested in adolescents all over the United States (or perhaps even all over the world). In practice, however, the researchers will probably obtain their subjects entirely from California and perhaps entirely from one or two high schools in the San Francisco Bay area. There are several methods for minimizing the threat caused by the inability to draw a random sample.

Broad Sampling. The goal of **broad sampling** is to obtain the widest possible sample within existing constraints. One way to do this involves maximizing the range of persons who will volunteer to participate. This can be done by making participation as convenient, inviting, and rewarding as possible. Researchers who ask participants to complete lengthy and tedious questionnaires will end up with a less representative sample than those who have reduced their measures to simple, quick, and easy formats.

As well as attempting to make participation as convenient as possible, there are other ways to increase the breadth of research samples. In endeavoring to solve the problem of generalizing beyond a specific sample, the investigator should take two steps: 1) *decide on an adequate definition of the population to which he or she is interested in generalizing*, and 2) *determine the degree to which the particular sample in hand differs from the population of interest*.

Defining the Population of Interest. Some investigators conducting research with child subjects may be interested in generalizing to all children. Of course, it is virtually impossible to randomly select subjects from such a broad population of interest. In this case the researcher should make every possible attempt to sample as broadly as possible within the existing constraints.

For instance, consider an investigation of teaching techniques in which the investigator can sample from three local grade schools. Every effort should be made to select subjects from all three, which will adequately reflect the population of those school districts. This will reduce the likelihood of further limiting generalizability by restricting the sample to one segment of the available population (for example, upper middle class white children who might comprise the student body of just one of the schools in question).

Another solution to the sampling problem is to increase representativeness through the use of specific sampling techniques. Cook and Campbell (1979) suggest two novel ways to do this: *haphazard sampling* and *impressionistic modal sampling*.

Haphazard sampling involves purposely taking every opportunity to get the widest range of subjects, experimenters, treatments, and settings represented in one's research. This strategy will surely increase representativeness relative to using a single subpopulation in a single setting with a sole experimenter. Many forms of **selection bias** will be reduced or canceled out by the sample's heterogeneity.

The limitation of this strategy is that such heterogeneity improves external validity at the expense of statistical power. That is, heterogeneity increases the amount of **random error variance** in the measures of interest, and thereby reduces the likelihood of detecting **systematic variance**.

Impressionistic modal sampling is applicable to situations in which the population of ultimate interest is comprised of institutional units (such as schools, hospitals, etc.), and cost or other considerations limit the researcher's access to more than just a few of them. For example, the elementary schools in a large city are likely to be quite diverse, and it would rarely be possible to sample randomly from all of them. One might, however, form an impression of what types of schools are most "typical" (that is, modal) by examining the dimensions on which they vary. Then several schools could be selected as "modal" cases.

For example, if the schools vary in racial composition and in the economic groups which they represent, we might select a middle-class white school, a lower-class school with many minority pupils, and a racially and economically mixed school as three modal cases. Taken together, these schools would represent reasonably well the range of elementary schools found in the city.

Assessing the Representativeness of Samples Used. As for the identification of plausible limits to generality, this is a somewhat more difficult problem. (It goes without saying, that if a random sample of the population could not be drawn for the investigation, neither is it available for a comparison with the sample used in order to identify any existing differences between the two!) Thus, this issue involves a degree of judgement on the part of the researcher, and the acceptability of his/her claims will be based in part on how far the results are to be generalized from the actual sample employed.

Ecological Validity

Ecological validity *refers to the question of whether the research findings can be generalized to all of the environmental contexts of interest.* Environmental context, or ecology, covers a wide range of factors, including the time, place, and people that surround and interact with the subjects.

Laboratory Versus Field Settings.   A **laboratory setting** is any situation or facility that is visibly or apparently devoted to research. A **field setting**, in contrast, is an environment or situation that the subject perceives as naturally occurring, so that the variables of interest can be observed or manipulated in an apparently spontaneous or unobtrusive way.

The advantage of administering treatments or making observations in the laboratory is that tight control over the situation can be maintained, and extraneous factors and distractions can be eliminated or at least minimized.

The disadvantages of a laboratory setting are that the research participants know they are in an investigation, and that the environment itself is novel and artificial. Critics are thus in position to argue that laboratory findings cannot be generalized to real-life settings.

In the early 1960s, psychologist Albert Bandura and his colleagues showed that preschool children who watched a film of an adult assaulting a plastic Bobo doll became more likely to yell at, hit, kick, and punch such a doll. Based on this work, Bandura (1963) published an article in *Look* magazine, entitled, "What TV violence can do to your child" in which he concluded that exposure to violent TV could make children more aggressive.

Critics from the television industry were quick to point out the "make-believe" nature of Bandura's experiments. They argued that a child's willingness to hit a plastic doll—a toy—in a laboratory setting did not mean that a TV performance could make young viewers more aggressive toward real people. This is a challenge to the external validity of Bandura's inferences.

The question of ecological validity can be raised about any laboratory experiment, for it challenges the artificiality that is inherent in the laboratory setting. The most obvious way to assure ecological validity is to conduct field experiments. One example of the power of field experiments over the laboratory setting can be found in the response to criticisms of Bandura's early study.

Subsequent studies by other investigators gradually moved toward a less artificial test of the television and aggression hypothesis. For example, studies were done in which the television programs viewed were selected from existing TV fare (instead of movies made in the laboratory), and in which the victims were other children and adults, rather than toys or dolls. Later studies went so far as observing childrens' spontaneous behavior in natural settings (such as school playgrounds) after exposure to televised violence. In all of these studies, a relationship between viewed violence and an increase in later aggression was found (Liebert & Sprafkin, 1988).

In this example we see that one way to argue for the external validity of laboratory findings is to demonstrate that the same principles operate in the field as in the laboratory. Field studies face some serious problems of their own, though. They can be costly to conduct and may also raise ethical concerns. They often involve observing participants without providing the opportunity for informed consent or debriefing.

Generalizing Across Experimenters.   Imagine that you are participating in a study, and the experimenter who greets you seems grumpy and unfriendly. If you are like most people, you will not be as cooperative or effective when given instructions by this person as you would have been if the experimenter had seemed warm and friendly. So, **experimenter characteristics** may influence psychological research findings. Results obtained by one experimenter or interviewer may not generalize to other experimenters or interviewers. There are two means of dealing with this problem.

One is to make all research personnel as "neutral" as possible. For example, it is good practice to write out scripts and rehearse procedures to reduce unnecessary variation. The other means available for controlling the influence of the experimenter characteristics is to employ more than one person to fill each public role in any piece of research, and rotate them regularly. These methods serve to increase generalizability by reducing the influence of personal characteristics on any particular group of subjects.

Temporal Generalizations.   Psychological research findings may be ungeneralizable to the extent that they are time bound. This raises the issue of **temporal validity**. For example, the results of a comparison of two types of teaching procedures, one of which is more likely to capture or focus a child's attention than another, might be very striking for groups of young children who participated in a nursery school in the late afternoon. However, the effects might not differ nearly so sharply if the experiment were conducted in the morning, when all children were better rested and more alert and attentive.

Likewise, many behaviors show seasonal or cyclical variations. Thus, measures taken at one time may not be generalizable to other times. College students, for example, appear to show considerably higher levels of anxiety and depression toward the end of the semester or quarter (when exams are imminent) than at the beginning. Their performance in experiments during these times (which is also when voluntary participation for extra credit is most likely to occur) may not even generalize to what the very same students would have done at other times of the year!

Similarly, laboratory animals demonstrate cyclical variations (e.g., circadian rhythms) in bodily functions that may make them respond to drug or environmental treatments very differently at one time than at another (Hunsicker & Mellgren, 1977).

When Is External Validity Relevant?

It is well to point out, before closing this section, that many laboratory investigations do not require external validity in the conventional sense, nor do they have empirical generalizations as their aim. Rather, the truly important laboratory experiment is one that achieves theoretical validity. To make this point, Mook (1983) used the example of Harlow's classic work with baby rhesus monkeys who were brought up with terry cloth and wire mesh "mother monkeys" rather than their real mothers. Mook observes:

> Were Harlow's baby monkeys representative of the population of monkeys in general? Obviously not; they were born in captivity and then orphaned besides. Well, were they a representative sample of the population of lab-born, orphaned monkeys? There was no attempt at all to make this so. It must be concluded that Harlow's sampling procedures fell far short of the ideal. . . .
>
> Real monkeys do not live within walls. They do not encounter mother figures made of wire mesh, with rubber nipples; nor is the advent of a terry-cloth cylinder, warmed by a light bulb, a part of their natural life-style. What can this contrived situation possibly tell us about how monkeys with natural upbringing would behave in a natural setting?
>
> On the face of it, the verdict must be a flat flunk. On every criterion of external validity that applies at all, we find Harlow's experiment either manifestly deficient or simply unvaluable. And yet our tendency is to respond to this critique with a resounding "So what?" And I think we are quite right to so respond.
>
> Why? Because using the lab results to make generalizations about real-world behavior was not part of Harlow's intention. It was not what he was trying to do. That being the case, the concept of external validity simply does not arise. . . .
>
> Harlow did not conclude, "Wild monkeys in the jungle probably would choose terry-cloth over wire mothers, too, if offered the choice." First, it would be a moot conclusion, since that simply is not going to happen. Second, who cares whether they would or not? The generalization would be trivial even if true. What Harlow did conclude was that the hunger-reduction interpretation of mother love would not work. If anything about his experiment has external validity, it is this theoretical point, not the findings themselves. (Mook, 1983, p. 381.)

Thus, there are times when psychologists may be less concerned with external validity than with **theoretical validity**.

THEORETICAL VALIDITY

Suppose a cognitive psychologist hypothesizes that reading false statements can raise uncertainty in our minds, even about things of which we are sure. As a first test of the hypothesis, he designs a simple experiment. Among a sample of volunteers from a subject pool, he randomly assigns half to read one of two statements, while the other half of his subjects reads the other (the independent variable). He then gives all the subjects a test (the dependent measure).

The experimental group is asked to read the following statement:

In the U.S. Civil War, the South came very close to winning.

The control group reads the following:

In the U.S. Civil War, many soldiers were killed.

The dependent measure is a one-item test, to be answered *true* or *false.* The test consists of a statement, flashed on a computer screen. The time it takes before the subject pushes an answer key (T or F) is recorded precisely. The statement is:

> The South won the U.S. Civil War.

Every subject answers *false* to this question, but the mean reaction times of those in the experimental group is more than twice as long (1.4 seconds) as the reaction time of those in the control group (.68 second). This difference is significant at $p < .01$. The researcher concludes that his hypothesis has been supported.

He reasons that the statement read by the those in the experimental group was false (the South *didn't* come close to winning the Civil War). And, as per the hypothesis, those exposed to this false statement should become less certain about a fact they knew to be true (the South lost). As a result of this uncertainty, their reaction times to the true/false question should be longer than those of the control group . . . and they were. Thus, the hypothesis has received support. Or has it?

Along comes a critic. This critic doesn't doubt the data or results, but she *does* doubt the interpretation. The researcher has assumed that *reaction time* (the actual dependent measure in the study) can be interpreted as reflecting *uncertainty*, which is the theoretical variable specified in the hypothesis. This may or may *not* be a valid assumption.

Perhaps, for example, reaction time in the experimental group was not protracted because of uncertainty about who won the Civil War, but rather simply because they were surprised to read yet another falsehood. (This may have made them wonder about the purpose or legitimacy of the experiment, so that it took them a moment more to "switch gears" when faced with a true/false question.)

Interpretive debates of this kind are not uncommon in the psychological literature. They reflect the imperfect relationship between the theoretical constructs in which the investigator is interested and the *operationalization* of these constructs in research. (See Chapter 1.)

In an effort to make a more convincing argument for one interpretation over another, multiple studies may have to be conducted, and **construct validation** techniques employed.

Construct Validation

Most of the phenomena studied by psychologists lack a single, definite criterion measure (or **operational definition**) with which they can be equated. The goal of **construct validation** is to define a complex psychological phenomenon by showing that its meaning resides in a *network* of relationships among directly measurable variables.

Typically, this means undertaking a **research program**, rather than just an isolated study. An example of how this can be done appeared in the literature on *test anxiety*.

Anxiety has been an important theoretical construct in psychology, at least since the provocative writings of Sigmund Freud. *Test anxiety* attracted a good deal of attention during the 1950s and early 1960s, and was presumed to refer to a single underlying factor: the motive to avoid failure (Atkinson & Litwin, 1960; Gorsuch, 1966). The predominant measure of test anxiety was a paper-and-pencil measure, the Test Anxiety Questionnaire (TAQ).

In the late 1960s a program of research was undertaken to address what the TAQ actually measured. This research was initiated by a hypothesized distinction between two components of test anxiety, *worry* and *emotionality* (Liebert & Morris, 1967). Thus, an effort was made to validate *two distinct constructs* that had formerly been presumed to be one.

The goal of the research program was to demonstrate the existence of both "cognitive concern over performance" (worry) and "physiological arousal" (emotionality). A modified Test Anxiety Questionnaire was developed, drawing on items from the original TAQ, which could be readily identified as tapping either worry (W) or emotionality (E). The goal was then to generate as many **testable implications** of the distinction as possible.

In the initial study, undergraduate students were given the modified TAQ (from which separate W and E scores could be computed) shortly before a major course examination. At the same time, the students also completed a questionnaire about how well they expected to do on the upcoming exam, from which an expectancy score was computed. Inasmuch as expectancy is a cognitive state, it should be predictable from W but *not* from E. This is precisely what was found. The higher a person's expectancy, the lower his/her worry scores. In contrast, emotionality scores were found to be unrelated to expectancy.

Next, it was hypothesized that W and E should relate differently to temporal factors. The reasoning was as follows:

> First, conceiving of E as a reaction to the stress of the testing situation itself, it was reasoned (Study I) that E scores would be lower following an examination than immediately prior to it. After turning in one's examination paper, the conditions producing immediate situational stress are gone and thus E should begin to dissipate quite rapidly. On the other hand, the major determinants of cognitive concern (W) are presumably left relatively unchanged until the individual actually receives a grade. . . . Hence, in contrast to E scores, no changes [in] W scores would be predicted as a result of merely completing the examination.
>
> [Second] predictions were extended to a third point in time. Specifically, it was hypothesized that E should be lower both *several days prior to* and *just after* an important examination than immediately before the stress-provoking situation. In the former instance the conditions that produce E have not yet occurred, and in the latter these conditions are no longer present. However, W should not show any systematic changes across this same time period. (Spiegler et al., 1968, p. 452)

To test these hypotheses, students were given the modified TAQ immediately before and immediately after a major exam. As predicted, E dropped substantially from pre- to postexam, whereas W remained unchanged. Similarly, another study showed that E rises markedly during the 5 days before a major exam, whereas W appears to decrease slightly.

A famous study of the 1950s had concluded that low-anxious persons do better on timed tests, whereas high-anxious persons do better on untimed tests (Siegman, 1956). The next study in the research program was designed to show that the worry-emotionality distinction could shed new light on these old data (Morris & Liebert, 1969).

A widely used general anxiety scale was modified to yield separate W and E scores. Subjects were then divided into four groups: high W/high E, high W/low E, low W/high E, and low W/low E. Low worriers were found to do better on timed tests than on untimed ones (regardless of level of E), whereas emotionality was unrelated to how well a subject did under timed versus untimed conditions. Thus, the pattern of effects previously ascribed to the interaction of anxiety and timing could now be understood more precisely as the relationship between worry and timing.

A final pair of studies in the program looked at the relationship between test anxiety and actual performance. For samples of both high school and college students it was found that W, but not E, predicted exam scores (Morris & Liebert, 1970). Taken together, the studies of this research program support and validate the theoretical distinction between cognitive and emotional components of test anxiety.

Here we have the essence of the construct validation approach. First, an idea is expressed in theoretical terms. Second, a research program is undertaken in which implications of the theoretical claim are derived and investigated empirically. The results of these empirical tests provide validation of the theoretical idea to the extent that they all come together to provide a *network* of converging evidence. The ultimate goal of much psychological research is to establish theoretical validity.

FOR REVIEW AND DISCUSSION

Key Terms
TEST VALIDITY
STATISTICAL TESTS
STATISTICAL CONCLUSION VALIDITY
STATISTICAL POWER
MATHEMATICAL ASSUMPTIONS (OF STATISTICAL TESTS)
RANDOM MEASUREMENT ERROR
TYPE I ERROR
TYPE II ERROR
TREATMENTS

PLAUSIBLE RIVAL HYPOTHESES
WITHIN-SUBJECTS COMPARISONS
BETWEEN-SUBJECTS COMPARISONS
MATURATION
RIVAL HYPOTHESIS
STATISTICAL REGRESSION
TRUE SCORE
MEASUREMENT ERROR
HISTORY
SELECTION BIAS
DIFFERENTIAL ATTRITION
DIFFUSION
COMPENSATORY EQUALIZATION
COMPENSATORY RIVALRY
JOHN HENRY EFFECT
RESENTFUL DEMORALIZATION
EXTERNAL VALIDITY
POPULATION VALIDITY
ECOLOGICAL VALIDITY
REPRESENTATIVE SAMPLE
SAMPLES OF CONVENIENCE
ACCESSIBLE POPULATION
RANDOM ASSIGNMENT
RANDOM SELECTION
POPULATION OF ULTIMATE INTEREST
COST-RESTRICTED SAMPLING
SELECTION BIAS
TEMPORAL VALIDITY
HAPHAZARD SAMPLING
RANDOM ERROR VARIANCE
IMPRESSIONISTIC MODAL SAMPLING
STATISTICAL SIGNIFICANCE
INTERNAL VALIDITY
VALIDITY OF SCIENTIFIC INFERENCES
THEORETICAL VALIDITY
CONSTRUCT VALIDITY
CORRELATION MATRIX
RANDOM MEASUREMENT ERROR
REPEATED TESTING
INSTRUMENT CHANGE
LABORATORY SETTING
FIELD SETTING
EXPERIMENTER CHARACTERISTICS
CONSTRUCT VALIDATION

Discussion Issues

1. Explain each term and indicate how it might be a source of internal invalidity:

   maturation
   testing
   instrument decay
   history
   statistical regression
   selection bias
   differential attrition

2. Diffusion, compensatory equalization, compensatory rivalry, and resentful demoralization are only threats to internal validity when subjects who do not receive a treatment know that others are receiving one. Under what circumstances are subjects most likely to obtain this knowledge? How can these threats be avoided?

3. In many ways, compensatory rivalry and resentful demoralization seem to be opposite effects; that is, one suggests an increase in the performance of subjects who do not receive a special treatment, whereas the other suggests a decline in performance. Under what circumstances is compensatory rivalry more likely? Under what circumstances is resentful demoralization more likely? Why?

4. How does the problem of external validity relate to the larger issue of whether induction is legitimate?

5. Explain how an internally valid causal inference can be subject to more than one explanation.

6. Discuss the role of subject selection and sampling alternatives in assuring and threatening external validity.

7. What would be the disadvantages of equating every theoretical construct with a single, explicit measuring procedure?

8. What is the relationship between internal validity and external validity?

THE TRUE EXPERIMENT

So far in our discussion we have emphasized the difficulties encountered in drawing causal inferences. We now turn to a simple and logically compelling way of accomplishing this goal: the true experiment.

CONCEPT OF THE TRUE EXPERIMENT

The hallmark of the experimental method is that variables of interest (as causes) are manipulated directly. Often one will hear lay persons (and even some psychologists) refer to a correlational study involving only classificatory variables as an "experiment"; however, from a technical point of view, this is an incorrect usage and can be misleading. In addition to the manipulation of relevant variables, the proper use of the experimental method involves two features: random assignment to treatments, and the use of comparison groups to eliminate the effects of extraneous variables.

Thus in our discussion we will speak of the **true experiment** as one in which causal inference is made on the basis of random assignment, manipulation of relevant variables, and direct control over irrelevant variables.

In the true experiment, the investigator administers or manipulates the hypothesized cause as a **treatment**, and thus can directly observe its effects. Properly executed and controlled, the true experiment can eliminate the third variable and directionality problems completely. What is more, the logical requirements of Mill's criteria are completely satisfied. (See Chapter 5.)

The Example of Experimentally Induced Compliance

To introduce the basic concepts and terminology associated with the true experiment, let's begin with a classic experiment in social psychology reported by Freedman et al. (1967). This experiment involved only between-subjects comparisons. In Chapter 8 we will consider several issues connected with within-subjects comparisons in the true experiment. But the basic logic of experimentation and all of the major concepts will remain the same.

Freedman et al. were interested in the question, "How can people be induced to do something they would not otherwise do?" As we already know, and as Freedman and his associates noted:

> One kind of answer to this question involves increasing the pressure on the individual until he is forced to comply. If a person is subjected to enough social pressure, offered enough reward, threatened with enough pain, or given enough convincing reasons, he will, under most circumstances, eventually yield and perform the required act. Inducement through pressure of this kind is one very effective means of producing compliance (1967, p. 117).

But there are many circumstances in which it is not possible or would be unethical to employ the amount of pressure required to produce compliance. In these instances it is important, both theoretically and practically, to identify other factors that may increase a person's willingness to comply with a request. One of these, which was the focus of the Freedman research, is guilt. The investigators suggested:

> Presumably when someone feels that he has done something wrong there will be a tendency for him to make up for his wrongful deed. He can do this by subjecting himself to punishment or by doing something good to balance the bad. Either of these processes might lead to increased compliance if the request is appropriate. Given the opportunity to engage in some extremely unpleasant behavior, the guilty person should be more likely to agree than the nonguilty since the former can use this as a form of self-punishment. Similarly, if he is asked to do someone a favor, pleasant or otherwise, the guilty person should be more likely to agree than the nonguilty because the former can view it as a good deed for the day, which will make up for the bad deed about which he feels guilty (pp. 117–118).

This argument forms the basis for a single, testable **experimental hypothesis**, namely that "guilt will lead to greater compliance [than nonguilt] in a wide variety of situations" (p. 118). At this point in the argument, the hypothesis is still untested. It is no more than an idea or possibility, but it has been sufficiently formulated to be tested subsequently in a **controlled experimental situation**.

The controlled experimental situation must meet all the conceptual demands of the basic hypothesis while controlling for all extraneous factors. What are the demands of the hypothesis of Freedman and his associates?

First, a situation must be created in which some subjects are made to feel guilty, while others are not. Second, all subjects must be exposed to a relatively demanding request with which they can comply or not as they choose. Finally, measurement of the *variable of interest* (in this case, compliance with the request) must be possible. To meet these requirements, Freedman and his associates performed a true experiment.

The principal experimental manipulation in this study was to induce some subjects, but not others, to tell a deliberate lie. Telling such a lie was presumed to induce guilt and, in turn, to increase subjects' willingness to comply with a subsequent request. In order to accomplish this, the researchers told male high school students that the experiment for which they had been recruited would first require that they spend a few minutes with another person. The "other person" was supposedly the previous subject but was, in fact, an experimental confederate.

The manipulation was extremely simple. As the subject and the confederate chatted, the confederate described to a randomly selected half of the subjects (those in the *lie condition*) the test they were going to take. Included in this description were examples of the items used and some of the previous subject's speculations about the purpose of the test and how to do well on it. Because this informant was, in fact, a confederate, his statements could be controlled precisely.

To the remaining subjects (those in the *nonlie* condition), no mention was made of the details of the test. Thus, the **independent variable**, *the condition or stimulus the experimenters manipulated or had under their control*, was whether or not the subject received advance information about the test he was about to take.

Subsequently, the experimenter returned to the waiting room, announced that she was ready to begin, and added, "This is a Remote Associates Test. . . . Since we are testing a slightly different hypothesis, *we must make sure that you have not taken this test before or heard about it from friends*". With a single exception, all subjects (including those who had heard a great deal about the test from the confederate just moments ago) stated that they had not heard about the test before. That is, they lied. And Freedman and his associates assumed that those who lied were feeling guilty about it.

A **dependent variable** (or dependent measure) *is that aspect of a subject's behavior that is measured after the manipulation of the independent variable.* (You can remember the term by noting that it is expected to *depend on*, or be controlled by, the conditions set up or manipulated by the experimenter.)

In this example, the dependent variable was straightforward. After taking the Remote Associates Test, the experimenter added that another member of the psychology department was doing a study without grant support. The subject was asked whether he was willing to participate in this "other study" without pay.

After the subject answered, the experiment was terminated. The subject's reply, compliance or noncompliance, was the dependent variable. The results themselves are shown in Table 7-1, from which it can be seen that the experimental hypothesis received clear support. Subjects who received the lie treatment were considerably more likely to comply than those in the control (nonlie) condition, as the experimenters had predicted.

To summarize briefly, in a true experiment subjects are assigned randomly to conditions in which they receive different treatments (the manipulated independent variable). Then scores on one or more measures (the dependent variable or variables) are obtained. Experiments may simply involve two groups (for example, an "experimental" or treatment group and a control group, as in the Freedman et al. study), or they may be considerably more complex, as we shall see.

TABLE 7-1   PERCENTAGE OF SUBJECTS COMPLYING ACCORDING TO EXPERIMENTALLY MANIPULATED GUILT

	Experimental (Lie)	Control (Nonlie)
Complied	64.5%	35.5%
Did not comply	35.5%	64.5%

Source. Data from Freedman et al. (1967).

In any event, the researcher must plan in detail any experiment so as to maximize the likelihood that he or she will be able to detect differences produced by differences in treatment. Such differences, if they are found, permit the researcher to infer a cause and effect relationship between the independent variable and the dependent variable.

The Rationale for Between-Subjects Comparisons

Underlying the rationale for the **between-subjects comparison** is the idea that *groups* (of massed data) rather than individual subjects will be compared. This introduces some issues not encountered in other designs.

To get a closer look at some of these issues, consider a hypothetical experiment designed to determine the effects of praise on children's classroom performance. Suppose that a particular teacher has 28 children in her classroom. She is asked to arbitrarily select 14 of these children (for example, by drawing their names out of a hat) and to praise them for every instance of classroom participation. In contrast, she is instructed *not* to praise the other 14 children when they participate in discussion.

Underlying the procedure for deciding which children will receive praise and which will not is the practice of **random assignment**. Specifically, each child had an equal chance of being assigned to either the praise or the no-praise group. The advantage of such a procedure over, for example, permitting the teacher to choose which of the children should receive praise and which should not, is that differences between the two groups on other factors should be minimized.

Once the children have been assigned randomly to one of the two groups, all children (those in both groups) must be dealt with in exactly the same way, *except* for the administration of the independent variable. Thus, the only difference between the two groups in this example would be in the presence or absence of the experimental treatment, that is, the administration of praise contingent on each instance of classroom participation.

Subsequently, another teacher[1] might be asked to take over the classroom for a day and carefully record the frequency with which each child participated in discussion. A tabulation of these frequencies, providing a single score for each subject (the number of times he or she participated during the *test* period), would then be prepared according to whether the children had received the praise or no-praise treatment. A hypothetical example of how this tabulation might appear is presented in Table 7-2.

In considering Table 7-2, note that *on average*, the children who received praise for their classroom performance from the first teacher were more likely to participate in class with the second teacher than were those who did not. When

---

[1] There are several advantages to using a second teacher. For example, the second teacher could be kept from knowing (that is, would be *blind* to) which children had received which treatment, and thus his/her own expectations would not influence the obtained results.

TABLE 7-2 HYPOTHETICAL EXAMPLE OF AN EXPERIMENT TO EVALUATE THE EFFECTS OF PRAISE ON CLASSROOM PERFORMANCE

Number of Responses in Class	
Group 1 (No praise)	Group II (Praise)
4	6
4	7
3	7
1	4
6	5
8	3
6	6
5	6
5	8
3	9
4	8
5	4
7	10
2	5
$\Sigma^* = 63$	$\Sigma = 88$
$M^\dagger = 4.5$	$M = 6.3$

*The sum of the scores in a group is customarily identified with the Greek letter Sigma (Σ).

†The average, or mean, of the scores in a group is customarily labeled M.

an experiment is conducted with groups of subjects, individual performance scores are combined to produce some measure of the overall performance of the *group*. This measure provides the basis for determining whether or not satisfactory evidence for a cause and effect relationship has been found in the form of reliable *between group* differences. To the extent that the two treatment groups differ or vary systematically, we may speak of finding an *experimental effect*.

Having found a difference with this one sample, the researcher wishes to know whether or not he or she can infer that a similar effect would be produced by teachers in other classrooms (the population in which the researcher is ultimately interested). How can such a determination be made?

The answer is provided by another concept we have mentioned often before: **variance**. We have already noted that the scores vary between the groups. The difference(s) between (or among) the groups in an experiment is referred to as **systematic variance**.

But it is also the case that *within* each of the two groups, not all of the scores are the same. (See Table 7-2). And some scores within each group may overlap with (be the same as) scores in other groups. How then, do we determine if the *between group* differences are meaningful?

In our hypothetical experiment, a substantial amount of participation (eight responses) was shown by a child who did not receive praise for his earlier participation. For this reason, one might wonder whether or not the average difference between the two groups occurred by chance, rather than as a result of praise. (Perhaps most of the more talkative children "just happened" to be the ones who received praise, and the praise itself did not produce the difference.)

Remember, however, that children were assigned to groups *randomly*. The use of **random assignment** should serve to minimize the threat of this possibility.

It is clear that scores among subjects vary regardless of whether the children did or did not receive praise. Some children simply spoke up in class more frequently than others. This variability (among subjects *within* a given group) is usually referred to as **error variance**. Error variance includes both **random measurement error**, which occurs in all psychological research (see p. 50), and other differences among subjects on factors not manipulated in the experiment.

It is through a careful examination of the variability (the average difference) *between* the two groups *relative to* the degree to which the scores differ *within* each group that we ultimately find an answer. The reasoning is as follows. The average difference between the two groups in an experiment will almost never be zero, even if the treatment given to one of them is totally ineffective. This is because not all the scores, even *within* one of the groups, will be the same.

In other words, *any two randomly selected groups from the same population will differ to some extent.* The degree to which individual scores differ, simply by chance, provides a basis for estimating whether the difference obtained *between* the groups is actually larger than would have been expected by chance alone. It is only through this type of analysis that we can be confident that our effects are reliable.

First, we must estimate how much difference we might expect between the groups by chance alone. The procedure involves measuring the variance within groups, that is, the degree to which each score is different from, or deviates from, the group's average. A particular statistic, the **variance statistic** (S^2), provides an index of this variability or dispersion. (Detailed instructions for calculating S^2 may be found in any standard statistics text, but they do not concern us here.)

The variance statistic is extremely important in calculating the actual effect of the manipulation of interest on the dependent variable. In our example (Table 7-2), we see that the group that received praise produced (on the average) 1.8 more instances of classroom participation than did the group in which no praise was provided. Is this difference large enough to warrant the conclusion that praise encourages participation?

To evaluate this question, researchers employ the concept of **statistical significance**, which refers to the likelihood or probability that relationships observed in a particular sample were due to chance alone. Statistical significance is usually assessed by comparing the systematic and error variance among the scores in an experiment.

In the most commonly used statistical procedure for this purpose, the analysis of variance (ANOVA), *F*-tests are used to evaluate the ratio of systematic variance (variance between groups, presumably reflecting the effect of treatment) to error variance (variance due to unknown sources). Conceptually, the formula for the *F*-test is straightforward:

$$F = S^2 \text{ systematic}/S^2 \text{ error}$$

Everything else being equal, as the *F* statistic becomes larger, the probability that the experimental results were due to chance alone decreases. This results from greater **systematic variance** relative to **error variance**. Thus, the obtained difference between groups is more likely to be due to some factor (other than chance) namely, the experimental treatment.

In reporting the results of research, the phrase **statistically significant difference** between treatment groups is often employed. Recall that a so-called statistically significant difference is one that has a low probability of occurring by chance alone, and thus reflects a difference that could be reliably expected in other samples, that is, a "real" treatment effect.

Thus, **between-subjects comparisons** involve examining the variance *between* versus *within* the groups in order to determine the meaningfulness of observed differences. Underlying this method is the assumption that subjects were **randomly assigned** to groups, and that the groups would therefore be expected to be very similar in the absence of a real treatment effect.

SELECTION OF SUBJECTS AND ASSIGNMENT TO GROUPS

No decision is more important in experimental research than selecting one's subjects and assigning them to treatment groups. In the ideal experiment, a sample of subjects would be selected randomly from the population in which the investigator is interested, and then these subjects would be assigned randomly to treatment groups within the experiment. We say "in the ideal experiment" because the first criterion, **random selection** of a sample, is rarely (if ever) achieved in psychological research. In essence, selecting a random sample entails all the problems involved in accurately surveying a population (see Appendix A) and is just too costly for most research.

Consider, for example, the psychologist interested in experimentally demonstrating that preschool children will benefit from a special form of preschool education. The psychologist will probably not draw a truly random sample of preschoolers in North America; rather, the children will likely be drawn from one or more local populations (for example, children in the county where the experimenter works).

Moreover, only those children whose parents consent to their participation will be sampled. Such a sampling procedure obviously is not random; all members of the population of interest do *not* have an equal chance of being selected. Many have no chance at all.

Can one generalize from samples chosen in this way? For the moment, it is sufficient to note that the question is finally one of the *representativeness of the sample*. If the sample can reasonably be considered to be representative of the population, it need not have been randomly selected. The thorny problem, of course, is that it can be difficult to convince a skeptic that a nonrandom sample is indeed representative.

Regardless of how the sample for an experiment is *selected*, subjects within the sample *must* be **randomly assigned** to treatment groups within the experiment, or no valid causal inferences can be drawn from the results. Let us explain why this is so.

The Necessity of Random Assignment

We had occasion to point out in our earlier discussion of threats to internal validity that one such threat is **selection bias**. As it pertains to subject assignment in true experiments, *selection bias is present whenever subjects have been assigned to treatment groups in such a way that initial differences between them, rather than a real experimental effect, may account for a post-treatment difference between groups.* Given this potential problem, how should subjects be assigned to the groups of an experiment in order to insure internal validity?

Recall that random assignment refers to any procedure in which subjects are assigned to groups in such a manner that every subject has an equal chance of being assigned to any of the experimental groups. Random assignment reduces the likelihood that differences among the groups after treatment are due to initial differences between the groups rather than to true experimental effects. Two general procedures can be used for subject assignment: **free random assignment** and **matched random assignment**.

Free Random Assignment.   In a two-group experiment, coin tossing could be used as the method of assignment. This is the simplest example of free random assignment, that is, random assignment without other restrictions.

When more complicated free randomization procedures are necessary (for example, when the design consists of more than two groups), it is often convenient to employ a *table of random numbers* (see p. 43). These tables are constructed from the digits 0 through 9, so that each digit is equally likely to occur in any spot on the table. The experimenter can then list the prospective subjects and assign them to the numbered conditions by consulting the table. A table of random numbers prevents errors and biases that might be introduced through experimenter–invented procedures for arbitrary assignment.

Imagine an experiment employing four conditions. The experimenter wrongly assumes that randomness means that two subjects will not be successively assigned to the same group. Thus, with the groups numbered from one to four, an assignment order such as 1, 3, 2, 3, 4, 1, 4, 2, and so on, seems random, whereas an order such as 1, 2, 2, 3, 3, 1, 4, 4, appears less random. However, a bias *against* repetitions may destroy the most important feature of or randomization—the assurance that each subject has an equal likelihood of being assigned to any one of the groups.

Matched Random Assignment.   Sometimes a researcher may know or suspect that certain preexisting characteristics of his or her subjects (such as their age, intelligence, number of prior hospitalizations, and so on) will be related to the dependent measure. It may be easier to detect an experimental effect if initial differences among the subjects on these dimensions are controlled. Some form of **matching** is typically used to accomplish this end.

Appropriate use of the matching technique involves three separate steps.

1. Rank order the subjects on the variable for which control is desired.
2. Segregate the subjects into matched pairs so that each pair member has approximately the same score on the variable to be matched[2] and
3. *Randomly assign pair members to the conditions of the experiment.*

The decision of whether or not to employ matched random procedures (as opposed to free random assignment) depends on a number of factors. Among these are the availability or cost of obtaining information on the variable to be matched (from existing records or through a pretest), the degree of relationship that is likely to exist between the matching variable and the dependent measure, and whether or not obtaining information on the matching variable can influence the subject's later performance in the experiment.

In general, *matching is most desirable when the influence of the matching variable is likely to be large enough to mask the experimental effect.* For example, if an investigator wishes to determine the effects of hypnotic suggestion on the ability to lift a heavy weight and has available only a small number of hypnotizable subjects, matching may be absolutely necessary. This is because initial differences among subjects in physical strength are likely to be considerable. On the other hand, it would be wasteful and costly to match for physical strength in an experimental study of perception.

Thus far, we have considered only **a priori matching** (matching before treatment). There is, however, another kind of matching procedure that is sometimes used, namely, **ex post facto matching**. (See Box 7.1.)

BOX 7.1   *THE DANGERS OF EX POST FACTO MATCHING*

> Suppose we want to show that completing high school will increase a person's earning power. We compare the incomes of high school graduates and high school dropouts when they are 25 years old. The graduates are making significantly more money than the dropouts. Can we conclude that finishing high school is the reason for the difference?
>
> No. Critics would be quick to point out that the groups might well differ on a **third variable**—IQ. It is plausible that (on average) more intelligent students finish high school, and less intelligent students drop out. It is also possible that more intelligent people will make more money later, regardless of their education. Thus we cannot conclude that a high school education (or diploma) per se increases earning power.
>
> Now suppose we are sensitive to this possibility. We identify a large number of students who did finish high school and a large number who did not. We also obtain information on each prospective subject's IQ. (IQ scores, or their equivalent,

---

[2]The principle may be extended to units larger than pairs. Three, four, or even more individuals may be matched and then randomly assigned to treatments.

are often available from school records.) We then test our secondary hypothesis and find that, indeed, the IQs of the graduates are higher than those of the dropouts. Is there any way to control for this difference?

It is at this point that we might consider **ex post facto matching**. (Ex post facto is Latin for "after the fact.") The idea is to create pairs of subjects matched on the third variable (IQ in this case), such that one member of each pair finished high school and the other did not. Suppose we do this and find that among the matched pairs, it is still true that those who finished high school earn more money at age 25 than those who did not. Now can we conclude that graduating from high school increases later income? The answer is still no. There are three problems with ex post facto matching.

The first problem is that the process dramatically shrinks the size of our usable sample. For instance, at least some students drop out of high school because they do not have the intellectual ability to complete this level of schoolwork. Most of these individuals will not have counterparts to be matched with in the completed high school group. As a result, the size of the remaining available sample will inevitably be smaller than the size of the original one.

The severity of this problem may be seen in a study by Chapin (1955), who employed the ex post facto design to explore the very question we have been discussing. Chapin began with a sample of more than 2000 students. However, in seeking appropriately matchable pairs in terms of grades in grammar school, parental occupation, age, neighborhood in which the students grew up, and the like, he ended up with only 46 cases that he judged to be usable (23 pairs). This subsample is less than 4% of the sample with which he began!

Second, and at least equally important, ex post facto matching, regardless of the number of variables on which matching occurs, can never guarantee that some other variable for which matching was not employed may be the important controlling factor in the difference in the incomes of the two groups in later life. As we pointed out earlier, the term "third variable" is partially a misnomer. The phrase actually refers to any variable other than the one of interest that might account for the effects we have observed.

The third problem is that **matching** on one variable may have the ironic effect of **systematically unmatching** on another variable. A relatively dull adolescent may finish high school because his parents place a great deal of emphasis on education. On the other hand, a bright adolescent may drop out of high school because his parents do not value education. Parental values, which clearly can be very important in later achievement, are not likely to appear in any of the records available to an investigator after the fact. They would remain as a potentially important but uncontrolled factor in an ex post facto design. Moreover, the problem does not end here.

A student with an IQ of 125 who has dropped out of school will, when matched with a student of like IQ who remains in school, produce a pair of individuals who (although alike on IQ) differ sharply from one another in motivation. Likewise, a student with an IQ of 90 who remains in school because he has been subjected to a strong achievement ethic by his family will likely differ on this second, and uncontrolled, variable from his matched 90 IQ counterpart, who did not experience family pressure and thus dropped out. The problem is illustrated in Table 7-3.

In both cases, the effect of matching has been to further "unmatch" or confound the presence or absence of a completed high school education with the presence or absence of exposure to parental emphasis on the value of education. It is in this sense that the effect of ex post facto matching can be particularly misleading.

TABLE 7-3 RESULTS OF EX POST FACTO IQ MATCHING OF YOUNGSTERS WHO DID AND DID NOT FINISH HIGH SCHOOL, SHOWING HOW MATCHING ON IQ SYSTEMATICALLY UNMATCHED ON MOTIVATION

Finished high school	Didn't finish
Normal motivation, High IQ	Low motivation, High IQ
High motivation, Low IQ	Normal motivation, Low IQ

Differences in later income between the *"Finished"* and *"Didn't Finish"* groups could be due to differences in schooling, differences in motivation, or an unknown combination of the two factors.

Employing A Control Group

At least two groups are necessary in any true experiment. In many experiments, an *experimental group* receives the treatment of interest, whereas an otherwise identical **control group** does not. Thus, the control group provides a **baseline** against which the effects of the experimental treatment may be evaluated.

For example, when a group of phobic patients is treated and found to be less fearful after than before treatment, no firm conclusion can be advanced as to whether the treatment (rather than, say, **history** or **maturation**) is responsible for the change. Had an untreated control group of equally phobic patients been included, data would be available for evaluating this **rival hypothesis**. If competing processes such as history and maturation were operating, they would presumably be equally likely to cause improvement in the control group as in the treated experimental group. With a control group, we would have reasonable confidence that differences between the groups after treatment were, in fact, due to the treatment.

Internal Validity of the Basic Experiment

The basic experiment, also called the **posttest-only control group design**, can be depicted as follows (using the notation introduced by Campbell and Stanley, 1966):

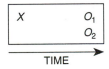

Here, the *X* represents the experimental treatment (or manipulation) and *O* symbolizes observation of the subjects. Temporal order is represented by the left-right progression, as indicated by the arrow. Thus, symbols directly above or below each other indicate events that occur simultaneously. The posttest-only control group design adequately controls for all eleven sources of internal invalidity discussed in Chapter 6.

Specifically, **history, maturation**, and **statistical regression** are all controlled in the sense that they will tend to affect both groups equally, and thus cannot provide a rival explanation for observed group differences.

Selection bias is controlled for directly, by proper random assignment.

Repeated testing, differential attrition, and **instrument change** present little problem because there is only one test per subject. And as long as the groups remain ignorant of each others' treatment, **diffusion, compensatory equalization, compensatory rivalry**, and **resentful demoralization** will not cause problems. However, the *effects* of several of these factors cannot be assessed without using a more complex design, as will be discussed in Chapter 8.

USE OF PRETESTS

The basic experiment (or **posttest-only control group design**) can be expanded to include a pretest for all subjects before the treatment is administered to the experimental group. This is called the **pretest-posttest control group design**.

There are two versions of the pretest-posttest design. They differ in the point at which the pretest is given. The two alternatives are depicted below, using the notation introduced by Campbell and Stanley (1966).

Type *RO*	$(M)^3$	R	O_1	X	O_3
	(M)	R	O_2		O_4

Type *OR*	O_1	M	R	X	O_3
	O_2	M	R		O_4

TIME

R in this notation indicates random assignment of subjects to groups. *M* signifies matching. *O* refers to the observation or measurement. *X* refers to the experimental treatment. Note that in the *RO* version of the design, random assignment is made *before* the first observation, that is, before the pretest. In the *OR* version, random assignment is made *after* the pretest.

Let's start with an example of the *RO* version. The hypothesis to be tested is that exposure to a violent TV cartoon will increase aggressive play by preschool children. We begin with 40 preschoolers, and randomly assign each child to ei-

---

[3]The parentheses signify that the matching procedure may or may not occur.

ther the violent cartoon or the control (no cartoon) condition. (This is the R in our notation.) Then we do a pretest that is identical for all the children. Specifically, we observe each child alone at free play for 5 minutes, counting instances of aggression. (In our notation, these observations correspond to O_1 and O_2.) Because we wish to control possible observer biases (see Chapter 10), we employ two independent observers who are blind to our hypothesis and unaware of the cartoon "treatment" we have planned.

After the pretest, each child watches either a violent cartoon or no cartoon, according to the random assignment we made at the outset. (This is the treatment, that is, the X in our notation.) Finally, each child is observed in the playroom again. (This is the posttest, corresponding to O_3 and O_4 in our notation.)

Suppose that the following data were obtained:

	Pretest	Posttest
Aggressive Cartoon	4	12
No Cartoon (Control)	6	5

Clearly, the children who observed the aggressive cartoon showed more aggression on the posttest than did the children who saw no cartoon. Assuming that these results are statistically significant, can we assume that the difference is attributable to the treatment itself? The pretest-posttest control group design provides a control for each source of internal invalidity, as follows:

History and **maturation** are controlled, inasmuch as effects due to either are equally likely to be present in the experimental and control groups. In our notation, factors that might produce an O_1–O_3 difference would also produce an O_2–O_4 difference. (Recall that group assignment was random.)

Likewise, the effects of **repeated testing** are controlled adequately because both groups of children received both the pretest and the posttest.

Instrument change is no problem as long as we are sure that the observers did not know which children saw the violent cartoon (as both groups would be affected equally).

Statistical regression poses no threat, even if both the experimental and control groups were randomly selected from an extreme population. We would still expect that both groups would show equal regression toward the mean, although the effect might be large.

Selection bias is effectively ruled out as a source of internal invalidity, because the groups were formed by random assignment.

We are assuming that no child dropped out of the experiment, so there is no **differential attrition**.

Finally, **diffusion**, **compensatory equalization**, **compensatory rivalry**, and **resentful demoralization** can be ruled out as long as the children in each group did not know what the children in the other group had done.

Note that the pretest-posttest comparison allows us to assess the amount of change (if any) that occurs from one test to another in the absence of the treatment (for example, history, maturation, or testing effects), by the O_2 versus O_4 comparison. Such changes cannot be assessed by posttest comparisons alone (e.g., in the basic experiment), although they are adequately *controlled for* in the O_1–O_2 comparison.

Now consider the alternative version of the pretest-posttest design (i.e., the *OR* version in our notation). In this design, the pretest would have come *before* assigning children to groups. This would have made it possible to use **matched random assignment.** If the children differed widely in their initial aggressiveness, as measured by the pretest, we could still insure no initial differences in our groups. We would do this by creating matched pairs in terms of initial aggressiveness and then, within each pair, assigning one member to the violent cartoon group and the other to the control group. In all other respects, the *RO* and *OR* designs are identical in their ability to control for each of the threats to internal validity.

Problems with Employing Pretests

From our discussion thus far, it might appear that it is always better to have a pretest. This is not so. One disadvantage of a pretest is, of course, the cost involved. Equally important, a pretest may actually affect the outcome of our experiment.

To explain this possibility, we must introduce the concept of **interaction** in experimental research. We say an interaction has occurred *when a particular outcome is obtained because of the **combined** effect of two or more events or experiences.* For the moment, we are concerned with *the interaction that may result between a pretest and a treatment.*

Imagine that subjects are given a paper and pencil questionnaire covering a wide range of topics, including several items about the degree to which they are racially prejudiced. Thereafter, half of the subjects (chosen randomly) are asked to read an essay explaining the social costs of prejudice. The control group does not read the essay. Later, both groups are asked to complete the questionnaire again. Suppose the experimental group shows a marked reduction in the frequency with which they agree with prejudicial statements, but not such change is found in the control group. Although it is tempting to attribute this change in expressed attitudes to the essay, there remains another possibility.

When the experimental subjects answer the questionnaire for the first time, they probably have no clue as to the purpose of the experiment. But when they read the essay against prejudice, they immediately guess that the purpose of the study is to see if the essay reduces prejudice. On the second administration of the questionnaire they do what they believe is expected of them. In this case, it is therefore the combination of having taken the questionnaire at the outset *and* receiving the treatment that gives rise to the change in responses on the questionnaire.

In other words, the change might not have occurred if a posttest-only design had been used. (In real-life situations, we normally do not test individuals before trying to persuade them via pamphlets, television programs, or the like.) Therefore, the results obtained from a posttest-only design might have been different *and might provide a more realistic assessment of the effect of the essay.*

So there are situations in which a pretest is desirable, and situations in which it is not. In general, a pretest is desirable when our sample is small and/or when we expect large individual differences (regardless of treatment) on our dependent measure. On the other hand, a pretest is always *un*desirable when it may interact with the treatment, as in the study of prejudice described above.

FACTORS THAT INCREASE THE POWER OF AN EXPERIMENT

*The **power** of an experiment is the degree to which it is able to detect the actual effects of the manipulated variable.* Just as a powerful microscope provides a high degree of resolution and thus permits the scientist to see things that might be missed with a weaker instrument, so a powerful experiment permits the investigator to detect real effects that might be missed if a less powerful experiment were conducted. Broadly, there are two ways of increasing the power of an experiment: maximizing systematic variance and minimizing error variance.

Maximizing Systematic Variance

Systematic variance is the extent to which the experimental manipulation leads the scores of the treated subjects to depart from the overall mean of the distribution of all other scores. It is reflected in the obtained mean differences between or among the groups of scores. Thus, *in experimental research it is **essential** to maximize the likelihood that manipulation of the independent variable will change the distribution of scores such that the distribution of (treated) scores can be discriminated from the original population of (untreated) scores.*

This principle is especially important in the early phases of research. For example, an investigator may have hypothesized that time spent rehearsing will increase recall of lines from a play. As an initial test of this hypothesis, she might compare recall of Hamlet's soliloquy in a group of actors who rehearsed the soliloquy 10 times with the recall of a group who rehearsed only once. Clearly, the experimental conditions differ widely and, if the hypothesis is correct, the expected difference should be detected.

With an initial test of a hypothesis such as this one, it would not have been desirable to compare recall of a group that had rehearsed ten times with a group that had rehearsed nine times. The variation between these conditions might not be great enough to produce changes in the dependent variable, but one would hardly be willing to conclude that amount of rehearsal is unimportant for learning one's lines.

In more advanced stages of research, smaller variations in an independent variable may be desirable. After demonstrating that actors who had rehearsed ten times recall their lines better than those who rehearse only once, the experimenter might want to refine or "map out" this relationship over increasingly smaller differences in the amount of rehearsal. For example, in a subsequent experiment, groups having rehearsed four, six, eight, and ten times might be compared.

Minimizing Error Variance

Error variance *refers to variability in the dependent measure generated by unknown factors.* There are five basic ways of minimizing error variance: applying stringent experimental control, employing reliable measures, aggregating data, using homogeneous samples, and increasing sample size.

Increasing Experimental Control.   To the extent that the experimenter provides identical conditions for all subjects, many possible sources of error variance will be eliminated. Obviously, the first step in achieving this goal is to be sure that all subjects within a particular condition of an experiment are treated in exactly the same way. If subjects within the same group are treated differently (for example, if an experimenter said words such as "right" more enthusiastically for some subjects than for others), this might contribute to within-group variability. The effect of permitting this to happen will be to reduce our ability to detect a difference *between* the groups that would achieve significance.

Using Reliable Measures.   The second major means of reducing error variance involves the notion of **reliability of measurement**. Any effort to measure a naturally occurring event, regardless of what that event is, is open to some error (see Chapter 3). For example, in measuring children's weight, some degree of error is introduced because the scales we use are manufactured to inexact specifications, and thus differ (at least slightly) from one another.

However, when we say a particular child weighs 60 pounds and another child weighs 54 pounds, it is reasonable to assume that most of the measured difference is due to an existing difference in the weights of the two children. A greater degree of error will doubtless be present when using a questionnaire to measure complex feelings, such as degree of marital satisfaction.

This issue illustrates the general concepts of the **true score** and **random measurement error**. (Recall that an obtained score may be thought of as having two parts: the true score, the score that would result if no error of measurement were present, and error.)

The fact that there is error in all measurement does not mean that the degree of error is uncontrollable. Reliable measures are those that contain relatively little measurement error; less reliable measures contain more error. Random measurement error will serve to increase the overall degree of error variance in an experiment and reduce our ability to detect reliable systematic variance. Thus, experimenters must insure that all measurement instruments and procedures are as reliable as possible.

Employing Aggregation.   Error is always present to some degree in any obtained score. The **principle of aggregation** has been suggested as a means of minimizing the error associated with individual scores by Rushton et al. (1983). The principle states that "the sum of a set of multiple measurements is a more stable and representative estimator than any single measurement" (p. 18). Simply put, the principle calls for obtaining several scores to represent each instance of the phenomenon of interest, rather than just one.

For example, in any study involving ratings by judges, random error can be reduced by employing several different independent judges and pooling or averaging their judgments. Or, in an investigation of reaction times, one may obtain the subjects' reaction times to a particular stimulus on several, dozens, or even hundreds of occasions, rather than just one. Averaging each subject's many scores will produce a better estimate of his or her true performance than would any single score. Error is reduced because random variations (positive or negative) from one judge to another or one response to another will tend to cancel each other out.

Using Homogeneous Groups of Subjects.   In any study involving a group of subjects (either animal or human), one can expect to find *individual differences* within the group. These individual differences will contribute to the error variance of an experiment. They can be minimized by employing **homogeneous groups**. Much animal research is done with highly inbred strains of rats, and much human research with subjects who share many characteristics—for example social class, age, and gender.

Increasing Sample Size.   In Chapter 3 we pointed out that larger samples provide more reliable descriptions of the populations they represent than do smaller samples, everything else being equal. One reason for the superiority of larger samples is that *as sample size increases, the effects of chance factors on individual subjects tend to cancel out.* Thus, a fifth way to protect oneself against excess error variance is to increase sample size.

In this chapter we have focused on the simplest expressions of the true experimental method. In fact, though, relatively few psychological experiments are this simple. Psychologists typically design more elaborate experiments to maximize both the amount of information they obtain and the degree of control they have over extraneous factors. We will discuss these more complex designs in the next chapter.

FOR REVIEW AND DISCUSSION

Key Terms
TRUE EXPERIMENT
TREATMENT
EXPERIMENTAL HYPOTHESIS
CONTROLLED EXPERIMENTAL SITUATION
INDEPENDENT VARIABLE
DEPENDENT VARIABLE
RANDOM ASSIGNMENT
VARIANCE
SYSTEMATIC VARIANCE
ERROR VARIANCE
VARIANCE STATISTIC

STATISTICAL SIGNIFICANCE
STATISTICALLY SIGNIFICANT DIFFERENCE
RANDOM SELECTION
SELECTION BIAS
FREE RANDOM ASSIGNMENT
MATCHED RANDOM ASSIGNMENT
BASELINE
POSTTEST-ONLY CONTROL GROUP DESIGN
HISTORY
MATURATION
STATISTICAL REGRESSION
DIFFERENTIAL ATTRITION
INSTRUMENT CHANGE
DIFFUSION
COMPENSATORY EQUALIZATION
COMPENSATORY RIVALRY
RESENTFUL DEMORALIZATION
POWER
RELIABILITY OF MEASUREMENT
TRUE SCORE
PRINCIPLE OF AGGREGATION
HOMOGENEOUS GROUPS
BETWEEN-SUBJECTS COMPARISON
RANDOM MEASUREMENT ERROR
MATCHING
CONTROL GROUP
RIVAL HYPOTHESIS
REPEATED TESTING
PRETEST-POSTTEST CONTROL GROUP DESIGN
WITHIN-SUBJECTS COMPARISON
BLIND
INTERACTION
SYSTEMATIC VARIANCE
A PRIORI MATCHING
EX POST FACTO MATCHING
THIRD VARIABLE
SYSTEMATICALLY UNMATCHING

Discussion Issues

1. A school psychologist wishes to test his idea that friendly teachers cause students to be more attentive.

   (a) State the hypothesis involved.

   (b) Put the hypothesis into testable form; that is, select an independent variable and a dependent variable.

2. Design experiments to test the following proverbs:
   (a) Haste makes waste.
   (b) He who hesitates is lost.
   (c) Love is blind.
   (d) Too many cooks spoil the broth.

3. An investigator wishes to determine whether the process of remembering and repeating a short story is influenced by different instructions to the subjects before they read it. Her subject population is college sophomores. How should they be assigned to groups? Suppose her subjects were preschoolers. Would she be more or less likely to use matched random assignment? Why?

4. In the following research design, specify any sources of internal invalidity and explain how they could have produced the results.

   The experimenter is interested in the effects of rate of presentation on the ability to learn a paired-associate list. She uses forty students from her introductory psychology class as subjects. Twenty students in the first three rows form group A, which sees each word for ten seconds; twenty students in the last three rows form group B, which sees each word for five seconds. Group A takes fewer trials to learn the list than group B.

5. Identify the weakness(es) in the following research design, and formulate recommendations for an improved experiment.

   An experimenter is interested in the effects of drug X on pre-school children's ability to learn a list of words. She takes forty pupils and randomly assigns them to either group A or group B. Subjects in group A are administered the drug, and those in group B are not given the drug. Group A is tested in the morning and group B in the afternoon. Group A learns the list more rapidly than group B.

6. Consider the following research description and identify the existing threats to validity.
   (a) An experimenter wishes to test the long-term effectiveness of a particular form of therapy. Students who apply to the university mental health clinic are assigned to the treatment groups, and students selected at random from the university student directory serve as controls. At the beginning of the study, all subjects are assessed through an interview. Through the entire study, the experimenter serves as both interviewer and therapist. At the end of 3 months of therapy, all subjects are reassessed and then assessed again after 5 years. Those subjects who have received other psychological help besides that offered in the study are included in the results. Students who received therapy improved most as measured by the interviews. Enough information has not been provided to evaluate some of the possible sources of internal invalidity. Which ones?
   (b) The researcher in problem 6(a) recognizes errors in his study and does it over. This time, students applying to the clinic are divided into two

groups—treatment and no treatment. They are all interviewed at the beginning of the study, after 3 months, and after 5 years. The experimenter again serves as both interviewer and therapist. Only subjects who have not received other psychological help are included in the results. Once again students who received therapy improved more than controls. Our experimenter repeated some mistakes and made new ones. What are they? What sources can you not evaluate from the information given above?

EXTENDING THE BASIC EXPERIMENT

8

❖ **FACTORIAL DESIGNS**
    Treatment Interactions
        Catalytic Interactions
        Terminative Interactions
        Antagonistic Interactions
        Synergistic Interactions
❖ **BLOCK DESIGNS**
    Uses of Block Designs
        Demonstrating the Generality of Experimental Effects
        Maximizing Statistical Power
        Identifying Limitations of an Experimental Effect
        Identifying Interactions Between Classificatory and
            Manipulated Variables
    Interpreting Block Designs: Fallacies in Causal Inference
    Selecting Groups for a Block Design
❖ **REPEATED MEASURES (MIXED) DESIGNS**
    Carryover Effects
    Counterbalancing

In the preceding chapter we introduced the basic experiment and described its underlying logic. Now we will consider the design of more complex experiments.

FACTORIAL DESIGNS

Most phenomena of interest to psychologists are multiply determined. An experiment in which a single treatment is employed (even with one or more control groups) fails to deal with this fact. To understand better a particular event or outcome, it is often desirable to identify and systematically manipulate several of the factors that might operate to influence the dependent variable of interest. The **factorial experiment** allows us this kind of flexibility.

In a factorial experiment, two or more different treatments are independently varied in a single study. The simplest possible arrangement for such a design is one in which only two treatments or factors are involved (customarily abbreviated A and B). Within each of the two factors, there are two levels (for example, the presence or absence of a particular treatment). Such an arrangement is referred to as a 2 × 2 factorial design.

For example, suppose we are interested in reducing fighting among nursery school children. One possibility is to punish the children whenever they fight. Another possibility is to reward the children whenever they engage in cooperative interactions with others. We are interested in the effects of both of these methods, and in what happens when they are combined. Posing the question in this way suggests the use of a 2 × 2 factorial design, creating the groups shown in Table 8-1.

Note that this 2 × 2 factorial produces an experiment containing four cells. We can determine the number of cells in any factorial experiment by multiplying the number of levels of each factor (2 × 2 = 4, 2 × 3 = 6, and so on). Instead of using the presence or absence of reward and the presence or absence of punishment, we could have used high punishment, moderate punishment, and no punishment (as factor A) and high reward, moderate reward, and no reward (as factor B). Then we would have three levels of each of the two factors, yielding a 3 × 3 factorial design. As seen in Table 8-2, the resulting experiment produces 9, or 3 × 3, experimental cells. This rule is infinitely generalizable.

TABLE 8-1   2 X 2 FACTORIAL DESIGN

Consequence for Prosocial Behavior	Consequence for Disruptive Behavior	
	Punishment	No Punishment
Reward		
No Reward		

TABLE 8-2   3 X 3 FACTORIAL DESIGN

Consequence for Prosocial Behavior	Consequence For Disruptive Behavior		
	High Punishment	Moderate Punishment	No Punishment
High reward			
Moderate reward			
No reward			

In addition, the factors can have any number of levels, limited only by the constraints of practicality. Thus, one can use a 3×4 design or a 2×6 design. Finally, any number of factors can appear in such a design (for example, a $3 \times 2 \times 2 \times 4$), limited only by the cost of generating all the cells within a reasonable sample size. (There are 48 subject groups [or *cells*] in a $3 \times 2 \times 2 \times 4$ design.) Also, the difficulties involved in interpreting all the possible combinations would be enormous.

Inasmuch as we have continually emphasized the importance of a control group in the true experiment, our first point should be that *in any factorial design in which one of the levels of each of the factors being employed involves the absence of treatment* (for example, punishment versus no punishment), *a cell in which none of the treatments is present inevitably appears.* This is the familiar untreated control group of simple (nonfactorial) experiments.

Another asset of the factorial design is its economy. Suppose, for example, that 60 children were available for an experiment on the effects of reward and punishment on tantrums. We might, using a nonfactorial design, divide these children randomly into three groups. One of the groups would receive reward for appropriate social activities, one would receive punishment for tantrums, and one would receive no treatment.

In this situation we would be able to determine the effects of reward for only 20 of the 60 children in the experiment. Likewise, the effects of punishment could be considered only for the 20 children who received that treatment, and we would get no information whatsoever as to the combined effects of reward and punishment. In contrast, the 2×2 factorial design would allow us to do all of the following: expose 30 of the 60 children to reward, expose 30 of the 60 children to punishment, provide 15 children who received both of the treatments, *and* leave 15 children who received no treatment.

One qualification should be noted. Only for the overall or "main" effect of reward do we have 30 children in the treated group of the experiment. To the extent that the reward operates in very much the same way (presumably to increase the likelihood of prosocial behavior) regardless of whether punishment is present or not, we can reasonably speak of the main effect of reward upon the 30 children.

There is, however, another possibility. The effects of reward (or punishment) may operate differently, depending on whether the remaining treatment is present or absent. For example, any one of the following possibilities might occur:

1. Reward and punishment are both effective in modifying the children's behavior, but the combination of these two treatments is no more effective than either would be alone.

2. Reward and punishment are each separately effective in modifying the children's behavior, but when they are combined their effects disappear entirely, so that the children's behavior is not changed any more than that found in the control group.

3. Reward and punishment are both effective in modifying the children's behavior, but their combination is even better than would be expected from the effects of either separately. (This would be the case if the children in the control group produced the most tantrums, both the rewarded and the punished children had fewer, but those who received both treatments became virtual paragons of good behavior after the experimental treatments.)

4. Finally, it is possible that neither reward nor punishment would have any detectable effect, but that the two together would produce a strong effect (in principle, in either direction) that would be totally unexpected from our knowledge of what either does separately.

Among the enormous benefits of employing a factorial design is the ability to detect, in a straightforward, statistical way, the presence of any one of these types of unique combinations or **interactions**.

Treatment Interactions

If two treatments each have an effect when considered separately, we might suppose that their combined effect would be the sum of their separate effects. This is the way calories work. If you have a candy bar (180 calories) and chocolate milk (180 calories) your caloric intake can simply be added up. You just treated yourself to 360 calories!

But when dealing with psychological phenomena, multiple causation rarely occurs additively. Many psychological variables *interact* when they combine, producing results that would not be anticipated from the effects of each factor considered separately. Somewhat more technically, *two factors (or variables) are said to interact whenever the effect of one factor is not the same at every level of the other factor.*

We will consider four patterns of interactions: catalytic, terminative, antagonistic, and synergistic.

Catalytic Interactions.   In any standard chemistry laboratory you will find two common reagents: potassium permanganate and glycerin. You can safely rub either of them on your fingers, with no ill effect (except for a purplish stain from the potassium permanganate). If, however, you are unlucky enough to get both of them on your fingers at once, you will get a nasty burn almost immediately. If you combine larger quantities of potassium permanganate and glycerin, you can make a volcano that sizzles, smokes voluminously, and spurts an extremely hot flame.

Cartoon 8-1   Beware catalytic interactions!

A novice chemist would, by simple observation of the separate effects of the two substances, be unable to detect that they could combine to catalyze a powerful oxidation reaction. *A **catalytic interaction** is one in which two or more treatments are effective only when they occur in combination.*

Suppose a health psychologist is interested in motivating heavy cigarette smokers to cut down on their smoking. She has two treatments in mind: 1) showing the subjects a film comparing the lung X-rays of heavy smokers and nonsmokers and 2) showing the subjects X-rays of their own lungs. Her experiment is a 2×2 design, such that one group sees the film *and* their own X-rays, one group sees just the film, one group sees just their own X-rays, and one group sees neither the film nor the X-rays.

The dependent measure is the number of cigarettes each subject smokes during the following week. The results show that neither the film by itself nor looking at their own X-rays by itself has much effect on smoking. However, subjects who see the film *and* their own X-rays (and thus can see that the lung damage portrayed in the film applies to them personally) cut down markedly on their smoking. This outcome, illustrated in Figure 8-1, is an example of a catalytic interaction.

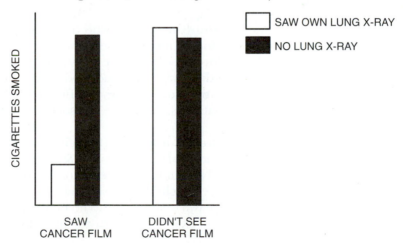

Figure 8-1   Results of hypothetical smoking study illustrating a catalytic interaction between treatments.

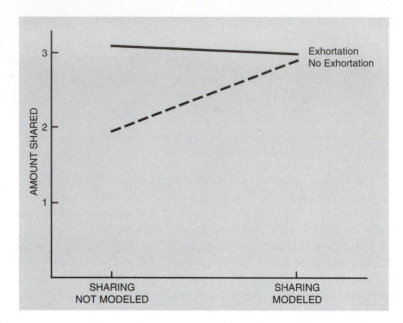

Figure 8-2   The effects of verbal exhortation and a sharing example on children's sharing. The pattern of results illustrates a terminative interaction (Poulos & Liebert, 1972).

Terminative Interactions.   *A* **terminative interaction** *is one in which two or more variables are clearly effective, but when combined, their effect is not increased over that of either one alone.*

During the 1960s child psychologists were studying two "socializing influences" on children: modeling and exhortation. Modeling refers to presenting children with another person (the model) who demonstrates the desired behavior. Exhortation simply means telling children what to do. Modeling studies repeatedly showed that children become more likely to share after being exposed to a sharing model. But studies that combined modeling with sharing exhortations suggested that this combination was no more effective than modeling alone. Does this mean that exhortation is ineffective as a socializing influence for children's sharing?

This question was addressed using a 2 (modeling, no modeling) × 2 (exhortation, no exhortation) factorial design (Poulos & Liebert, 1972). The results, shown in Figure 8-2, revealed a terminative interaction between these two factors. Exhortation alone *did* increase children's sharing. So did modeling alone. But the combination of these two treatments was no more effective than using either of them alone. This is an example of what we mean by a terminative interaction.

Antagonistic Interactions.   Let's return to the chemistry laboratory for an example of an **antagonistic interaction**. The following demonstration was used (years ago) when one of us taught undergraduate chemistry:

> I poured a carefully measured quantity of hydrochloric acid into one beaker and a carefully measured quantity of sodium hydroxide into another. From the first beaker I then poured a small quantity of hydrochloric acid into a shallow glass tray. I asked a student to give me a copper penny, which I then dropped into the acid. Great billows of smoke emerged as the penny was rapidly eroded. Soon the penny was completely gone.
>
> Then I dropped a small piece of beefsteak into a tray containing some of the sodium hydroxide. This fluid, too, proved to be highly destructive. The caustic sodium hydroxide consumed the meat completely in a short time. When I challenged my students to drink the remaining contents of either of the beakers, no one ever volunteered. Then I announced that I was "twice as brave" as any of the students, poured the contents of both beakers into a larger third beaker, and immediately drank its entire contents.
>
> Instead of destruction of my mouth and internal organs, I suffered no ill effects (except for a marked increase in thirst). Although both substances are, separately, extremely dangerous, they combine in an antagonistic way to yield nothing more than salt water.[1]

Antagonistic interactions also appear in social behavior. For example, people are more likely to conform to group norms in public than they are in private. People are also more likely to adhere to group norms when they are offered money to do so. But if you offer someone money in public for going along with a group, they may feel that going along will appear to be accepting a bribe, and therefore refuse.

Synergistic Interactions.   A synergistic interaction is one in which the effects of one variable are *potentiated or altered* through the addition of a second variable.

Muscle pain can be reduced by prescription analgesics. It can also be reduced by minor tranquilizers, which serve as "muscle relaxants." But analgesics can potentiate the effects of tranquilizers, so the combination of even small doses of the two can produce a near stupor in some people. This is an example of a **synergistic interaction**.

Psychologists interested in helping people lose and keep off excess pounds have found a synergistic interaction between exercise and dieting. Exercise makes some contribution to weight control, as does reduced caloric intake. But a proper combination of the two has a synergistic effect; that is, it is far more effective than would be expected, even from "adding up" their separate effects.

So far, our discussion has focused on designs in which all factors were manipulated as independent variables, and all the comparisons were made between-subjects. Experimental designs of this type are sometimes called **fully randomized designs**. Assignment to each cell of the design is on a random basis. There are two other major types of factorial designs: block designs and repeated measures (or mixed) designs.

---

[1]$HCl + NaOH \rightarrow NaCl + H_2O$.

BLOCK DESIGNS

Until the introduction of the Salk vaccine in the 1950s, polio was one of the most frightening diseases of childhood. It was responsible for 5% of the deaths of children between the ages of 5 and 9, and left many others severely crippled or totally paralyzed.

Researchers did not come to understand the disease until they asked the question: Which groups of young children were most likely to be stricken? Surprisingly, this inquiry revealed that polio was far *more* prevalent among those who were better off hygienically (those with better housing, better diets, better sanitary conditions, and so on). Indeed, in countries with the poorest standard of living, polio was virtually unknown. How could this be?

The explanation turned out to be that there is an abundance of the polio virus in impoverished regions. So, almost every infant gets the disease, but so early in life that he or she is still protected by the natural immunity passed from the child's mother. As researcher Paul Meier explained, "Everyone [living in poverty] had had polio, but under protected circumstances, and, thereby, everyone had developed his own immunity." (Meier, 1978, p. 4) It was this observation that led to the idea of general immunization at an early age, which was accomplished with the Salk vaccine. Without observing that polio had a differential effect on different groups, its virtual elimination as a health threat might not have occurred.

In essence, the research on polio and the development of a vaccine to prevent it represent a triumph for integrating two different approaches to research: experimental and correlational. This can also be accomplished with **block designs**.

*A **block design** is one in which subjects from two or more different populations are assigned to each treatment.* Thus, a block design always includes at least one classificatory variable and one manipulated variable.

Suppose that the researcher is interested in the effects of special training on young children's motor skills. Recognizing the possibility of a gender difference in motor skills, the investigator decides to use a block design. A sample of boys and girls is obtained, and then half the boys and half the girls are randomly assigned to the special training. The remainder get no special treatment. Table 8-3 illustrates the design.

This design is *blocked* because the first factor of the investigation (gender) is a **classificatory variable**, not a treatment. The second variable (exposure to the special training) is, however, a treatment, that is, a **manipulated variable**.

TABLE 8-3   SCHEMATIC OF A MIXED DESIGN WITH TWO FACTORS, GENDER AND TRAINING IN MOTOR SKILLS

	Boys	Girls
Training		
No training		

Gender is the classificatory variable, training the experimental one.

Block designs may involve three, four, or more factors, and each of the factors may have more than two levels. Subjects might, for example, be divided on the basis of whether they show high, moderate, or low anxiety (anxiety level serves as the classificatory variable). Then, persons from each of the three groups could be assigned to three different levels of treatment that vary in the degree to which they are stressful (manipulated variable). This factorial block design produces nine cells.

Block designs can use more than one classificatory variable. In a study of the effectiveness of different methods of teaching, children could be classified into groups based on both gender and age. When the divisions among subjects on the classificatory variables are potentially of practical or theoretical significance, the block design has many features to commend it over simpler "straight" experimental designs. We consider some of these features next.

Uses of Block Designs

All block designs permit the researcher to obtain correlational and experimental evidence simultaneously, as two separate sources of variability on a given measure. Such a design may be used primarily for this purpose, but it can also either disclose the generality of treatment effects *or* illuminate their limitations. As we shall see, in either case the sensitivity of the significance test in a block design is maximized through a reduction of **error variance**. (Recall that reducing error variance increases the **power** of a statistical test.)

Demonstrating the Generality of Experimental Effects.   Block designs can demonstrate the generality of an experimental effect across variables such as age, gender, or socioeconomic status. Suppose, for example, that two methods of teaching a foreign language are being compared: a traditional method and a new one. The investigator might combine this experimental manipulation (type of language training) with four ages of students (5, 7, 9, and 11) in a 2×4 block design. One possible outcome of this study appears in Figure 8-3. The new teaching method was superior to the traditional one regardless of a student's age.

Maximizing Statistical Power.   As noted earlier, block designs can increase the sensitivity of an experimental test. An investigator may fail to detect an experimental effect because of large within-group variability (or error variance). (Recall that the power of a statistical test is *maximized* when error variance is *minimized*, enabling the researcher to more readily detect **systematic variance**.)

Consider an investigation of the effects of viewing a prosocial television program on the behavior of first grade children. Both boys and girls are randomly assigned to either a prosocial or neutral TV condition, and their prosocial behavior is subsequently monitored.

The data from this hypothetical study are presented in Table 8-4. Let us suppose that the investigator, believing that gender will not be important, ignores it and analyzes the data for an effect attributed to the treatment. A graphic representation of this analysis, shown in Figure 8-4, demonstrates considerable

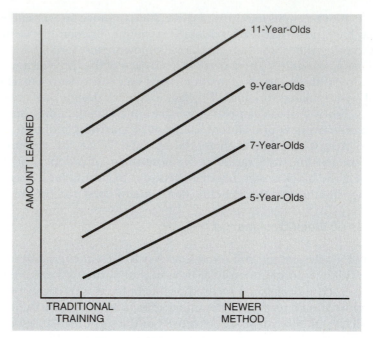

Figure 8-3 Effects of two methods of teaching on children of varying ages, illustrating the generality of an experimental effect. For all ages, the newer method is superior.

overlap between the two treatment groups (the shaded area in the figure) and little effect of the treatment.

Table 8-4 shows, though, that there is a considerable difference between girls and boys. The data, plotted separately for each gender, are shown in Figure 8-5. The inclusion of the classificatory variable reduces the amount of overlap between groups. Comparing Figures 8-4 and 8-5, we see that the latter has a considerably smaller shaded area; therefore, the block design provides a more sensitive test of the hypothesis under consideration by *reducing error variance*.

Identifying Limitations of an Experimental Effect.   One of the most valuable uses of block designs is to disclose the limitations of an experimental effect. Consider an investigation by Poulos & Davidson (1971). These investigators were interested in determining the effectiveness of a short film, "The Red Toothbrush," on children's attitude toward the dentist. The film, which was designed primarily to reduce fear of dental examinations in children, depicts two children visiting a dentist's office.

One child, an 8-year-old boy, is fearless throughout. He enters the dentist's office, seats himself in the dental chair, and is the subject of a dental examination and cleaning. At the end of the session, he receives a reward: a red toothbrush.

The second child, a 4-year-old girl, is depicted as initially fearful. The film shows her observing the behavior of the fearless older child. As she watches the

TABLE 8-4 RESULTS OF A HYPOTHETICAL INVESTIGATION OF THE INFLUENCE OF EXPOSURE TO PROSOCIAL BEHAVIOR ON TELEVISION ON CHILDREN'S PROSOCIAL BEHAVIOR

Females		Males	
Neutral	Prosocial	Neutral	Prosocial
TV	TV	TV	TV
3	5	7	9
4	6	8	10
4	6	8	10
5	7	9	11
5	7	9	11
5	7	9	11
6	8	10	12
6	8	10	12
6	8	10	12
6	8	10	12
7	9	11	13
7	9	11	13
7	9	11	13
8	10	12	14
8	10	12	14
9	11	13	15

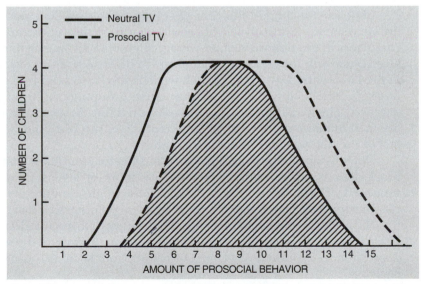

Figure 8-4 Effects of exposure to prosocial TV on children's prosocial behavior, illustrating a large amount of overlap between the two treatment groups.

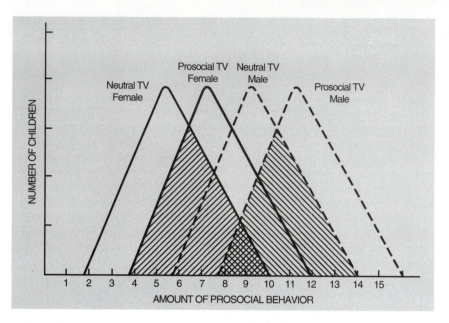

Figure 8-5   Effects of prosocial TV on behavior in male and female children, illustrating how the inclusion of a classificatory variable makes the study more sensitive by accounting for some of the overlap seen in Figure 8-4.

procedure, her fear gradually decreases. Afterward, she calmly hops into the dental chair and willingly undergoes the same dental procedure.

The fearful child in this film was expected to provide a model with whom the viewer, even if initially fearful, could identify. However, because both of the characters in the film were quite young, one possibility was that the film would be effective only for very young children. To determine if this was true, children in the Poulos and Davidson research were divided into two age groups: 1) those under 7 and 2) those over 7. Within these groupings, some of the children watched "The Red Toothbrush," and others did not. As seen from Figure 8-6, an interaction between film and age of the observer was obtained. The positive effect of the film was indeed limited to children under 7.

Identifying Interactions Between Classificatory and Manipulated Variables. Block designs can show that a treatment is more or less useful than had been supposed. These designs allow researchers to detect interactions between classificatory and manipulated variables that might otherwise have been masked.

Consider an investigation of the effectiveness of three anti-depressant drugs. The patients have been divided into two groups on the basis of the severity of their depression. A hypothetical pattern of results from such a study is presented in Figure 8-7.

Figure 8-7(A) shows that treatment 3 produces the greatest improvement when patients with symptoms of low and high severity are not segregated. Hence,

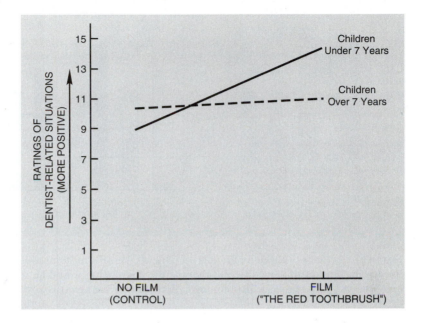

Figure 8-6 Data from Poulos and Davidson (1971), illustrating that the effects of a particular modeling film were limited to children under the age of seven.

in the absence of any information about characteristics of the patients, treatment 3 would be preferred. *But when the severity of the patients' depression is considered, treatment 3 would no longer be the therapeutic approach of choice for any of the patients!* As seen in Figure 8-7(B), for patients with mild depression, treatment 1 is most effective. For patients with severe depression, treatment 2 is best. Thus, there is a clear treatment by block interaction not detected by the previously massed data.

Finding such an interaction can go hand in hand with increasing the **power** of an experimental test. For example, we might fail to obtain an "overall" effect for some treatment, yet obtain a significant interaction that clearly identifies a subset of the population that will benefit from it.

Interpreting Block Designs: Fallacies in Causal Inference

Most block designs are analyzed using the same statistical procedures that are employed with pure experimental designs. Thus, it is tempting to interpret the results of a block design as if all the factors were manipulated variables. This, however, would be a mistake.

Suppose there were two kinds of people: those who wear pink shirts and those who wear blue shirts. All these people suffer from occasional headaches, but none has tried aspirin for relief. We now wish to determine if aspirin is an effective treatment for their headaches.

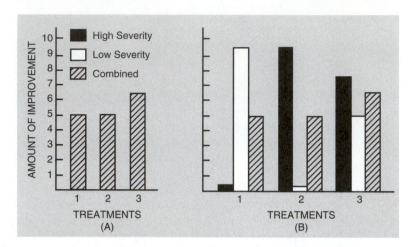

Figure 8-7   Effects of three treatments on patients whose symptoms are either high or low in severity, illustrating how different therapeutic approaches would be selected depending on absence (A) or presence (B) of information concerning severity.

Recognizing that we are confronted by two distinct groups, we decide to employ a block design, blocking on shirt color. Now half of our pink shirt people are randomly assigned to treatment with aspirin for their next headache, as are half of our blue shirt people. The remaining subjects receive no treatment.

Our results indicate that aspirin did indeed provide headache relief, but only for the blue shirt group. We may now conclude that aspirin is an effective treatment for the headaches of blue shirt people. However, we can *not* conclude that shirt color determines aspirin effectiveness. (We do not know, for instance, if having a pink shirt person wear a blue shirt and *then* take aspirin would increase the effectiveness of the aspirin.)

Shirt color in this example is merely a classificatory variable. It was not under experimental control, and you as the researcher do not know what underlying factors cause these people to wear the shirt colors they wear. Thus, you can not draw causal conclusions from classificatory data. Put another way, *categories are not causes.*

There are actually two steps in interpreting effects associated with classificatory variables (such as gender or age or shirt color) in block designs. First, the investigator must describe the relationship between the classificatory and manipulated variables (for example, by noting the presence of an association between shirt color and aspirin effectiveness). Second, the researcher must try to *explain* the association. This is done by hypothesizing underlying mechanisms that can then be tested through further research.

Ultimately, many classificatory variables can be construed as reflections of several underlying processes. Consider, for instance, the classificatory variable, age. Differences observed between age groups in response to a treatment might result from any of several age-related processes (for example, greater linguistic ability, greater motor skills, and so on), many of which might be controlled for experimentally.

Selecting Groups for a Block Design

Block designs always entail formation of classificatory groups. Sometimes the classification is straightforward, as in the case of gender. Often, however, the investigator must divide the sample on the basis of some continuously distributed information, such as previous test scores or economic background.

For instance, a researcher might be interested in the effects of stress on college students' performance on a cognitive task. He or she might also be interested in whether general anxiety level, a classificatory variable, is related to performance on the task. In such an investigation, one is interested in both the experimental and the classificatory factors, as well as in the possible interaction between the two. The question arises: How should subjects be selected from the distribution of initial anxiety test scores so as to maximize the value of the research?

There are several ways a sample might be divided. In one strategy, the **median-split technique**, subjects are divided at the median (middle) of the distribution of the classificatory variable. Thus, all the subjects are used, with those above the median forming the "high anxiety" group and those below the median forming the "low anxiety" group. The problem with the median-split is that two very similar subjects, one with an anxiety level just above the median, and the other with an anxiety level just below the median, will be put in contrasting groups. At the same time, a person with a score just above or below the median will be grouped with others whose scores are very extreme.

Another strategy is the **extreme groups technique**. Here, only subjects from the ends of the distribution (e.g., the highest and lowest 10%) are used. This procedure is appealing because it appears to maximize the difference in which we are interested.

However, this approach has problems of its own. For a concrete illustration, consider a study of the effects of anxiety on learning. Four groups of subjects are constructed by factorial combination of anxiety level and amount of stress induced. The results of this hypothetical study are presented in Table 8-5. Note that high- and low-anxiety subjects differ only in the stressful learning task. From

TABLE 8-5   EFFECTS OF ANXIETY ON NUMBER OF ITEMS LEARNED IN STRESSFUL AND NONSTRESSFUL SITUATIONS

	No Stress	Stress
High anxiety (top 10%)	8.4	2.7
Low anxiety (bottom 10%)	8.3	8.8

these data it might be concluded that on stressful learning tasks, there is a general relationship between anxiety and learning (the higher the anxiety, the poorer the learning).

Suppose, however, that the high- and low-anxiety subjects were selected from the upper and lower 10% of a distribution of scores, whereas the relationship between anxiety and learning is curvilinear in the total population. This possibility is illustrated in Figure 8-8.

The figure shows that learning is optimal in subjects with moderate levels of anxiety. This discovery could not have been made from an extreme-groups study, because the most relevant subjects were thrown out before the investigation began! Hence, *when extreme groups are employed, conclusions about the overall relationship between the classificatory and dependent variable cannot be legitimately drawn.*

One solution to the classification problem involves **multiple discrete leveling**. In this approach, the total distribution of the classificatory variable is broken into several levels, rather than just two (as in the median split). For example, in a study of the influence of anxiety on academic performance, the distribution of anxiety scores could be divided into *quartiles* (i.e., equal quarters). Such a design allows both nonlinear main effects and nonlinear interactions to be de-

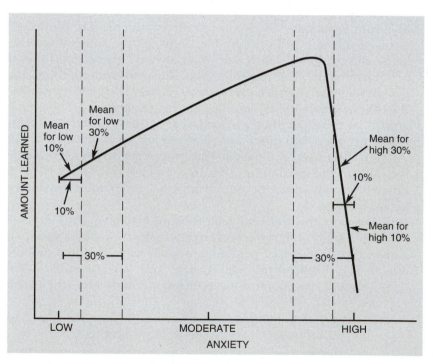

Figure 8-8 Effects of anxiety on learning, illustrating a curvilinear relationship in which differences are detected for the very extreme (10%) but not for the less extreme (30%) comparisons.

tected. To illustrate this advantage, consider two alternative analyses of a study of the relationship between need achievement and persistence on a solvable versus an unsolvable task.

In the first analysis, subjects were split at the median (dichotomized) on the need achievement variable. As can be seen from Table 8-6(A) there were no differences for either the classificatory or the manipulated variable. However, in the second analysis, a quadripartite (four-level) division of subjects was employed, and an interaction between type of test and need achievement level was obtained. As can be seen from Table 8-6(B), subjects who are very low or very high in need achievement persisted less than the remaining groups, but only on the insoluble task. From a consideration of the A and B parts of the table, it can be seen how the median split masked the interaction.

In sum, block designs can clearly be used to serve many research purposes. Although they are open to certain pitfalls of interpretation, they can amplify the amount and type of information gathered in experiments. They also play a vital role in examining the external validity of research.

REPEATED MEASURES (MIXED) DESIGNS

To move a step beyond simple blocking, we will now consider the **repeated measures**, or **mixed design**. Experimenters may sometimes choose to make **within-subjects comparisons** as well as **between-subjects comparisons**. This can be

TABLE 8-6 DICHOTOMIZED AND QUADRIPARTITE SPLITS IN A HYPOTHETICAL EXPERIMENT ON TASK PERSISTENCE, ILLUSTRATING THE ADVANTAGE OF A MULTIPLE DISCRETE LEVELING PROCEDURE

(A)

Dichotomous Break

Soluble Task		Insoluble Task	
High n Ach[*]	Low n Ach	High n Ach	Low n Ach
10	10	10	10

(B)

Quadripartite Break

Soluble Task				Insoluble Task			
Very High	High	Low	Very Low	Very High	High	Low	Very Low
10	10	10	10	5	15	15	5

[*] n Ach, or need for achievement, is implicated in many interesting relationships. For an extensive review the reader is referred to McClelland. Atkinson, Clark, and Lowell (1953) and Birney (1968). A brief summary can also be found in Liebert and Spiegler (1982).

accomplished only by obtaining more than one measure from each subject. Thus, all within-subjects comparisons involve **repeated measurement**. (Recall the advantages of the pretest-posttest control group design mentioned in Chapter 7.)

Repeated measurement may be woven into factorial experiments, in combination with between-subjects comparisons, to form one of a number of **repeated measures designs**, commonly known as **mixed designs** (because of the "mixing" of both between- and within-subjects comparisons).

The primary purpose of mixed designs is often to control for **individual differences** on the **dependent measure**. Often, the responses of different people to the same experimental treatment are quite variable. If this source of variability is not removed, the ability to detect between group differences may be very limited (due to the high degree of error variance relative to systematic variance). Repeated measures designs can minimize this problem by measuring the responses of an individual subject to each of the treatments *relative to that subject's average responsiveness to all of them*. To put it another way, the subject becomes his or her own control. In this way, variability due to **individual differences** in general responsiveness can be eliminated.

Imagine we wish to know whether a display of three red lights to indicate STOP produces faster reaction times than a conventional one-light display. We might do a simple between-subjects experiment. In this experiment, subjects would be randomly assigned to either a one-light *or* a three-light display, and their reaction times would be measured. The major drawback of this approach is that reaction times vary enormously from one person to another. In between-subjects comparisons, these variations will become unaccounted for (or error variance), and will limit severely the power of our experiment.

The alternative, using a repeated measures design, with a within-subjects comparison, would be to present each subject with *both* displays. Now we are in a position to *compare each subject's reaction to each condition*. However, for the comparison to be valid, we must control for possible **carryover effects**.

Carryover Effects

Whenever making within-subjects comparisons in which each subject is given more than one treatment, one must insure that subjects are not all given the same treatments in the same order. This principle recognizes the fact that exposure to one manipulation or test may produce persistent consequences, called **carryover effects**, that influence the subject's response to any subsequent manipulation.

Let's return to our example of reaction times to one- versus three-light displays. As we've said, to determine whether responses are quicker to the three-light display, the psychologist would very likely choose a repeated measures design. This is because effects produced by the number of lights would be expected to be quite small relative to existing **individual differences** in reaction time. That is, people will vary in alertness, coordination, motivation, and a variety of other factors that could make them generally fast or slow. These variations might completely mask the effects of the lights if subjects were only compared in a between-subjects design.

An experimental psychologist working on a problem like this would probably present each subject with a number of trials on each display (e.g., 30) and use the average of these trials under each condition as the person's score in that condition.

Averaging over many trials in this way helps to minimize the influence of chance factors (such as temporary distraction) on the scores and therefore further reduces error variance. This is an application of the **principle of aggregation** discussed in Chapter 7.

Suppose, now, that each subject in the study first received his or her 30 trials in the one-light condition, and then received thirty trials in the three-light condition. Would this procedure be acceptable? No. Very likely individuals would improve as they became more familiar with the procedure, more comfortable with the experimental setting, and more practiced in the task.

A general improvement resulting from experience with a task or experimental procedure, usually called a **practice effect**, must *not* be confounded with the experimental conditions. All the subjects might be expected to respond a bit faster in the second 30 trials because they would be more practiced, but we would not want to attribute this improvement to a difference in the number of lights. *The general problem is therefore to avoid confounding the order in which treatments are presented with the different treatments themselves.*

Table 8-7 illustrates three potential consequences of permitting the carryover effect to enter our hypothetical experiment. (To simplify the discussion, we have assumed that the practice effect would be the same for everybody and would decrease reaction time approximately 0.20 second.) Table 8-7(A) is a case in which the true difference between conditions is 0; that is, the number of lights does not affect reaction time. However, the practice effect makes it appear as though reaction time is faster to three lights than to one light (0.55 versus 0.75 second). In Table 8-7(B) a potential real difference, in which reaction times to the one light are faster, is actually masked by the practice effect. And finally, in Table 8-7(C), a potential real difference, in which reaction times to the three lights are faster, is magnified by the practice effect.

A very similar argument can be made for the contamination of the data by a carryover effect referred to as the **fatigue effect**. People may get tired or bored during the course of a challenging or long experimental procedure. If one condition always follows another, this fatigue effect will contribute more to our estimate of performance under one condition than the other. In the light example, a fatigue effect would produce a systematic tendency to overestimate reaction time for the three-light condition.

Practice and fatigue are fairly common processes, but there are numerous other carryover effects that may also threaten particular types of within-subjects comparisons. When comparing two drugs, for example, one must be sure that the first drug administered is not still active when the second is given. In actual research situations, it is often very difficult to specify all the possible carryover

TABLE 8-7   SOME POTENTIAL CONSEQUENCES OF CONFOUNDING
THE ORDER OF CONDITION WITH THE CONDITIONS THEMSELVES

Subject	(First) One	(Second) Three (Real)	Real (three lights) Plus Practice Effect
		(A)	
1	0.50	0.50	0.30
2	0.75	0.75	0.55
3	1.00	1.00	0.80
M	*0.75*	*0.75*	*0.55*
		(B)	
1	0.50	0.70	0.50
2	0.75	0.95	0.75
3	1.00	1.20	1.00
M	*0.75*	*0.95*	*0.75*
		(C)	
1	0.70	0.50	0.30
2	0.95	0.75	0.55
3	1.20	1.00	0.80
M	*0.95*	*0.75*	*0.55*

*Data are reaction times in seconds, and we have supposed that practice decreases
reaction time by 0.20 for every subject.

Source: Adapted from Johnson and Liebert (1977)

effects, and it is virtually impossible to assess the relative contribution to scores
of carryover effects (such as practice and fatigue) that exert their influence in
opposite ways. Then, too, we do not usually know the true difference between
conditions before conducting the research.

Carryover effects are very similar to **repeated testing** effects, and they constitute a threat to the internal validity of all within-subjects comparisons. One
way to deal with possible carryover effects is through counterbalancing.

Counterbalancing

To guard against potential erroneous conclusions that result from carryover effects in within-subjects comparisons, investigators commonly use a procedure
called **counterbalancing**. The general purpose of counterbalancing is much like
that of assigning subjects randomly to treatment conditions: Potential error resulting from carryover effects is distributed equally across all conditions of the
study, thereby tending to cancel out.

When subjects in a within-subjects experiment are run in a counterbalanced way, an equal number receive the treatments in A-B order and in B-A order. All the problems illustrated in Table 8-7 would have been avoided if half the subjects had seen the lights in the order three-one, and the other half had seen them in the order one-three.

A major limitation of counterbalancing is that it becomes quite complicated whenever more than two treatments are involved. For example, although there are only two possible orders of two treatments (A-B and B-A), there are *six* possible orders of three treatments (A-B-C, B-C-A, C-A-B, C-B-A, B-A-C, and A-C-B) and 24 possible orders of four treatments, too many to list here.

One solution to this problem is to pick randomly a few of the possible orders and then, again randomly, assign subjects in equal numbers to each of the selected orders. Another alternative is to create a randomized order of treatments for each subject. In either case, by using the powerful tool of random assignment, one can effectively control for many carryover effects.

Here a word of caution is needed. *Counterbalancing the order of administration of treatments across subjects in a within-subjects experiment is an effective way to deal with carryover effects only when we are reasonably certain that the carryover effect from treatment A to treatment B is the same as the carryover effect from treatment B to treatment A.* For example, if one treatment is more fatiguing than the other, counterbalancing the order of presentation will not equally distribute the carryover effects to the two conditions. Thus the decision whether to use within-subjects experimental designs must be based on knowledge of the likely magnitude of possible carryover effects.

In our discussion so far, we have assumed a change of treatment on the within-subjects factor from one measure to another. In some research, however, it is of interest to obtain repeated measures *without changing* treatments. In studies of depression, for example, patients may be assessed at the end of treatment, and again at several follow up points. Here within-subjects comparisons are being used to examine the stability or durability of treatment effects, and can provide information that is entirely straightforward.

In our next chapter we will examine some viable research designs that can be used in situations where the control of a true experiment is not possible.

FOR REVIEW AND DISCUSSION

Key Terms
INTERACTIONS
FACTORIAL EXPERIMENT
CATALYTIC INTERACTION
TERMINATIVE INTERACTION
ANTAGONISTIC INTERACTION
SYNERGISTIC INTERACTION
REPEATED MEASUREMENT

REPEATED MEASURES DESIGNS
INDIVIDUAL DIFFERENCES
CARRYOVER EFFECTS
PRACTICE EFFECT
FATIGUE EFFECT
COUNTERBALANCING
MIXED DESIGN
BETWEEN-SUBJECTS COMPARISONS
WITHIN-SUBJECTS COMPARISONS
CLASSIFICATORY VARIABLE
ERROR VARIANCE
POWER
MEDIAN-SPLIT TECHNIQUE
EXTREME GROUPS TECHNIQUE
CURVILINEAR RELATIONSHIP
MULTIPLE DISCRETE LEVELING
FULLY RANDOMIZED DESIGNS
BLOCK DESIGNS
MANIPULATED VARIABLE
DEPENDENT MEASURE
REPEATED TESTING

Discussion Issues

1. Suppose that an experimenter is investigating the effects of social deprivation on the power of social reinforcers such as praise. Children are placed in a small room with toys for 15 minutes. In the social deprivation condition, the subjects are left alone. In the control, or no social deprivation, condition subjects are joined by an adult female who plays with them for the entire 15 minutes. Then a second adult female gives each subject a dull task, such as bead stringing, and praises the child for each 60 seconds of performance.

   The dependent variable is total time spent on the task. Subjects are 6-year-old males and females, and 10-year-old males and females. Given the following sets of data, should the experimenter block the subjects on age, sex, or both? (Note: In practice, the experimenter should choose the variables on which to block *before* collecting the data.)

(a)   6-YEAR-OLD   10-YEAR-OLD

	M	F	M	F
Social Deprivation	8	14	11	9
	5	9	8	13
	10	10	9	11
	12	12	10	13
	8	8	5	8

Control	12	6	10	9
	8	8	8	13
	10	11	12	8
	7	9	6	6
	9	10	9	10

(b)

	6-YEAR-OLD		10-YEAR-OLD	
	M	F	M	F
Social Deprivation	10	8	6	9
	13	7	8	11
	11	10	10	10
	8	11	11	13
	10	7	9	12
Control	10	12	11	9
	7	8	8	7
	6	13	11	11
	9	9	10	6
	11	11	13	11

2. Does the following design employ blocking? If blocked, identify which variable is classificatory and which is manipulated experimentally.

   College sophomores were given a short course in speed reading. Three groups had courses lasting for 5, 15, or 25 sessions. Then all subjects were asked to read a passage and given a test of comprehension. Within each group, one third of the subjects were offered no money, one third $1, and one third $10, contingent on a certain level of performance. Dependent measures were time taken to read the passage and number of items correct on the comprehension test.
   Blocked (yes or no) _____
   Classificatory variable(s) _____
   Experimental variable(s) _____

3. An investigator is interested in the effects of various types of information on changing attitudes toward former communist countries. She divides her subject pool into three groups based on socioeconomic status. Each group has the same original *mean* rating of Russia. She then assigns subjects to one of four treatment groups: reading books about Russia; exposure to panel discussions by members of the Russian embassy; viewing films about Russia; and a no treatment control. She finds significant differences between socioeconomic groups: high-status subjects showed the greatest increase in liking; low-status the least increase. She also finds significant difference between treatment conditions: The panel discussion produces the greatest change, no treatment the least; films produce more change than books, but less than the panel discussion.

    (a) What conclusions can the investigator draw from these results?

    (b) How else could the investigator have classified her subjects?

4. Give a brief definition of each technique for selecting groups, and give a general rule for when it should be used.

    (a) Median split (full range)

    (b) Extreme groups

    (c) Multiple discrete leveling

5. You wish to evaluate the effects of watching "Sesame Street" at age 5 on reading ability at age 6 (the end of first grade). You suspect that level of intelligence may influence the response to "Sesame Street," but you don't know the nature of the relationship. You give all your 5-year-olds the WPPSI (Wechsler Preschool and Primary Scale of Intelligence), divide them into groups on the basis of their IQ scores, and assign them to experimental conditions.

    (a) What method do you use to select your groups on IQ score (remember, you don't know if the relationship is linear or curvilinear)? Why?

    (b) If the relationship is curvilinear, what effects would another method of selection (for example, extreme groups) have on your results? Graph a set of data that demonstrates the different results that might occur using the two different methods of selection.

6. On TV you see the following commercial: the announcer shows a "before" picture of 10 Saint Bernard puppies and 10 beagle puppies all weighing approximately the same. He says that he has been feeding the Saint Bernards Grow Fast Puppy Chow and the Beagles Brand X. Next, he shows a picture taken 6 months later in which the Saint Bernards clearly outweigh the Beagles. The announcer concludes that Grow Fast is superior to Brand X. After receiving a barrage of letters from critical social scientists, the Grow Fast Company has become concerned over the quality of their research program. They come to you for consultation and advice. Point out the problem with their research and design a study that will adequately test their claim (use a block design).

7. What is a mixed design? Under what circumstances is it used?

9

SINGLE-SUBJECT AND QUASI-EXPERIMENTAL DESIGNS

In the last two chapters we have been discussing true experiments, in which treatment effects are examined between (or among) groups formed by random assignment. Now we turn to another broad class of designs, called *quasi-experiments*.

Quasi-experiments are like true experiments in that they employ the same units of analysis; that is, they involve one or more manipulated independent variables (as treatments) compared by considering subjects' performance on one or more dependent variables (outcome measures). *The major difference between quasi-experiments and true experiments is that the scores compared in a quasi-experiment are not based on the performance of groups formed by* **random assignment**. As a result of lifting this requirement, quasi-experiments become more feasible than true experiments in many applied or field settings where random assignment of individuals to treatment groups is not possible.

On the other hand, the lack of random assignment robs the quasi-experiment of the logical force of the true experiment and leaves it a weaker tool for drawing solid casual inferences. In addition, whether any useful conclusion can be drawn from a quasi-experiment often depends on the specific pattern of outcomes obtained. With some patterns, interpretation is relatively straightforward; with others, interpretation is uncertain or impossible.

Well-designed true experiments, in contrast, are interpretable under a much wider range of possible outcomes. But there are many circumstances in which the quasi-experiment is the only feasible approach. For this reason, it has proven quite useful to research psychologists.

There are two broad classes of quasi-experimental designs: interrupted time series designs and nonequivalent control group designs. **Interrupted time series designs** involve within-subjects comparisons, that is, repeated observations of the same individuals as they are exposed to a succession of changes in the independent variable. **Nonequivalent control group designs** involve actual or simulated between-subjects comparisons. Our discussion begins with interrupted time series designs.

INTERRUPTED TIME SERIES DESIGNS

Interrupted time series designs *are those in which the ongoing flow of events is interrupted by the introduction of a treatment at some specific point in time.*

All interrupted time series designs employ within-subjects comparisons. That is, they involve **repeated measurement** of the same subjects. (See Chapter 8.) The important data are changes in the dependent variable occurring between successive treatments. All such designs face six different threats to internal validity.

First, subjects' response to a second treatment or condition may be influenced by some residue of the first treatment (a **carryover effect**). Second, some experience irrelevant to the experiment (**history**) may have occurred between the successive treatments. In addition, **maturation**, **statistical regression**, **repeated testing**, and **instrument change** also pose serious threats to this class of designs under some circumstances. If any of these threats is plausible, then the internal validity of the interrupted time series design is seriously compromised. (See Box 9.1.)

BOX 9.1 *DO SPEED LIMITS SAVE LIVES?*

Campbell and Ross (1968) reported an intriguing example of how interrupted time series can be misleading. In 1955 the State of Connecticut began a severe crackdown on speeding with the intent of reducing traffic fatalities. No formal research plan was developed, but in 1956 the governor reported the data shown in Figure 9-1 and concluded that the program had saved 40 lives and had therefore been highly successful.

The governor had made a strong causal inference, and Campbell and Ross wondered whether it was valid. As a test they used the naturally occurring interrupted time series design and plotted the number of traffic deaths for several years before and after 1955. These data are shown in Figure 9-2. This figure dramatically illustrates that the drop in fatalities from 1955 to 1956 is only part of wide year-to-year fluctuations in the number of traffic deaths. An even greater drop in the number of fatalities occurred in a year when there was no change from low to high enforcement of speeding laws (1957 to 1958). The drop from 1955 to 1956 could be simply a part of a larger (but unexplained) trend toward fewer fatalities over the years 1955 to 1958.

Another point that can be raised is the possible operation of **statistical regression**. Notice in Figure 9-2 that the crackdown began when traffic deaths were at their highest. Thus, it might be expected that the next year's figure would be lower, simply due to regression.

In sum, when more data are examined, the validity of the causal inference "reducing speeding causes fewer fatalities" is certainly not well substantiated.

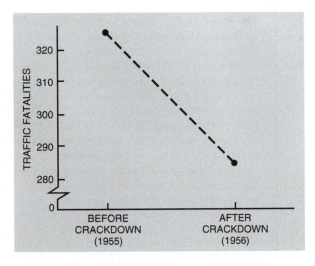

Figure 9-1 Connecticut traffic fatalities, 1955–1956. Data from Campbell and Ross (1968).

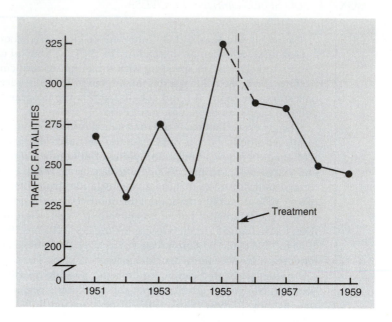

Figure 9-2   Connecticut traffic fatalities, 1951–1959. Data from: Campbell and Ross (1968).

The drop in traffic deaths between 1955 and 1956 could be due to *statistical regression*, to unusually dry weather, to fewer cars on the road, to new safety devices, or to any of a large number of other uncontrolled factors.

   To examine the possible operation of some of these other variables, Campbell and Ross compared the data from Connecticut with those of neighboring states that did not initiate a crackdown. The idea is that such variables as dry weather, improved safety features, or the like *would* likely be operating in these states as well. Thus, the hypothesis that some variable other than the crackdown produced the drop would be supported if the other states' data showed a drop similar to Connecticut's. These data are shown in Figure 9-3.

   Notice that Rhode Island, Massachusetts, and New Jersey also showed declines in fatalities between 1955 and 1956. This information supports the notion that the Connecticut decline cannot be attributed to the crackdown alone. But Connecticut also shows a greater persisting decline over the years 1957, 1958, and 1959. These data suggest that the crackdown may have had a genuine effect. In sum, we are left with a somewhat ambiguous array of data. Some, but not all, of the decline of traffic deaths in Connecticut may have been due to the crackdown. The interrupted time series analysis has revealed the complexity involved in trying to draw causal inferences from simple interrupted time series designs.

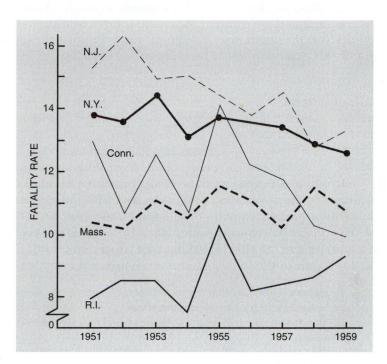

Figure 9-3   Traffic fatalities for Connecticut, New York, New Jersey, Rhode Island, and Massachusetts (per 100,000 persons). Data from: Campbell and Ross (1968).

Interrupted time series designs can be employed with either small or large groups of subjects, or they can be employed as **single-subject designs**. In general, the logic of these designs is the same, regardless of whether one or many individuals are involved. However, using these designs with a single subject has some unique advantages and disadvantages, as we shall see.

Simple Interrupted Time Series Designs

The simplest way to use interrupted time series is to take a measure of the dependent variable of interest, introduce a treatment hypothesized to cause a change in the dependent variable, and take a second measure of the dependent variable after the treatment has been introduced. This design is called an **A-B design**, in which the measurements taken under "A" occur before the treatment, whereas the measurements taken under "B" occur after treatment. When employed with single subjects, the simple interrupted time series design is often called a **clinical trial**. Clinical trials are fairly common as initial reports of treatment effects in clinical psychology, psychiatry, and medicine.

To illustrate, let's begin with a simple example. Assume that an investigator has designed a treatment to reduce the self-abusive behavior of an autistic child. Using the notation we have employed previously, the simplest experimental test of this treatment would be represented as follows:

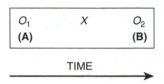

In this quasi-experiment an initial baseline period of observation, O_1, was followed by the application of punishment (X) contingent on these behaviors. Subsequently, the frequency of self-abuse was reassessed (O_2). If the frequency of self-abusive behaviors declines from O_1 to O_2, is the investigator justified in concluding that the effect was due to the treatment? No. Such a result could also be due to any of the following sources of internal invalidity.

1. **History**: Other specific events between O_1 and O_2, for example, a change in ward personnel could have produced the effect.
2. **Maturation**: The self-abusive behaviors could have decreased because of **spontaneous remission**. If the change produced by the treatment was rapid, maturation becomes less likely as an alternative hypothesis. On the other hand, *maturation is most likely to be a threat when the treatment is protracted and the change is gradual.*
3. **Instrument change**: The observer may have become less diligent in recording the behaviors on O_2 versus O_1, *or* might have become more capable or efficient over time.
4. **Statistical Regression**: If the child being studied was selected for an extremely high base rate in O_1, the frequency of self-abusive behavior can be expected to regress toward the mean, that is, to decrease on a second assessment (O_2) regardless of treatment.
5. **Repeated Testing**: Testing effects are unlikely in this case because of the nature of the test used (direct observation). However, repeated testing would be a serious threat if self-reports were taken before and after treatment. (Recall that people tend to appear more "normal" when taking a personality test a second time.)
6. **Interactions** among the aforementioned threats to internal validity can occur.

In the preceding example there was only one pretreatment measure and one posttreatment measure. However, with interrupted time series designs, any number of observations can be made before or after the treatment. The simple interrupted time series design is strengthened considerably by taking multiple measures before and after introduction of the treatment.

Consider the hypothetical example in which a child who is enuretic (a bed-wetter) is treated with a urine alarm.[1] Suppose, too, that a record is kept of the number of nights per week the child wets the bed for 4 weeks before the intro-

---

[1]The urine alarm has been successfully employed for simple bedwetting (primary nocturnal enuresis) since the late 1930s. See Houts and Liebert (1984) for a further discussion of types of bedwetting and their treatment.

duction of the treatment and for 4 weeks during which the alarm is used. The design is represented in Campbell's notation as follows:

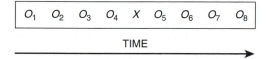

$$O_1 \quad O_2 \quad O_3 \quad O_4 \quad X \quad O_5 \quad O_6 \quad O_7 \quad O_8$$

TIME

Figure 9-4 shows a fairly typical pattern of results. If the child is 10 years old and has never had 3 dry nights in a row before, the results appear quite compelling.

Another way to strengthen the simple interrupted time series design is to select the point at which the treatment is introduced on a random basis.

The Random Interruption Design.   Suppose that an investigator develops a treatment for a child's fear of the dark. She wishes to evaluate its effectiveness with a single youngster. The investigator might assess the child's fearfulness, administer the new treatment, and then test the child again. But as we have seen, maturation, history, or repeated testing might explain any observed improvement.

One possible solution can be found in the **random interruption design**. If it were decided to test the child on seven separate occasions, the point at which

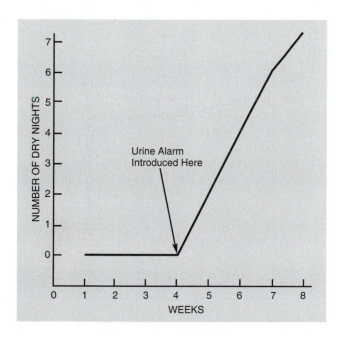

Figure 9-4   Hypothetical example of the effects of a urine alarm on the bedwetting of a 10-year-old illustrating an interrupted time series design with multiple pretreatment and post-treatment measures.

the treatment is introduced could be selected randomly; for instance, by drawing one of the "internal" numbers (2–6) from a hat and administering the treatment after the interval drawn.

Suppose that the number 4 were selected. There would then be four pretreatment assessments followed by three posttreatment assessments. If the procedure were effective, data such as those shown in Figure 9-5 would be expected. Should these results occur, the likelihood of this particular pattern occurring by chance or by history, testing, or maturation would be very low.

Thus far we have seen that *the major issue in simple interrupted time series is how the time of introduction of treatment is determined.* If the decision to introduce the treatment is based on the dependent measure (for example, if patients seek treatment when their symptoms are most acute, or businesses institute new practices when their sales or productivity is at its lowest), seasonal trends or statistical regression can mimic a treatment effect. That is, *an improvement might have occurred at about the same point in time, even if no treatment had been introduced.*

On the other hand, if the time at which the treatment is introduced can be decided randomly, and its apparent effects endure across all posttests, the results are quite compelling. In these circumstances we expect to see a sharp discontinuity in the dependent measure occurring immediately (or very shortly) after the introduction of treatment.

However, not all problems are as consistent as our bedwetting example, and many treatments may have a real effect that is delayed rather than immediate.

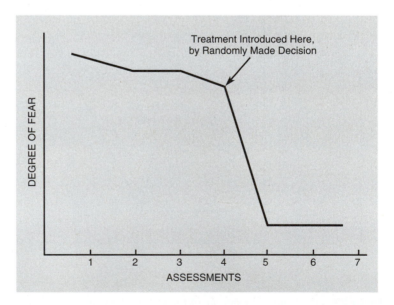

Figure 9-5   Hypothetical data from a fearful child, illustrating the random time series single-subject design.

In such cases, more powerful designs are necessary to assess treatment effects adequately.

Interrupted Time Series with Reversal (A-B-A and A-B-A-B Designs)

Reversal designs involve careful measurement of some aspect of the subject's behavior during a given time period (as a **baseline** or control procedure), the introduction of some environmental modification or treatment during the next (*experimental*) time period, a return to the conditions that prevailed during the control period, and often, a second introduction of the experimental manipulation.

The intent of this procedure, sometimes referred to as an **ABA design** or **ABAB design**, is straightforward. Suppose behavior changes from A (the control period) to B (the experimental period), returns to baseline when the experimentally manipulated conditions are removed (that is, returned to A), and "re-reverses" when B is again introduced. If this pattern occurs, there is little doubt that it is the manipulation, and not chance or uncontrolled factors, that have produced the change. And logically, the design itself satisfies Mill's two requirements for demonstrating sufficient causality (see Chapter 5).

The *ABAB* single-subject design was used by Tate & Baroff (1966). These psychologists treated the self-injurious behavior of a 9-year-old boy, Sam. Sam, who had been diagnosed as psychotic, engaged in self-injurious behavior, including ". . . banging his head forcefully against floors, walls, and other hard objects, slapping his face with his hands, punching his face and head with his fists, hitting his shoulder with his chin, and kicking himself." Such acts were "a frequent form of behavior observed under a wide variety of situations" (p. 281).

Despite his self-injurious behavior, Sam was not entirely asocial. In fact, it was noted that ". . . he obviously enjoyed and sought bodily contact with others. He would cling to people and try to wrap their arms around him, climb into their laps and mold himself to their contours" (p. 282). It was this observation that gave rise to the treatment. Specifically, the investigators demonstrated the effects of punishing Sam's self-injurious outbursts by the contingent withdrawal of physical contact. Their hope, of course, was that this "time-out" from human contact would reduce the frequency of the behaviors that produced it.

The study, run for 20 days, involved a daily walk around the campus for Sam. Two adult experimenters talked to him and held his hands continuously. During the control days, Sam was simply ignored when he engaged in self-injurious behavior. However, during the experimental days, the adults responded to any self-injurious actions by immediately jerking their hands away from Sam. They maintained this time-out until three seconds after the last self-injurious act.

The results of the systematic reversal of these procedures, shown in Figure 9-6, illustrate the dramatic effects of contingent punishment for reducing undesirable behavior in this case. The bars show the relative frequency of self-injurious acts during each of the four periods of the experiment. The data clearly

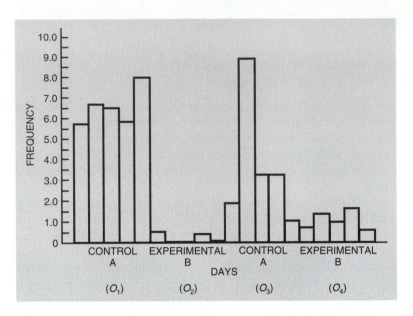

Figure 9-6   Effects of the contingent punishment proceedure in Tate and Baroff's study, illustrating experimental effects within a single-subject design. (The individual bars are data for each day of the experiment). Source: Adapted from Tate and Baroff (1966).

suggest that the major changes are due to the punishment rather than to chance or accident. Moreover, the side effects of the punishment procedure appear to be positive rather than negative. Tate and Baroff note:

> On control days Sam typically whined, cried, hesitated often in his walk, and seemed unresponsive to the environment in general. His behavior on experimental days was completely different—he appeared to attend more to environmental stimuli . . . there was no crying or whining, and he often smiled (1966, p. 283).

It should be apparent from the Tate and Baroff study that the single-subject design can serve as a well-controlled investigation and demonstrate convincing relationships. The investigators purposely reinstated the original (premanipulative) circumstances to determine whether the subject's behavior would also return to its baseline under these conditions at time O_3. Employing this procedure, they demonstrated that the behavior under observation was indeed controlled by the systematic withdrawal and reintroduction of consequences.

If the change in frequency from O_1 to O_2 had been due to **history, maturation**, **instrument change**, **statistical regression**, or **repeated testing**, the removal of the treatment would not have been expected to produce a difference between O_2 and O_3. The conclusion that the treatment was directly related to the decrease that occurred between O_1 and O_2 is yet further attested to by the difference that again appears between O_3 and O_4. Thus, the evidence is extremely convincing; the single-subject design clearly can produce compelling causal inferences. Tate and Baroff used the design to demonstrate a principle of behavior through the systematic treatment of one individual under tightly controlled conditions.

Interrupted Time Series with Replication (The Multiple Baseline Design)

Sometimes use of the reversal technique is not possible. Subjects' initial state may not be recoverable, as, for example, in the study of learning. Or, as in psychotherapy studies, it might be possible to reinstate the initial condition of the subject or patient, but to do so would be unethical. Who, for example, would be willing to reinstate a severe depression to demonstrate the effectiveness of a treatment?

In such circumstances, a **multiple baseline** or replication is often employed. With this procedure, two or more behaviors are chosen for study. For example, a child who is having "learning problems" may be chosen, and both math and reading performance selected as the two areas for treatment. Baseline data are collected on the degree of inattentiveness during *both* math and reading lessons. Subsequently, reward is introduced for attention in math lessons, but not for reading. A second observation then occurs. Finally, in the third phase of the study, reward is introduced for reading as well as mathematics. A hypothetical pattern of results using this procedure is shown in Figure 9-7.

Such a pattern provides support for the inference that reward, and not other factors, modified the child's behavior. If one of the threats to internal validity were operative, it should affect inattention during both math and reading

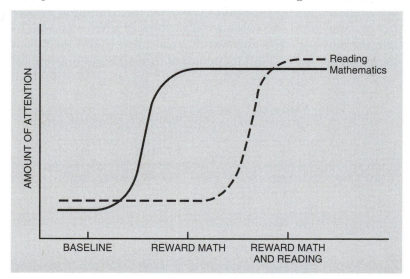

Figure 9-7 Effects of reward on attention during mathematics and reading lessons, illustrating the multiple baseline procedure.

lessons. Hence, rewarding the child's attention during math would not markedly change math *relative to reading* if some other factor were operating. Employing *two* baselines makes it possible to minimize certain threats to internal validity.

There is one important *dis*advantage of the multiple baseline procedure. The behaviors under study may not be independent; for example, the experimental treatment for math may also indirectly influence reading. If this is so, the investigator will be unable to distinguish among **history, maturation**, or **repeated testing** and true experimental effects.

The use of multiple baselines is by no means limited to single-subject designs. An analogous procedure can also be used in group studies. The difference is that, instead of employing a second dependent measure (e.g., math after reading), the group version of the design involves introducing the treatment for a second group (the "replication") after a longer baseline than was used for the first group. In group applications it is often possible to have several replications, each with a baseline of different length.

An example of a group multiple baseline study is found in the work of Sulzer-Azaroff and Consuelo de Santamaria (1980). These investigators were interested in reducing the number of safety hazards in each of six departments of a large industrial organization. The treatment involved giving department supervisors a "feedback package." The package included information as to the number and location of hazardous conditions in their departments, along with specific suggestions as to how each hazardous condition might be corrected.

Before administration of the treatment, a baseline measure of hazardous conditions was taken. The duration of the baseline was 3 weeks for two of the departments, 6 weeks for two other departments, and 9 weeks for the remaining two departments. As expected, each department showed a relatively stable number of hazards for the baseline (regardless of whether it was 3, 6, or 9 weeks in length) and a marked decrease in hazardous conditions shortly after the treatment was administered. The design of this study is shown in Table 9-1.

TABLE 9-1   THE SULTZER-AZAROFF AND CONSUELO DE SANTAMARIA (1980) MULTIPLE BASELINE DESIGN

	O_1	O_2	O_3	O_4
First two departments	A	B	B	B
Second two departments	A	A	B	B
Final two departments	A	A	A	B

A is baseline; B is treatment.

The Changing Criterion Design

One quasi-experimental design developed specifically for single subject research is the **changing criterion design**. This design is a variant of the multiple baseline (replication) design. However, it involves changing the criterion for reinforcement of a single target behavior over time, rather than initiating reinforcement for two or more different behaviors at different points in time. This design thereby eliminates the possibility of **carryover effects** that plague single subject multiple baseline designs.

In this design, one begins by taking a baseline of the target behavior. Then reinforcement (or punishment) is introduced for a different level of the desired behavior (higher or lower than the baseline). Once the new level of performance is reached, the reinforcement criterion is tightened, so that a yet higher or lower level of the target behavior is required for reinforcement. *The reinforcement criterion is thus progressively tightened until some desired final criterion is reached.* The unique strength of the design is that it *uses each step as a baseline for the next step.*

As an illustration of the changing criterion design, consider a study by Hall and Fox (1977), in which a "behavior disordered" boy, Dennis, was permitted to play basketball (a favorite activity) at recess contingent on doing an ever-increasing number of arithmetic problems in his math sessions. As seen in Figure 9-8, Dennis' math accomplishments increased steadily to accommodate the increasing demands of each new criterion. The overall pattern of results leaves little doubt that it was the contingent reinforcement that was responsible for the dramatically improved performance during math sessions.

Complex (Multiple Treatment) Interrupted
Time Series Designs

There are many possible extensions and elaborations of the basic interrupted time series design. Each is applicable to a special set of hypotheses or circumstances, or helps to further reduce the threats to internal validity that are faced by simpler designs. In this section we provide a few illustrative examples of these more complex designs. For a wider survey, the interested reader is referred to Barlow and Hersen (1984), Cook and Campbell (1979), and Kratochwill (1978).

The A-B-C-B Design.   Single subject interrupted time series designs have been widely used by researchers interested in behavior modification, a family of therapy techniques that relies heavily on contingent reinforcement.

One challenge that can be raised to the A-B-A-B reversal design as used in behavior modification studies is that the subjects' response to reinforcement does not necessarily demonstrate that contingent reinforcement is required for behavior change. The administration of noncontingent reinforcement might produce the same change (e.g., by diverting the subjects' attention). One way to handle this challenge is to employ the **A-B-C-B design,** in which A is the baseline period, B is contingent reinforcement, C is *non*contingent reinforcement, and B is a return to contingent reinforcement.

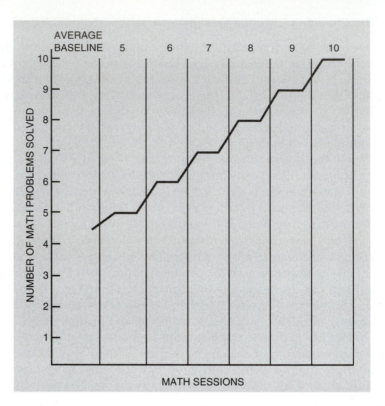

Figure 9-8   The number of math problems solved by Dennis in Hall and Fox's (1977) study, illustrating the changing criterion design. Source: From data reported in Hall & Fox (1977).

This design was used by Miller, Hersen, Eisler, and Watts (1974) with a 48-year-old alcoholic. The dependent measure was the patient's blood-alcohol level (determined from breathalyzer samples). After eight biweekly baseline measures (A), reinforcement (consisting of treats at the hospital canteen) was administered contingent on a low blood-alcohol level (B). This resulted in a sharp drop in blood alcohol level. The same reinforcement was then given noncontingently (i.e., regardless of the results of the breathalyzer test), whereupon the patient's blood-alcohol level began to rise (C).

Finally, contingent reinforcement was again introduced, whereupon the patient's blood alcohol soon dropped back to 0 again. The pattern of results, depicted in Figure 9-9, shows convincingly that it is the reinforcement contingency and not the mere presentation of reinforcement that accounts for the change.

Decomposition Interrupted Time Series Designs.   Investigators have also developed interrupted time series designs to analyze a complex treatment into component parts, to see which are the truly active or necessary ingredients. An example is a study of a classroom of hyperactive children in a university laboratory school (Rosén, O'Leary, Joyce, Conway, & Pfiffner, 1984). The dependent measure,

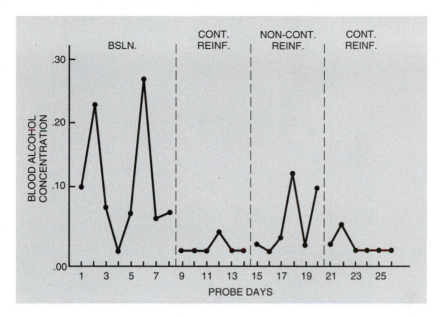

Figure 9-9   Biweekly blood alcohol concentrations of an alcoholic treated with contingent and noncontingent reinforcement for abstinence, illustrating the A-B-C-B design. Source: From Barlow and Hersen, (1984, p. 171).

recorded unobtrusively by highly trained observers, was the percentage of time which the children spent "on task," defined as "sitting and working quietly, listening to the teacher give group lessons, and working on any other task approved by the teacher" (p. 584).

The baseline here was not a no-treatment condition; rather, it was taken under the teacher's usual behavior, which included both praise for on-task behavior (positive consequences) and reprimands for off-task behavior (negative consequences). After the initial baseline, negative consequences were withdrawn and the teacher simply ignored all inappropriate behavior, whereupon the percentage of time the youngsters spent on-task plummeted. The third phase was a return to baseline (i.e., reinstituting both positive and negative consequences); this quickly brought on-task behavior up again to its previous level.

Next, the positive consequences were removed while the negative consequences continued. In sharp contrast to what happened when the negative consequences were withdrawn, removing the positive consequences did not decrease on-task behavior. In the final phase, the teacher's usual practice of both positive and negative consequences was restored. The overall pattern of results, shown in Figure 9-10, suggests that a willingness to reprimand off-task behavior is the critical ingredient in managing hyperactive children.

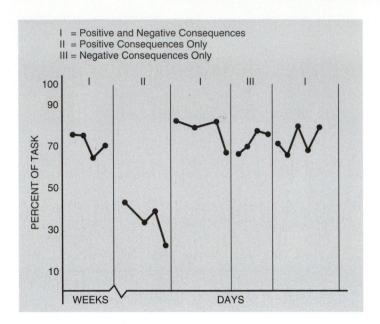

Figure 9-10   Percent of on-task behavior in Rosén et al's study as a function of positive and negative consequences, illustrating the decomposition interrupted time series design. Source: From data reported in Rosén et al. (1984).

Evaluating Single-Subject Interrupted Time Series Designs

For years a controversy has raged about the advantages and disadvantages of single subject interrupted time series designs. Our aim in this final section is to give you a sense of the issues involved.

Advantages: Sidman's Arguments.   Sidman (1960) advanced several arguments that single-subject research is *preferable* to between-groups experiments. We will consider some of these.

Among the most compelling of the points made by Sidman is his criticism of the manner in which data from between-groups studies are analyzed. As you may recall, between-groups differences are typically evaluated for **statistical significance**, against the likelihood that the obtained finding would have occurred by chance. The inclusion of *chance* as a basis for evaluating experimental hypotheses forms the basis of Sidman's objection. He argues that chance, in essence, represents ignorance (that is, **error variance**, or that variability we are unable to successfully attribute to any specific factor). By evaluating results against "chance," we are passively accepting our ignorance.

Sidman's argument is that *the between-group design can mask the weakness of a treatment*. The between-groups investigator is satisfied at having produced a significant difference and is unconcerned that considerable variance may still be unaccounted for.

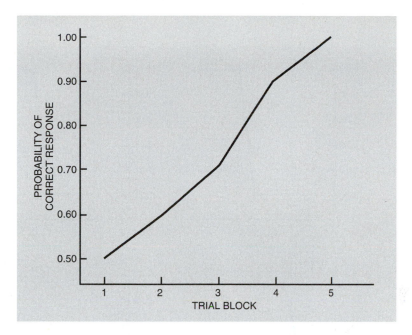

Figure 9-11   Results of hypothetical learning experiment with five children, illustrating a continuous increase in probability of correct response when the data are averaged over children. The smooth curve, though, may not tell us how individual subjects actually learn over time.

Sidman's second major criticism concerns the artificiality of pooling data. This is an attack on the general practice of averaging results over a group of subjects.

Consider, for example, a study in which children are asked to predict which of two lights will illuminate on a given trial. Five children are tested in five trial blocks of 10 trials each. The experimenter presents them with a double alternation pattern of lights (the left light illuminates twice, then the right light twice, and so on). The results of this hypothetical study, averaged over all five children, are displayed in Figure 9-11. There is a smooth increase in the probability of correct responses from the first to the 5th block of trials. From data such as these, it might be concluded that learning is a gradual or *continuous* process. But an examination of the data from individuals shows that this conclusion is *totally wrong*.

In Figure 9-12, the data for each individual child are plotted separately. When individual children are considered, the learning process appears to be *discontinuous*. For each child the probability of correct responding jumps from .50 (chance performance, since there are only two alternatives) to 1.00. It is only because the transition occurs at different times for different children that the averaged curve appears continuous and smooth.

Limitations of Single-Subject Designs.   One obvious drawback of single-subject designs is that they are suitable only for evaluating treatments that are discrete, or for responses that can be expected to reverse fairly rapidly.

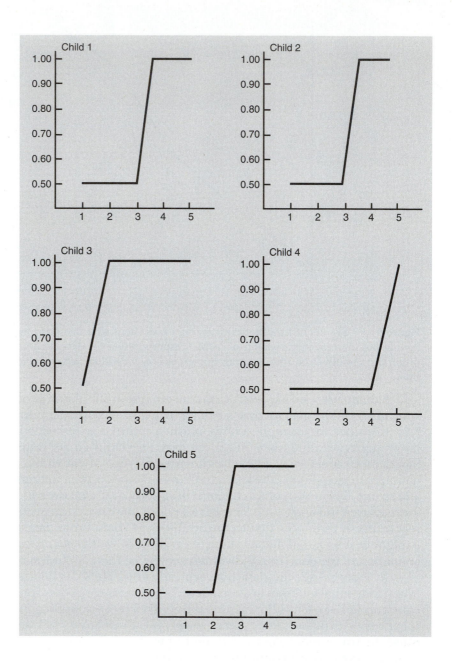

Figure 9-12   Results of the same hypothetical learning experiment as in Figure 9–11. These graphs reveal that learning was, in fact, discontinuous rather than smooth, as seen when we look at the data for each child individually.

Further, these designs yield only the *pattern* of directional changes. In turn, this means that a good ABA reversal shows only a change from A_1 to B and an opposite change from B to A_2. The probability of each of these directional changes is .50, so the likelihood of obtaining the expected pattern is $.50 \times .50$ or .25. It would, therefore, occur by chance in one-quarter of all cases in the absence of a real experimental effect. If only two or three single-subject quasi-experiments of 10 show the expected *ABA* effect, it is easy to see why the result can be faulted as weak or invalid. Such a problem is by no means inevitable, but it is one that single-subject researchers must be on guard to avoid.

Finally, the single-subject design, like the case study, may produce data of little generality. Even though such designs may appear to be internally valid, the results may not be generalizable to the population; hence, the results may have little *external validity*.

NONEQUIVALENT CONTROL GROUP DESIGNS

In real life, people are often grouped for social, educational, or economic purposes. For example, children in school are grouped into grades and classrooms, patients in hospitals are grouped into wards, and workers in many industries are grouped into shifts or work teams. These assignments are institutionally made, and ordinarily researchers cannot tamper with them. Instead it is often necessary to compare preexisting or intact groups, where some groups have received the treatment of interest and others have not.

Two new threats to **internal validity** exist with nonequivalent control group designs that we have not encountered before: selection-maturation and local history.

Selection-maturation *is a threat to internal validity whenever it is plausible that the groups being compared are developing at different rates on any dimension correlated with the dependent variable.*

Local history *is a threat whenever some experience that might be related to the dependent variable has occurred for one of the groups, but not for the other.*

The internal validity of nonequivalent control group designs is also at considerable risk of **compensatory rivalry** and **resentful demoralization**. This is true whenever those in the control group are aware of special or different treatment received by the experimental group. The problem is made worse by the fact that many pre-existing groups have traditional rivalries that may be brought out by giving special treatment to one group.

As seen with single-subject designs, quasi-experimental designs can take on different forms. We next describe the five basic configurations and forms of nonequivalent control group designs and explain the advantages and limitations of each.

The Posttest Only Nonequivalent Peer Control Group Design

Suppose a computer manufacturer has two workshops in which computers are assembled and wants to see if a bonus system will increase productivity of work teams. The manufacturer flips a coin to decide which work team is to receive a bonus for increased productivity, institutes the bonus plan for that group, and uses the number of units produced by both the bonus and no-bonus groups for the next 4 weeks as the dependent measure.

This design can be diagrammed as shown below, with the broken horizontal line indicating that the two groups were employed "intact," rather than being formed by randomly assigning individuals to the bonus and no-bonus conditions:

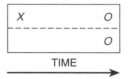

Suppose the bonus group produces twice as many units as the no-bonus group in the 4 weeks following the introduction of the bonus scheme. This is a difference which the manufacturer considers very impressive. Can we conclude that the bonus was effective in raising productivity? No.

In the absence of a *pretest* it remains completely plausible that the bonus group had much higher productivity than the no-bonus group even before the bonus plan was introduced. Thus **selection bias** is a **plausible rival hypothesis** for the observed posttest difference. Selection bias *always* poses a serious threat to the posttest only nonequivalent control group design. In fact, results obtained with this design are uninterpretable in most cases.

The Pretest-Posttest Nonequivalent Peer Control Group Design

Suppose a fourth-grade math teacher has two math classes. He wishes to determine if a new method for teaching math is more effective than the traditional method. The teacher gives the children in both classes a mathematical achievement test at the beginning of the year. By the flip of a coin, he chooses one class for the new method. In the other class, he uses the traditional method. The mathematical achievement test is readministered to all the children at the end of the year. The teacher has used the **pretest-posttest nonequivalent peer control group design**, as diagrammed below:

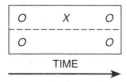

Whether the results obtained with this design are interpretable depends on the pattern of results obtained. Figure 9-13(A) shows a pattern of results in which the new method group was superior to the traditional method group at *posttest*.

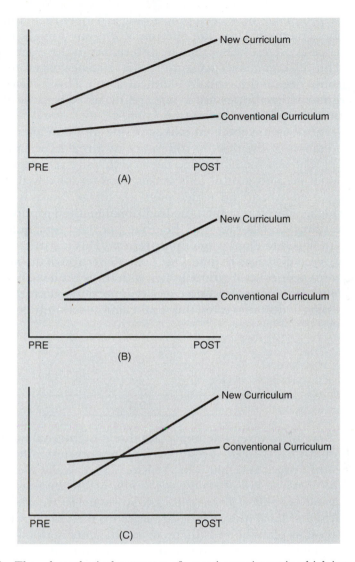

Figure 9-13   Three hypothetical outcomes of a quasi-experiment in which intact classrooms receive either a new or the conventional math curriculum. A is uninterpretable because the posttest difference may arise from selection-maturation. B is less likely to be an artifact of selection, and C is even more convincing as a real treatment effect. All three outcomes nonetheless may still be open to the threat of local history.

However, the children in the new method group also did somewhat better than the traditional method group at *pretest*.

This outcome cannot be interpreted unambiguously. It is seriously threatened by the possibility of **selection-maturation**. That is, the children in the new method group may have been progressing at a more rapid rate than those in the traditional method. Thus, the difference at posttest might be explained by the difference at pretest rather than by differences in the teaching methods.

The outcome shown in Figure 9-13(B) is somewhat more interpretable. The two groups began with virtually identical scores. This reduces the plausibility of the argument that the posttest differences occurred because of initial differences in aptitude or achievement.

If the outcome obtained is like the one shown in Figure 9-13(C), then the interpretation of the posttest difference as a real experimental effect is even stronger. The new method group began with lower achievement scores than the traditional method group. This makes it quite unlikely that the new method group started out with an achievement advantage. Nor is it likely that they were maturing at a faster rate than the traditional method group.

A valuable elaboration of the pretest-posttest nonequivalent peer control group design is to employ **multiple pretests**. This is particularly powerful if the tests are equally spaced in time. One possible version of the multiple pretest non-equivalent peer control group design, with three pretests, is diagrammed below. The multiple pretests provide a check on selection-maturation. If the groups are progressing at different rates, this would almost certainly be apparent across the pretests.

O	O	O	X	O
O	O	O		O

TIME

There is, however, one important threat to internal validity that cannot be ruled out by *any* pattern of results in a pretest-posttest nonequivalent peer control group design, and that is local history. Specifically, local history *refers to the possibility that some experience that might influence the dependent variable occurred between pretest and posttest for one of the groups, but not for the other.*

Whether local history is in fact a serious threat in any particular study will depend on its plausibility. Is there, or might there reasonably have been, some intervening experience for one group but not the other that could be relevant to scores on the dependent measure? Answering this question in any real instance depends on intimate knowledge of the situation and context in which the research occurred.

The designs we have considered so far are threatened by selection bias and selection-maturation. This is because we ordinarily have no way of arguing that the groups being compared are sufficiently alike in all relevant respects except for the treatment. Simulated designs, to which we turn next, endeavor to increase the likelihood that the comparison groups are in fact sufficiently alike. They do this by simulating the kind of equivalence between groups that is produced by random assignment in the true experiment.

The Simulated Posttest Only Design with a Cohort Control

Recall that a **cohort** is any group that passes through experiences together at the same time. For example, all the children who were in the first grade in 1984–85 form a cohort. All the children who were in the first grade in 1994–95 form another cohort.

Contiguous cohorts *are those which pass through an institution in immediately adjacent time periods.* The class of 1994 and the class of 1995 are contiguous cohorts. Contiguous cohorts are of interest in nonequivalent control group designs because they are generally highly similar to one another. In some cases it is possible to capitalize on this similarity by comparing contiguous cohorts that seem to differ only in that one of them has received a treatment of interest, while the other has not.

Suppose a research psychologist is interested in the impact of a new educational TV program designed to promote reading skills. Suppose, too, the investigator can identify a reading test that is commonly administered in standardized form to first-grade children all over the country.

If these reading scores can be obtained for a large random sample of children who passed through the first grade in the year immediately before the new TV program was introduced and in the year after the program was introduced, any difference in reading scores favoring the younger cohort might be interpreted as an effect of the new TV series. The design can be diagrammed as shown below. The wavy line designates the use of presumably equivalent cohorts.

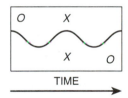

Selection-maturation is unlikely to contaminate a design involving contiguous cohorts whose members were selected on a random basis. However, the possibility of a **local history** effect still cannot be ruled out logically (though it may be shown to be implausible under some circumstances).

The Simulated Pretest-Posttest Control Group Design

Suppose that a major public information campaign on energy conservation is about to be instituted in a particular community. A team of research psychologists sets out to determine the campaign's effectiveness (i.e., the degree to which it lowers energy consumption). Plainly, it will not be possible to use any of the true experimental designs; there is no practical way of controlling people's access to newspapers, radio, and television. Therefore random assignment to the campaign is not possible. However, **random selection** may be possible.

The investigator can identify the relevant population—all the households in the community—and draw two random samples from it. Using the **simulated control group design**, we would compare the energy consumption of one group of households *before* the campaign is introduced with the energy consumption of the other group *after* the campaign has been completed. In this way we have simulated a comparison between two presumably equivalent groups (both were drawn randomly from the same population), who differ only on whether they have been exposed to the campaign at the time the measurement takes place.

This design is quite sophisticated, but like all other quasi-experimental designs involving nonequivalent control groups, the possibility of local history masquerading as a treatment effect cannot be ruled out. For instance, in the foregoing example we cannot be sure that the two groups were completely comparable at the time their energy consumption was measured. In the interim between the time the "control" group was measured and the time the "experimental" group was measured, experiences that might influence energy consumption other than being exposed to the campaign itself may have occurred. For example, the cost of energy might have gone up.

The Regression Discontinuity Design

In many applied settings, a treatment may be available only to those who have a pretreatment status above or below some cut-off point. For example, it is common in many colleges and universities to put students who have reached or exceeded a particular grade point average for the semester on the "dean's list." Similarly, sales personnel who exceed a certain number of sales may be given an end-of-the-year bonus. We may wonder in such situations whether these special treatments improve recipients' performance in the following time period. That is, does being put on the dean's list for good grades during semester 1 cause students to do better during semester 2 *than would otherwise have been predicted from their semester 1 grades?*

One approach to such questions is to generate a **regression equation** (as explained in Chapter 4) to predict semester 2 grades from semester 1 grades. If semester 2 grades are higher than expected for those on the dean's list, it may mean that being put on the dean's list contributes to higher grades. This would be true if the regression line was *dis*continuous, showing a "break" at the dean's list cutoff point, but was generally linear both before and after that point. (See Figure 9-14.)

Unfortunately, valid causal inferences can only be drawn from the **regression discontinuity design** when the relationship between semester 1 and semester 2 grades follows a simple linear (straight line) pattern across the entire distribution of semester 1 grades. In fact, however, it is plausible that the true underlying regression line is **curvilinear**. For example, students with higher grades during semester 1 may be developing their study skills at a faster rate than those

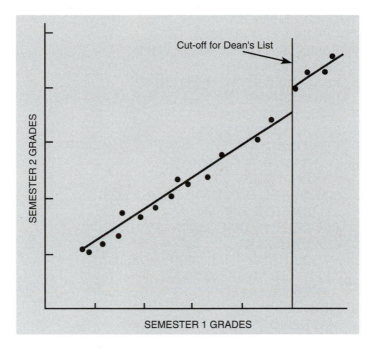

Figure 9-14   Regression of semester 2 grade point average on semester 1 grade point average for dean's list and nondean's list groups. Source: After Cook and Campbell (1979).

with lower grades, independent of whether there is a dean's list or not. In this case the true regression line may be curvilinear. Fitting a linear regression line to the data would give the impression that the dean's list award had contributed to semester 2 grades when in fact it had not.

This is another example of the problem of **selection-maturation** in quasi-experiments. The problem is further compounded by the fact that those selected for special awards, bonuses, or attention typically form only a small percentage of the total sample (i.e., only a few students make the dean's list). This makes it especially problematic to estimate the true shape of the distribution on the short (top) side of the cutting point.

FOR REVIEW AND DISCUSSION

Key Terms
    QUASI-EXPERIMENTS
    NONEQUIVALENT CONTROL GROUP DESIGNS
    INTERNAL VALIDITY
    SELECTION-MATURATION

LOCAL HISTORY
COMPENSATORY RIVALRY
RESENTFUL DEMORALIZATION
SELECTION BIAS
PLAUSIBLE RIVAL HYPOTHESIS
PRETEST-POSTTEST NONEQUIVALENT PEER CONTROL
   GROUP DESIGN
MULTIPLE PRETESTS
COHORT
CONTIGUOUS COHORTS
RANDOM SELECTION
SIMULATED CONTROL GROUP DESIGN
REGRESSION EQUATION
REGRESSION DISCONTINUITY DESIGN
CURVILINEAR
INTERRUPTED TIME SERIES DESIGNS
REPEATED MEASUREMENT
CARRYOVER EFFECT
HISTORY
MATURATION
STATISTICAL REGRESSION
INSTRUMENT CHANGE
REPEATED TESTING
SINGLE-SUBJECT DESIGNS
A-B DESIGN
CLINICAL TRIAL
SPONTANEOUS REMISSION
INTERACTIONS
RANDOM TIME SERIES SINGLE-SUBJECT DESIGN
BASELINE
A-B-A DESIGN
A-B-A-B DESIGN
MULTIPLE BASELINE
CHANGING CRITERION DESIGN
CARRYOVER EFFECTS
A-B-C-B DESIGN
STATISTICAL SIGNIFICANCE
ERROR VARIANCE
RANDOM ASSIGNMENT

Discussion Issues

1. Suppose you are interested in teaching a retarded boy to dress and feed himself. Your treatment will employ reinforcement of appropriate behavior. What kind of single-subject design would you use? Why?

2. In what ways is the single-subject reversal design an improvement over the simple case study approach? Include a discussion of how the *ABAB* design controls for sources of internal invalidity.

3. Devise a set of results for a hypothetical study in which the pretest-posttest nonequivalent peer control group design produced relatively unambiguous results. Using your hypothetical data, explain how each of the threats to internal validity can be ruled out by the pattern of data you have devised.

4. A number of drugs have been used in the treatment of schizophrenia. An investigator wishes to know which drug is most effective in reducing schizophrenic behavior. Each subject is given drug X for 3 days, drug Y for 3 days, and drug Z for 3 days. What kind of design is this? What are its advantages and disadvantages?

5. Discuss Sidman's argument that analysis of group data causes one to accept one's own ignorance. Do you agree or disagree with this position? Why?

6. The sales manager of a large automobile dealership institutes a 2-week vacation bonus in Hawaii for sales people who sell at least 10 cars during the month of June. Only two of the 20 sales people who work at the dealership achieve this goal. The sales manager wants to examine the number of cars sold by each sales person during August to see if the bonus increased sales. What design(s) could be used? Supposing there is no apparent bonus effect, could compensatory rivalry have masked the possible effect of the bonus? How?

PITFALLS FOR THE UNWARY

A young lawyer, freshly arrived at his new job as associate in a big law firm, was invited over for dinner by one of the firm's senior partners. When he arrived for dinner, his host greeted him at the door and announced: "We are going to have *chicken chambourg* for dinner. I hope it turned out. I worked on it all day."

In due course, the chicken appeared and was served. It tasted awful. Dry. Tough. Stringy. And it smelled a little like burnt fruit. Inevitably, the host popped the question: "How do you like it?"

The young lawyer is in the *role of guest*. A guest feels considerable pressure to be "polite." So it is not surprising that our young associate cheerfully replied, "The chicken was fine." (The truth is, he considered saying "It was wonderful," but couldn't bring himself to do it.)

Besides the threats to validity already discussed in Chapter 6, there remain five pitfalls awaiting the unwary psychological researcher. These pitfalls arise from the participants acting out their roles in the research enterprise. The focus of this chapter is on these remaining threats to the validity of research conclusions, and some suggested methods of minimizing them.

In psychological research, each of the participants plays a role. Like the guest in the story, these roles exert pressure on what they say and do. Broadly speaking, three roles are involved in any psychological research: subject, experimenter, and investigator.

The **subject role** is held by the person(s) whose behavior is actually being studied.

The **experimenter role** is held by those who make direct contact with the subjects, including the administration of treatments (if any), testing and/or observing subjects' responses, and scoring and recording the data gathered from tests or observations. (Note that the term experimenter is used in a broad sense, to include research personnel in any study, regardless of whether an experimental manipulation is involved.)

The **investigator role** is filled by those who design, analyze, interpret, and report the results of research. In any given study, the role of investigator may be played by a single individual or by several individuals working in collaboration.

Note, too, that the investigator and experimenter roles can be filled by the same person. However, in practice, a person in a "senior" position will typically play the investigator role while research assistants administer the treatments and carry out the data collection.

In this chapter, we discuss five specific "pitfalls." Four of these involve ways in which subjects may distort or bias the outcome of research. The fifth involves the way in which experimenters may bias research. We begin with an examination of **volunteer bias**.

VOLUNTEER BIAS

Regardless of how extensive the subject recruitment effort is, *participation* is always voluntary. Thus, because of **volunteer bias**, we end up with an actual group of subjects who are different from the population of ultimate interest (which includes those who *do not* volunteer as well as those who do).

Volunteer bias is a special case of **selection bias**. The presence of such bias is suggested by systematic analyses of the special characteristics of research volunteers. Rosenthal and Rosnow (1969) found that those who volunteer tend to be (1) higher in educational level, (2) higher in occupational status, (3) higher in need for approval, and (4) higher in IQ than the general populations from which they came. Clearly, there would be ample opportunity for any of these characteristics to *interact* with an experimental treatment. So, research with volunteers may not be generalizable to the population of interest.

Volunteer bias can play some interesting tricks on our data. Consider the story of Claire, a graduate student who developed a computer simulation of a nuclear power plant to study "operator error." In Claire's study the subjects were volunteers from an undergraduate subject pool, in which introductory psychology students select the studies they will participate in from "sign-up sheets" describing what each study requires of subjects.

At the time of Claire's study, about 50% of the students in the pool were female, *but* the sample who volunteered to operate a simulated nuclear power plant was 90% male. When the study was over, Claire compared the performance of her male and female subjects, and found the female subjects were significantly better operators than the male subjects. Is the conclusion that women undergraduates (in general) are better system operators than men warranted? No. The large sample of women who *did not* volunteer for this experiment might well be much less good as operators than those who did volunteer.

The widespread use of **self-identified clinical populations** (that is, people who present themselves to psychologists for treatment) also invites volunteer bias problems. This possibility is clearly illustrated in a study by Schachter (1982).

The study was inspired by psychologists' many attempts to help people quit cigarette smoking—attempts that have been notoriously *un*successful. Schachter quotes numerous sources as concluding that the overwhelming majority of people treated for smoking, between 80 and 90 percent, relapse and return to their smoking habit within 12 months of treatment termination. And yet, Schachter notes, "virtually everyone knows large numbers of people who have quit smoking, apparently permanently" (1982, p. 435). A similar contrast, he adds, holds for obesity.

Why does a disparity exist between findings in the clinical literature and personal experience? One answer is that *people who can cure themselves do not go to therapists.* Thus:

> Our view of the intractability of the addictive states has been molded largely by that self-selected, hard-core group of people who, unable or unwilling to help themselves, go to therapists for help, thereby becoming the only easily available subjects for studies of recidivism and addiction (Schachter, 1982, p. 437).

To demonstrate his point, Schachter set out to study the "cure" rates for smoking and obesity in two very different populations, namely, all the people in the Psychology Department at Columbia University (including faculty, graduate students, secretaries, and technicians—a total of 84 people, 83 of whom agreed to be interviewed as part of the study) *and* all the people working in shops in the center of Amagansett, Long Island (a total of 48 people in 19 shops, of whom 47 consented to be interviewed).

The interviews, which were done with painstaking care to reduce the possibility of interviewer bias, revealed that almost 64% of those who once smoked and had tried to quit succeeded; likewise, almost the same percentage, 63%, of those who tried to lose weight and "keep it off" had done so. Thus,

> . . . . in nontherapeutic populations the rates of successful self-cure of cigarette smoking and of obesity are considerably higher than anything yet reported in the therapeutic literature. This conclusion is based on virtually 100% samples of two different populations—an urban university psychology department and a geographically defined portion of the entrepreneurial and working population of a very small town. The fact that the rates of self-cure are so similar in these two populations is taken as evidence that these findings are generalizable beyond any single demographic group. (Schachter, 1982, pp. 441–442)

There is no completely adequate solution to the problem of volunteer bias in research with human subjects. Ethical constraints require that subjects be informed about research before participating, and that they be permitted to decline or withdraw at any time. What researchers *can* do is be aware of the possible limitations of their conclusions whenever participation in a study has much more appeal for some potential subjects than for others.

REACTIVITY: THE EFFECTS OF BEING OBSERVED

In most human behavioral research, the participants know that they are serving as subjects in an investigation. The act of observation can produce changes in the phenomenon being observed, a problem not unique to psychological research. In physics, the celebrated Heisenberg principle of uncertainty makes a similar point. Heisenberg (1958) wrote:

> One could argue that it should be at least possible to observe the electron in its orbit. . . . The electron [will be] practically at rest before the observation. But *in the act of observation* at least one light quantum of the gamma ray must have passed the microscope and must first have been deflected by the electron. Therefore, the electron has been pushed by the light quantum, it has changed its momentum and velocity, and one can show that this change is just big enough to guarantee uncertainty. . . . (p. 47).

In psychological research, the problem caused by knowing that one is in the role of "subject" is particularly acute. Subjects are likely to behave differently than they might when unobserved. The presence (or possible presence) of such reactions may make the obtained results unrepresentative of the natural situation in which the investigator is ultimately interested. When observations or test scores are influenced by the act of measurement, they are said to be **reactive**.

   While most measures used in psychological research are potentially reactive, with creativity adequate unobtrusive measures can be devised. For some interesting examples, see Box 10.1.

BOX 10.1   *NONREACTIVE MEASURES*

Unobtrusive measures *are those that do not intrude upon, and therefore cannot interfere or interact with, the observations being made.* There are two broad classes of unobtrusive measures: *physical traces* and *archives*.

Physical Traces

The term **physical traces** refers to those measurement procedures that examine the durable residue of earlier events as evidence for the occurrence of particular actions or processes. There are four types of physical traces.

   Erosion measures involve inspection of the relative "wear and tear" of various objects and facilities as an index of their degree of use. For example, inspection of library books acquired at approximately the same time can serve as a useful index of the reading preferences of library users. This measure might be markedly more accurate than others, such as questionnaires.

   Respondents to a questionnaire might indicate a strong preference for intellectually oriented or other high-status volumes, but an inspection of the books themselves might reveal that these erudite pieces are rarely checked out and their pages almost never turned. In contrast, although novels featuring excitement, adventure, or sex might rarely appear on the respondents' questionnaire listings of their favorites, the books' dog-eared pages might attest to their actual popularity.

   Natural accretion refers to the remnants of past behavior that have been laid down naturally, without the investigator's intervention. Under some circumstances, it can be both a powerful and durable source of evidence. Sawyer (1961) estimated liquor consumption in a supposedly dry town by examining trash containers and counting the number of empty liquor bottles that were found. (Not surprisingly, very few dry towns are really dry.)

   Natural accretion is also used in police work. Modern criminal investigations often employ complex analyses of natural accretions such as soil from shoes and clothing to demonstrate that a suspect was at the scene of a crime. The fact that Napoleon died from poisoning (in 1821) was discovered 140 years later on the basis of arsenic traces found in the remains of his hair.

   A third type of physical trace, **controlled erosion**, involves a predetermined plan to measure some form of erosion. For example, researchers have measured children's activity level by having them wear self-winding wristwatches adapted to record body movement.

   In advertising research, one popular technique is to use a "glue-seal record," in which a pair of magazine pages are bound together by a small spot of glue that does not re-adhere after the seal has been broken. It is then possible to determine the popularity of particular magazines by counting the number of broken seals in samples of a particular issue. (The method was devised because earlier attempts with questionnaire responses had suggested that individuals would claim falsely that they had read or looked at particular advertisements when they had not.) With imagination and perseverance, one could devise many such measures for a variety of purposes.

Finally, there are measures of **controlled accretion**. These are measures of traces left behind after the environment has been intentionally prepared or "primed" to collect them. Again with imagination, the possibilities are almost limitless. Here is a particularly clever example of the use of controlled accretion:

> The relative popularity of exhibits with glass fronts could be compared by examining the number of noseprints deposited on the glass each day. . . . This requires that the glass be dusted for noseprints each night and then wiped clean for the next day's viewers to smudge. The noseprint measure has fewer content restrictions than most of the trace techniques, for the age of the viewers can be estimated as well as the total number of prints on each exhibit. Age is determined by plotting a frequency distribution of the heights by age (minus, of course, the nose to top of head correction) (Webb et al., 1966, pp. 45–46).

Archives

Archives are the ongoing and continuing records of society. Archival records of birth, marriage, and death may be used to test various hypotheses in an unobtrusive manner. For example, investigators who hypothesized that people can extend their lives for at least short periods of time by "will power" have related dates of death in public records to birth dates and religious holidays. People are less likely than would be expected by chance to die shortly before their birthdays or shortly before holidays related to their own religious beliefs.

In an early use of archival records, Galton (1872) used longevity data to measure the efficacy of prayer, reasoning that if prayers were effective in preserving life, then members of royal houses (who were probably among the most prayed-for individuals, witness the British anthem "God save the Queen") should live longer than other groups with comparable medical attention. Contrary to the "efficacy of prayer" hypothesis, Galton found that members of royal families had, on the average, shorter life spans (64.04 years) than did men of literature and science (67.55 years).

Political and judicial records, weather reports, items appearing in the mass media, and a variety of other sources may also be related to meaningful hypotheses. The major problem with archival records as a source of evidence is that they are produced *by* someone else and *for* someone else. The investigator must be wary of selectivity in both the material that is deposited and the material that survives, particularly when looking at records over a long span of time.

If, for example, a full set of newspaper issues is not available, those that remain may not adequately characterize the time from which they are taken. Decisions made by some unknown clerk, at an unknown time, as to what was "worth saving" and what was not may bias our conclusions. For example, if newspapers containing reports of murders and mayhem are more likely to be saved than those reporting no violent events, our estimate of the homicide rate would be falsely inflated.

Obviously there are practical constraints in using nonreactive measures. But it is remarkable what one can think of with a bit of imagination. And certainly, research psychologists must continually be aware of the possibility that ordinary laboratory observations can be distorted by reactivity.

DEMAND CHARACTERISTICS

Subjects entering a test situation are not merely passive recipients of the manipulations or instructions they are given. Rather, they will develop their own hypotheses about the nature and purposes of the investigation. These hypotheses, together with the subjects' "reading" and interpretation of the circumstances in which they are placed, constitute the **demand characteristics of the situation**. The concept of demand characteristics, introduced into the methodological literature by Martin Orne (1962), recognizes the fact that subjects often care about the outcome of the investigation and/or try to show the investigator that they are sophisticated individuals and shrewd problem solvers.

A subject's **role behavior** is behavior elicited by the demand characteristics of the situation. When subjects respond according to what they judge to be an appropriate role in the situation, the study's findings may be misleading or worthless.

A demonstration of how demand characteristics can operate was provided in a classic study by Orne and Scheibe (1964). Before this study, there had been a number of reports on the effects of *sensory deprivation*. In these studies, subjects were isolated and deprived of external stimulation as much as possible (for example, by having them wear translucent goggles and cardboard "gloves" as well as by restricting movement). Dramatic effects, apparently due entirely to sensory deprivation, were typically reported: hallucinations, disorientation, and deterioration in intellectual and emotional behavior.

Orne and Scheibe's work aimed at demonstrating the possibility that some of these effects were due, in part, to demand characteristics. They asked how much of the bizarre behavior of subjects in sensory deprivation experiments was caused by cues that communicated the *expectancy of bizarre behavior.*

Subjects were randomly assigned to one of two conditions. In the first condition a medical history was taken, and a tray of drugs and medical instruments, labeled the "emergency tray," was placed in full view. During the instructions it was stressed that the subjects should report any unusual experiences. Finally, they were shown a red button marked "Emergency Alarm," which they could press if they could no longer tolerate the situation.

In the second condition, subjects were told that they were a control group for a sensory deprivation study. These subjects were *not* exposed to suggestive cues. They saw no panic button or emergency tray, and did not undergo a medical interview.

Afterward all subjects were treated identically, spending three hours in an isolation room. The demand characteristic group showed far more sensory deprivation symptoms than the controls, including bizarre reports such as "the walls of the room are starting to waver."

Problems in Assessing Situational Demands

One possible way of assessing demand characteristics is through a detailed postexperimental interview with subjects, to determine whether they guessed the experimental hypotheses and then "played along." However, as Orne (1969) observed, this strategy has its own pitfalls. The greatest danger is in the **pact of ignorance**

> . . . which all too commonly characterizes the postexperimental discussion. The subject knows that if he has "caught on" to some apparent deception and has an excess of information about the experimental procedure he may be disqualified from participation and thus have wasted his time. The experimenter is aware that the subject who knows too much or has "caught on" to his deception will have to be disqualified; disqualification means running yet another subject, still further delaying completion of his study. . . . *Hence, neither party to the inquiry wants to dig very deeply* (1969, p. 153).

There are potential means of managing the threat posed by demand. One involves the use of **counter demand**, in which subjects are told *not* to expect the predicted effects. For example, a researcher interested in the effects of a stimulant drug on productivity might tell subjects to expect a change in their sleeping patterns at night, but tell them (contrary to the researcher's expectation) that their daytime activities will be unaffected.

Another alternative is simply to prepare subjects not to expect any change for a period of time exceeding the lag that is actually expected between administration of the treatment and changes on the dependent measure. For instance, a new tranquilizer that is expected to produce results within one hour might be described as slow acting. Subjects could be told not to expect to begin to experience relief for several hours, or even days, after administration of the first dose.

By including a counter demand condition (as one independent variable) for comparison with subjects given no counter demand instructions, some reasonable assessment of the effects of demand can be made. This allows a researcher to remove the demand effects statistically, or at least to separate demand effects from effects due to the experimental treatment.

We now turn to a discussion of the placebo effect, which can be considered a special case of demand characteristics.

THE PLACEBO EFFECT

Pilgrimages to Lourdes, religious conversion experiences, ingesting "magical" potions, and the like can all apparently produce therapeutic effects. Similarly, pharmacologically inert substances (e.g., sugar pills) can sometimes lead to improvement in conditions such as ulcers, headaches, warts, and psychiatric illness (Frank, 1961). These therapeutic effects are genuine, but the changes are due not to any "real" healing power in the treatment. Rather, they are due to the **placebo effect**.

In medicine a *placebo* is defined as a pharmacologically inert substance. The **placebo effect** refers to the therapeutic gains produced by the ingestion of a placebo. It is thought to result from the patient's expectation that the treatment will yield improvement.

Placebo effects are so pervasive and powerful that proof of the effectiveness of new medicines is now expected to involve a true **double blind experi-**

ment. In such an experiment, neither the patient nor the physician knows who is getting the placebo and who is getting the "real" medication. The placebo medication is made to look, taste, and "feel" like the real medication. Actually, though, it is either an inert substance or one that produces irrelevant side effects to convince patients in the placebo control condition that they have gotten real medicine. (In the latter case we speak of **active placebos**.)

Placebo effects are not limited to medical research. In fact, placebo effects may appear in any type of research in which subjects are exposed to a "treatment." Thus, specific instructions aimed at improving performance in a learning experiment may produce real effects, even if the researcher construed these instructions as inert or meaningless. For some examples of the problems introduced by placebo effects, and some means of addressing them, we turn to the literature on psychotherapy research.

Placebo Controls in Psychotherapy Research

By the 1950s psychotherapy researchers had picked up on the importance of including placebo controls in their research (Rosenthal & Frank, 1956). By the 1960s, placebo controls in psychotherapy research had become commonplace. Many researchers confirmed that those given placebos showed significantly more improvement than those given no treatment.

Paul (1966), in a study of the effectiveness of systematic desensitization (a psychotherapeutic treatment for anxiety) required a control group for comparison. He gave speech-anxious college students what was purported to be a "fast-acting tranquilizer," but which was in fact a two-gram capsule of sodium bicarbonate (which has no anxiety-related properties). The sodium bicarbonate group showed significantly more improvement than a no-treatment control group. Improvement was evident both in their self-reported feelings *and* in independent measures of apparent anxiety reported by observers. (The systematic desensitization treatment proved more effective than the placebo treatment in this case.)

Analog Versus True Psychotherapy Research.   The widespread use of placebo controls in the late 1960s and early 1970s led to several important critiques that cast doubt on both the methodological and ethical appropriateness of this practice. The most cogent analysis was offered by O'Leary and Borkovec (1978).

They began their analysis with the observation that efforts to test and contrast types of psychotherapy fall on a continuum, depending on the nature and severity of the subject's problem and the length of the treatment. At one extreme the treatment is only an analog to therapy, involving one or a very few sessions, and a "target problem" of no real consequence to the subject. Numerous methods for treating minor or inconsequential phobias, such as snake phobias, fall into this category.

At the other extreme are those studies in which the participants have debilitating or life-threatening problems, such as severe depression. These problems often require substantial and lengthy treatment. O'Leary and Borkovec note that analog studies are basically laboratory experiments involving analysis of behavior change processes for theory development. In these studies placebo controls are ethically appropriate and methodologically useful. On the other hand, in true therapy studies such treatments may be methodologically unsound and ethically dubious.

Methodological Problems with Placebo Controls.   The methodological problem can be understood by asking what, exactly, placebo controls are supposed to control *for*. Presumably, they are supposed to control for **plausible rival hypotheses**, such as subject and experimenter expectancies and demand factors in this situation. In true psychotherapy research, placebo treatments do not effectively control for these threats.

For one thing, **double blind** studies, though quite feasible in drug research, are virtually impossible in psychotherapy research. Psychotherapists must know what they are giving and clients must know (at least up to a point) what they are getting. Moreover, psychotherapists can hardly have the same expectations for treatments they believe to be useful and those they believe or know to be irrelevant or inert.

Ethical Problems with Placebo Controls.   Ethically, too, the placebo control is problematic in true psychotherapy research. This is because placebo therapy often involves serious **deception**. Moreover, it may also serve as a deterrent to seeking alternative treatment by suffering individuals.

What are the alternatives? O'Leary and Borkovec (1978) discuss several. One is to employ **best possible comparisons**. For example, new and promising therapies may be compared with the prevailing established alternatives. Thus, cognitive therapy for depression has been compared with commonly used pharmaceutical antidepressants (Rosenhan & Seligman, 1984).

Second, there are **component control comparisons**. For example, many psychotherapy treatments consist of several components. It is often possible to "dismantle" them, thereby identifying the effective ingredients. Houts and Peterson (1985), for example, analyzed Houts and Liebert's (1984) Full Spectrum Home Training for bedwetting (which consists of a urine alarm, practice in urine retention, and an "overlearning" procedure). Specifically, they compared the relapse rates of children who received only the urine alarm, the urine alarm and retention control training, and the full treatment. (Results showed the full package provided the best protection against relapse.)

We now turn our attention to the problem of bias introduced by the experimenters themselves.

EXPERIMENTER BIAS

Robert Rosenthal and his colleagues have performed many studies to demonstrate that the researcher's expectations regarding the outcome of a particular investigation may influence the data collected—the so-called **experimenter bias effect** (Rosenthal & Rosnow, 1984).

Most studies done by research psychologists are designed with clear expectations of the likely or predicted outcome. If it can be shown that these ex-

Cartoon 10-1   Expectancies affect outcomes!

pectations make the data collected more favorable to the investigator's hypotheses, psychological research may be faced with a serious problem.

Consider the classic demonstration of the experimenter bias effect (Rosenthal & Fode, 1963). In this study, undergraduate students served as experimenters in a simple maze problem, using rats as subjects. Half of these student experimenters were told that their rats were bright and should therefore learn quickly. The remaining half were told that their rats were dull and should show "little evidence of learning." In fact, the rats assigned to both groups were drawn randomly from a relatively homogeneous population of rodents. The only systematically manipulated difference between the groups was whether the student experimenters expected their animals to do well or poorly.

The expectancy manipulation *did* produce a marked difference in the data reported. Students working with the presumably "bright" animals presented data suggesting that their rats performed approximately 59% better than did the animals who were presumed to be dull!

It is now well-documented that at least under some circumstances the expectancies of an investigator can bring about the results he or she expects: the so-called **self-fulfilling prophecy**. Nonetheless, the question of the degree to which this phenomenon actually pervades psychological research still remains.

To determine whether self-fulfilling prophecy effects influence data, Rosenthal (1978) reviewed data from 21 studies involving more than 300 observers and 140,000 separate observations, looking for recording errors. He found that there was a marked tendency for even quite simple recording tasks to lead to errors that favored the hypothesis held by the observers. Thus, investigators must be continuously on guard to prevent any form of bias from affecting their results and research reports.

There are a number of specific ways to handle the problem of potential experimenter bias. First, investigators should employ experimenters or data collectors who are **empirically blind**, that is, *unaware of the hypothesis being tested*. However, this is often easier said than done. For experimenters to fulfill their role adequately, they will generally need to know something about the purpose of the investigation. Even where they need not be told the purpose, they are likely to speculate about it and form their own hypotheses (much like subjects do).

For these reasons, experimenters are often kept **blind to group assignment**. (This procedure is sometimes referred to as a **single blind**, or **blind experimenter** technique.) An extension of the single blind technique is the **double blind** procedure mentioned earlier, in which neither the subjects nor the experimenters have any knowledge of group assignment. This is particularly common in medical research where a new pharmaceutical is being compared to a placebo for effectiveness.

While subjects must be informed in advance about the nature of the research and any possible risks associated with participation, it is common practice to reveal to them all they would need to know about *any* group involved in the study, and then inform them only at the end of their participation about which group they were actually assigned to.

For instance, in a drug study subjects might be told in advance that two active drugs are being compared to a placebo, and informed of all the potential side effects of both drugs. They can then be asked to consent to participate *regardless* of which group they be assigned to. In this way, subjects are fully informed of all potential risks without being told which medication (or placebo) they will actually receive until the conclusion of the study. (This helps to minimize placebo effects, as well as the influence of any expectations on the part of the subject.)

Another means of minimizing the possible influence of experimenter bias is to limit the degree of contact between experimenter and subject. This can often be accomplished through **automation**; that is, the actual procedures involved in the research can be automated (instructions delivered via audio tape, videotaped or computerized data collection procedures, and the like).

Experimenters should also be led to believe that their behavior will be carefully monitored throughout the entire data collection period. And finally, Rosenthal has suggested that the potential effects of expectancy may be *assessed* by employing two groups of experimenters who have been led to have opposite expectancies about the outcome of the research.

Assessing and Controlling Experimenter Bias

How can we tell whether bias effects have undermined the adequacy of observations made in a particular investigation? Perhaps the best way of determining the empirical worth of observations is to assess the degree to which two or more observers witnessing the same events would agree about their description. *In any study in which the data might be subject to interpretation or misperceptions, it is the responsibility of the investigator to demonstrate that independent observers would agree on the observations being reported.*

Usually such demonstrations involve assessing **inter-rater reliability** (see Chapter 3). However, high inter-rater reliability is not sufficient evidence of agreement unless the check is carried out very carefully. In many studies claiming to have checked inter-rater reliability, two observers were present only for some portion of the period of data collection.

If the observers are in substantial agreement for this portion of the data, it might be assumed that they would also have been in agreement for the remainder of the data collection period. From a sampling point of view, this is a reasonable assumption. However, this also assumes that the presence of a second observer (or knowing that a second observer is to be used) does not influence the accuracy of observation. There is evidence to suggest that this second assumption is *not* sound.

Reid (1970) recruited seven undergraduate women to assist in the coding of mother-child interactions from videotapes. The women were informed that some of the tape content had been precoded so that their accuracy could be assessed; this was the **overt assessment** condition. The women were also told that after they had reached a certain criterion, their scoring would never be checked again. In fact this was false. Coding was monitored throughout the entire study. The latter period, during which the women were unaware they were being checked, represented the **covert assessment** condition. From a comparison of these conditions, Reid concluded:

> The results of the present investigation do not lend support to the hypothesis that overt reliability estimates accurately describe data collected by unmonitored observers. In the present situation, the estimates consistently exaggerated the reliability of [observers] in the covert-assessment condition by about 25 percent. The drop observed in observer performance was not gradual, but occurred suddenly as [the observer] made the transition from overt to covert assessment. . . . It is quite possible that other strategies for the collection and assessment of observation data are immune to the effect observed in this study. However, this would seem to be a question that could be better answered on an empirical rather than a priori basis (pp. 1149–1150).

The finding that reliability of observations is significantly higher when observers know reliability is being checked than when they believe they are the sole observers was later confirmed by another team of investigators (Romanczyk, Kent, Diament, & O'Leary, 1973).

Our conclusion is that *it is always desirable to employ two independent observers when the recording of ongoing behavior is the goal.* Or, if employing two or more independent observers is not possible, observers should at least be led to believe that their data can be checked in some way. The need for independent reliability checks is especially important when the observations to be made involve judgments that are difficult or open to ambiguity. In investigations particularly sensitive to bias, it is also desirable to employ observers who are blind to the treatments that individual subjects have received.

In considering the possibility of experimenter bias, keep in mind that the obligation of the critic is merely to show the *plausibility* of some rival hypothesis. In contrast, the investigator making the original causal claim must be able to show that his or her causal inference *is* empirically valid. This can only be done if the investigator has used a research design that effectively rules out or discredits all plausible competing explanations.

FOR REVIEW AND DISCUSSION

Key Terms
       SUBJECT ROLE
       EXPERIMENTER ROLE
       INVESTIGATOR ROLE
       REACTIVE MEASURES
       DEMAND CHARACTERISTICS OF THE SITUATION
       ROLE BEHAVIOR
       PACT OF IGNORANCE
       UNOBTRUSIVE MEASURES
       PHYSICAL TRACES
       EROSION MEASURES
       NATURAL ACCRETION
       CONTROLLED EROSION
       CONTROLLED ACCRETION
       ARCHIVES
       SELF-FULFILLING PROPHECY
       EXPERIMENTER BIAS EFFECT
       EMPIRICALLY BLIND
       OVERT ASSESSMENT
       COVERT ASSESSMENT
       SINGLE BLIND
       BLIND EXPERIMENTER
       INTERRATER RELIABILITY
       AUTOMATION
       VOLUNTEER BIAS
       SELECTION BIAS
       SELF-IDENTIFIED CLINICAL POPULATIONS
       COUNTER DEMAND
       PLACEBO EFFECT
       DOUBLE BLIND EXPERIMENT
       ACTIVE PLACEBOS
       PLAUSIBLE RIVAL HYPOTHESES

DECEPTION
BEST POSSIBLE COMPARISONS
COMPONENT CONTROL COMPARISONS
BLIND TO GROUP ASSIGNMENT

Discussion Issues

1. One possible measure of people's attitudes toward some newsworthy event (like the energy crisis) would be examination of the letters to the editor in major newspapers. What is this type of measure called? In what ways is it or is it not a good measure?

2. A business woman is building a new drive-in theater. She wants to determine her customers' parking preferences so that she can design the drive-in to satisfy their desires—location of the concession stand, exits, playground, and so forth. Using nonreactive (unobtrusive) measures, how would you go about providing the needed information?

3. Explain how the roles of investigator and experimenter are different. What problems exist when the two roles are played by the same person?

4. Subjects are given a large cup of coffee which they are told is "very strong." In fact, though, the coffee is decaffeinated. When questioned about the degree of "lift" they experienced, most say this cup of coffee affected them more than usual. How can we explain these results?

5. After a notorious murder trial, the local newspaper invites its readers to send written comments to the editor. How are those who write in likely to differ from the general population of readers?

6. A group of senior citizens decides to monitor the amount of sex depicted on TV. Each member of the group chooses one "typical" television program to watch for 2 weeks. Based on their observations, the group concludes that there is too much sex on TV. Describe all the possible pitfalls associated with this conclusion.

7. Discuss the problems associated with the use of placebo controls in psychotherapy research.

8. What is meant by the term "pact of ignorance?" How does this threaten the validity of research conclusions?

CULMINATION OF RESEARCH: THE JOURNAL ARTICLE

This chapter has two purposes. First we will introduce and describe the journal article and other outlets for psychological research. In this context we will explain how to access and search the psychological literature. Then we will examine the journal article for a second time, in order to explain in detail how to prepare an APA-style research report.

SEARCHING THE LITERATURE

Whether you are undertaking a research project of your own or merely wish to learn about the research others have done, sooner or later you will probably need to do a **literature search**.

The purpose of such a search is to bring together in your own hands most or all of the research and thinking of others related to your topic or problem.

Research Outlets

There are three broad outlets for psychological research: journal articles, scholarly books and monographs, and conventions and meetings.

Journal Articles.   The most important outlet for the publication of scientific findings in psychology is the *journal article.* Although some professional journals publish reviews and commentaries, most are devoted to the publication of research reports.

A journal article is a formal report of one or more pieces of original research. When psychologists decide their findings are clear and important enough to justify a formal communication to other psychologists, they are most likely to submit a report to one of the professional journals for publication.

After choosing an appropriate journal, the researcher(s) will write a report. Once the article has been prepared and double-checked for accuracy, it is formally submitted to a journal and mailed to the journal's editor. The rule is that an article may only be submitted to one journal at a time. Further, by submitting an article to a given journal, authors enter into an implicit contract. If the report is accepted for publication by the journal, the authors are committed to publish it there.

When an editor receives an article, he/she gives it an initial reading. If it appears generally appropriate, the editor of a **refereed journal** will send the article out for review by two or three consultants who are experts in the area of the study. These reviewers serve as referees in the sense of helping the editor decide which articles should be accepted for publication.

Each consultant prepares a written review of the prospective article, assessing its strengths and weaknesses and recommending publication, revision, or rejection. These reviews are sent to the editor, who will weigh the opinions, seek reviews from additional experts if necessary, and then decide whether the article is accepted.

Researchers typically wait 2 or 3 months (sometimes considerably more) before learning whether their article has been accepted. Worse yet, the lag between acceptance and actual publication may be as much as 2 years, and is almost never less than several months. (For this reason, when an article is accepted some researchers prepare **preprints** of their research reports and distribute them to interested colleagues.)

After an article is published, the importance of its contribution is determined by the general community of researchers who read it. Articles judged to be important will subsequently be cited by other researchers and scholars. Sometimes an article will also generate a direct reply; that is, someone writes an article that offers a different interpretation of the study than was offered by the original researchers.

Scholarly Books and Monographs. Occasionally, a researcher or research team will have conducted a project important or extensive enough to warrant a full, detailed report. These works typically run between 100 and 300 pages in length. Unlike textbooks, some are highly specialized on a particular topic and/or original research project. Other scholarly books are less focused on a specific project, and instead provide a theoretical and empirical analysis of an important topic.

Scholarly books and monographs have been written on most of the major topics in psychology. To determine quickly if a given volume is relevant to your interests, it is useful to begin with the summary chapter that typically appears at the end of these works.

Conventions and Meetings. The major limitation of books and journal articles as sources of information is that there is usually a substantial **publication lag.** An article or book submitted for publication in 1995 may not actually appear in print until 1997 (or later).

As a way of shortcutting the publication lag of the printed word, many psychologists first present their most important findings at conventions or professional meetings. For example, hundreds of such presentations are made every year at the annual meeting of the American Psychological Association. Announcements of upcoming meetings relating to psychology are made in the back of the monthly publication, *American Psychologist.*

Meetings of major associations are often accompanied by catalogs listing the authors and titles of each presentation. You can usually obtain one by mail. Many psychologists use these catalogs to write away for copies of presentations which they were unable to attend. You can do the same.

Using the Library

Most college libraries will have ample material for a review of the psychological literature on any major topic. The first question you will encounter is how to identify and locate the relevant research. A good place to start is with *Psychological Abstracts.* Published monthly by the American Psychological Association, this periodical informs you of what articles have been written on specific topics and in which journals these articles appear. It also contains abstracts (or summaries) for each article cited. In addition to citing journal articles, it may include listings of books, chapters of books, or other publication outlets.

Psychological Abstracts is divided into two sections: a *subject index* located in the back of the book and the *abstracts* located in the front of the book, arranged alphabetically according to categories.

To use *Psychological Abstracts* effectively, you must first determine what subject heading you wish to search. The *Thesaurus of Psychological Index Terms* (a guide to the subject headings used in *Psychological Abstracts*) can assist you. For example, if your topic was "test anxiety," you would simply look it up in the *Thesaurus*. If it is listed, it would be an appropriate heading to search in *Psychological Abstracts*. In some instances, your subject may not be listed at all, or it may be listed with the instruction to "use . . ." underneath it. This notation will direct you to a term that can be used instead of the one you chose initially.

Table 11-1 illustrates the information that the *Thesaurus* provides, including: The index term with the date it was first entered (the subscript); a post note (PN) indicating the number of times the term has occurred in the text over the years; a unique 5-digit code (SC); a scope note (SN) that provides a definition and/or the proper use of the term; a "used for" term (UF) that lists frequently encountered synonyms, abbreviations, alternate spellings or word sequences; broad terms (B); narrow terms (N); and related terms (R).

After choosing an appropriate heading, you would then return to *Psychological Abstracts* and look it up in the subject index. The heading will be pre-

TABLE 11-1   SAMPLE THESAURUS ENTRY FOR "ANXIETY"

Anxiety 67

PN   9342   SC 03310

SN   Apprehension or fear of impending actual or imagined danger, vulnerability, or uncertainty. Prior to 1988, also for anxiety disorders.

UF	Angst
	Anxiousness
	Apprehension
B	Emotional States 73
R	Anxiety Neurosis 73
	Emotions/ 67
	Fear of Success 78
	Guilt 67
	Jealousy 73
	Panic 73
	Panic Disorder 68
	Phobias 67
	Stress 67

This information is reprinted with the permission of the American Psychological Association, publisher of *Psychological Abstracts* (copyright 1988 by the American Psychological Association) and may not be reproduced without its prior permission.

ceded by an *item number*. This number corresponds with a numerical listing in the abstracts section. The abstract of interest can now be located by turning to the appropriate page in the first section of the book.

Table 11-2 illustrates the information to be found in the *Psychological Abstracts*: The abstract number; the author(s) or editor(s); the affiliation of the first-named author or editor only; the title of the article, book, or chapter; the publication title and bibliographical data (year, month, volume, issue number, pages); and the summary text.

Another available resource is the *Social Sciences Citation Index* (*SSCI*). It is divided into three sections: The *Permuterm Subject Index*, the *Source Index,* and the *Citation Index*. The SSCI has an advantage over *Psychological Abstracts* in that articles can be identified by linking concepts or key words.

In the *Permuterm Subject Index* section, key words are taken directly from the cited article titles and listed in alphabetical order. Immediately under these key words are other key words that are linked to the main term in a title. For example, if you were searching "anxiety" and "women," you would look up the main term "anxiety" and look for "women" underneath it. If both terms appear, this indicates that an article has been cited that includes both of these concepts. The author's name will be listed beside the term (see Table 11-3). With the author's name in hand, you can now proceed to the next section, the *Source Index*.

The *Source Index* is an alphabetical listing of the authors cited. By looking up the author's name, which you have previously located, you will find the corresponding article title, journal name, and bibliographical data, as well as a list of references cited in that article. (See Table 11-4).

The last section of the SSCI is the *Citation Index*. It differs from the previous sections in that you can search out a specific article and identify all subsequent ar-

---

TABLE 11-2   SAMPLE ABSTRACT ENTRY

31158.de Man, Anton F., Hall, Vincent & Stour, Dale (Bishop U. Lennoxville, PQ, Canada) Neurotic nucleus and test anxiety. Journal of Psychology, 1991(Nov), Vol 125(6), 671-675.-103 undergraduates participated in a study of the relationship between test anxiety, self-esteem, locus of control, mental ability, and gender. Results indicate that people who appraise situations as threatening, who feel inadequate, and who doubt their personal control generally suffer from test anxiety. Further analyses revealed independent relationships between the worry component of test anxiety and the variables of trait anxiety, internality, chance, and mental ability. There were independent associations between the emotionality aspect of test anxiety and the measures of trait anxiety and chance.

TABLE 11-3   SAMPLE PERMUTERM ENTRY

Permuterm® Subject Index

To find articles on a specific topic:

1. Locate any one of the words (Primary Terms) that describes the topic. If you want every unique title that includes that primary term, select only the articles marked with an arrow (◗). This eliminates repetitive examination of the same title.

2. To narrow selection, use any of the other words (Co-Terms) listed below that Primary Term. When using co-terms always disregard arrows.

3. Using authors' names consult the *Source Index* for the full titles and bibliographic data.

Sample Display

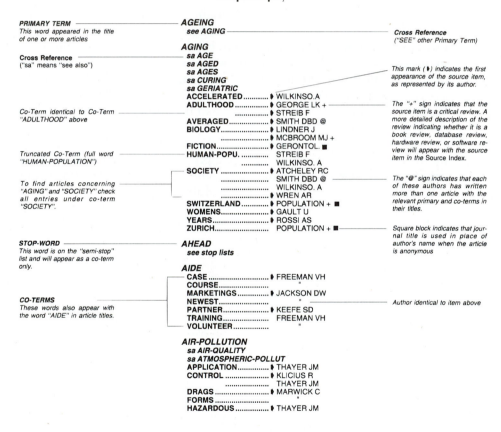

Reprinted from *Social Sciences Citation Index Life Sccience,* 1994 with the permission of the Institute for Scientific Information (ISI) copyright 1994.

TABLE 11-4   SAMPLE SOURCE INDEX ENTRY

Source Index

To locate a full description of a source item, look up the first author. Under a given name, publications of primary authorship are described first. Items of secondary authorship follow, cross-referenced to the first author by a SEE reference.

Sample Display

first source author ———

ADAMS DM
  HAYNES RW DUTROW GF BARBER RL ——————— coauthors
  VASIEVIC.JM—PRIVATE INVESTMENT IN FOREST
  MANAGEMENT AND THE LONG-TERM SUPPLY OF TIMBER ——— source item title
    AM J AGR EC   64(2):232-241   94   14R   **CR816**
      OREGON STATE UNIV, CORVALLIS, OR 97331, USA

(ANON)	80	FOREST PRODUCTIVITY		
◆USDA	68	17 REP		
"	73	20 REP		
"	80	REV DRAFT AN TIM SIT		
ADAMS DM	77	OREGON STATE U FORES	19	
"	80	FOREST SCI MONOGRAPH	22	1
BARBER RL	79	THESIS OREGON STATE		
BERCK P	79	BELL J SC	19	447
HOUGH FB	1878	REPORT FORESTRY	1	
KING RA	72	21 N CAR STAT U DEP		
LARSON RW	74	USDA FOR SERV TECH B	1908	
MCKILLOP WL	67	HILGARDIA	30	1
RAHM M	80	FOREST POLICY PROJECT		
ROBINSON VL	74	FOREST SCI	20	191

listed references from the bibliography of the source item (Note: anonymous authors are listed first.) — (bracket pointing to the reference list)

year, journal abbreviation, volume and page of reference ———

ADAMS EK
  THE FISCAL CONDITION OF THE STATES
    PHI DEL KAP   63(9):598-600   94   2R   **DG141**
      EDUC COMMISS STATES, ON EDUC PROGRAMS, DENVER, CO, USA

source journal title ———

first source author's address ———

| ◆US BUR EC AM | 81 | SURV CURR BUS | | |
| GOLD SD | 82 | 1982 NAT COUNC STAT | | |

cross-referenced secondary author ———

ADEY M
  see YESAVAGE JA   J PSYCH TR   3   545   86

first source author ———

source item from a selectively covered journal ———

ADLER DA
  ■ **A FRAMEWORK FOR THE ANALYSIS OF**
  PSYCHOTHERAPEUTIC APPROACHES TO
  SCHIZOPHRENIA
    YALE J BIOL   58(3):219-225   94   4R   **FA006**
      NEW ENGLAND MED CTR, DIV ADULT PSYCHIAT, BOX 1007,
      171 HARRISON AVE., BOSTON, MA 02111, USA

source journal year ———

number of references ———

ADLER DA	81	HOSP COMMUNITY PSYCH	32	387
ANTHONY WA	77	AM PSYCHOL	32	658
FRIEDSON E	66	SOCIOLOGY REHABILITA		71
MCGLASMAN TH	83	ARCH GEN PSYCHIAT	40	905

language of the book being reviewed ———

source item language code ———

author of book being reviewed ———

AEBLI H
  (GE) GOAL-DIRECTED BEHAVIOR-GERMAN-
  VONCRANACH, M, KALBERMATTEN, U
  ◆**BOOK REVIEW**
    PSYCHOLOGIE   40(2):161-162   94   1R   **DZ697**

term indicating type of item ———

AHARONI Y
  PERFORMANCE EVALUATION OF STATE-OWNED
  ENTERPRISES—A PROCESS PERSPECTIVE
    MANAG SCI   27(11):1340-1347   94   8R   **CC559**
      TEL AVIV UNIV, RAMAT AVIV, ISRAEL

Article can be purchased from ISI®'s The Genuine Article® service. Refer to this ISI accession number when ordering. ———

◆HEBR U JER	70	REP COMM PREP GOV CO		
◆PRIV COUNC OFF	77	CROWN CORP DIR CONTR		
◆UK GOV	61	CMND 1337		
JENSEN MC	76	J FINANCIAL EC	3	305
MARRIS R	64	EC THEORY MANAGERIAL	40	
PHATAK A	69	ANN PUBLIC COOPERATI	2	
SIMON H	79	AM EC REV	69	495
TURVEY R	71	EC ANAL PUBL ENTER	49	253

(◆) corporately authored references ———

source journal volume, (issue): and pagination ———

Reprinted from *Social Sciences Citation Index Life Scicnce,* 1994 with the permission of the Institute for Scientific Information (ISI) copyright 1994.

TABLE 11-5   SAMPLE CITATION INDEX ENTRY

Citation Index

To use the *Citation Index*, look up the name of the first author of a work which you know to be relevant to your topic. Any of the author's works cited during the period covered by this issue of the *SSCI®* will appear in this index. You can use the names of the citing authors to enter the *Source Index* for descriptions of citing works. When the same reference has been cited by more than one source item, the source citations are arranged alphabetically by first author. Though only first authors are given in the *Citation Index*, all authors will be listed in the *Source Index*.

Sample Display

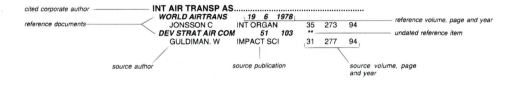

cited author	**RENOUX G**					reference volume and
	73 B WORLD HEALTH ORGAN		48	661		page
	THELIN A	SC J S MED	1980	1	94	
cited reference year and	**74 MED MAL INF**	4	159			
journal	CHANTAL J	REV MED VET	132	35	94	source journal
	76 PUBLIC POLICY MARKET	53				
	WESTBROO. RA	J RETAILING	57	68	94	volume, page, and year
						of source (citing) item
	RENZULLI J					
undated item	**** UNPUBLISHED**					Codes indicating type of source item:
	BALDWIN AY	EXCEPT CHIL	47	326	94	
	77 ENRICHMENT TRIAD MOD					**Blank** articles, reports, technical
source (citing) author	CASSIDY J	READ TEACH	35	17	94	papers, etc.
	FOSTER W	GIFT CHILD	25	17	94	**B** book reviews
	ROGERS VR	"	25	175	94	**C** corrections, errata, etc.
						D discussions,
	RERRICK EG					conference items
	72 J MENTAL DEFICIENCY 16		84			**E** editorials, editorial-like items
	PITCHER D	CRC C R LAB	13	241	94	**I** items about
						individuals (tributes,
	REVELMACDONALD N					obituaries, etc.)
	75 HOMME ANIMAL 317					**K** chronology—a list of events
	78 ASEMI 9 243					in sequence.
	78 PALAWAN PHONOLOGIE C					**L** letters, communications, etc.
	SEE SCI FOR 1 ADDITIONAL CITATION					**M** meeting abstracts
	OBUKHOV GA	SOC SCI INF	19	971	94 D	**N** technical notes
additional citing item						**R** reviews
indicator	**REVILLE**					**RP** reprint
	1802 REV HIST	50	1			**W** computer reviews
reference year earlier	GOHN JB	GEORGET LAW	70	943	94	(hardware reviews,
than 1900						software reviews,
						database reviews)

E.G. RERRICK's 1972 article in the Journal of Mental Deficiency was cited by D. PITCHER in an article published in CRC Critical Reviews in Clinical Laboratory Sciences in 1994.

G.A. OBUKHOV cites three publications by N. REVELMACDONALD.

A complete description of each source item code appears in the Conventions Used In The Citation Index *section of the instructional material.*

Corporate Author Citation Index

The format of these items is the same as that of the *Citation Index* except that the reference year is transposed to follow the title (and volume and page, if appropriate) of the cited document.

cited corporate author	**INT AIR TRANSP AS**..					
	WORLD AIRTRANS	19 6 1978				reference volume, page and year
reference documents	JONSSON C	INT ORGAN	35	273	94	
	DEV STRAT AIR COM	51 103	**			undated reference item
	GULDIMAN. W	IMPACT SCI	31	277	94	

source author   source publication   source volume, page and year ticles that make reference to it. This information can be extremely valuable when seeking articles related to a topic of interest. By identifying a single article relevant to your topic, a host of other, more recent articles may also be uncovered.

Table 11-5 shows the information you will find in the *Citation Index* upon locating a specific article. It is as follows: the author cited; the article cited; the author(s) who are doing the citing, and the bibliographical information on their articles.

An alternative to the manual search method is the *computerized search.* If this option is available to you, it may be your best choice. Computerized searches enable you to scan multiple headings, and cover a vast time span with minimal effort and greater efficiency than you could achieve alone. These searches typically yield printed results. There are two basic types of computer searches: The On-Line Search and the CD-ROM Search.

On-Line Searching allows you access to hundreds of data bases. However, an appointment is typically necessary because the process requires the aid of a trained librarian. On-Line searches require several days to complete, and there is generally a fee for this service (usually under $25.00). The advantages of the On-Line search far outweigh the delay and small fee.

CD-ROM (Compact Disc-Read Only Memory) Searching can access only a single data base. On the plus side, it is a walk-up service that requires only minimal assistance from a librarian. Moreover, it provides instant printed results and there is no fee. Despite its limited range, a CD-Rom search is often sufficient in the early stages of research development.

There are many CD-ROM systems in use today. You should inquire at your campus library for information regarding computerized search services available to you.

Regardless of how you choose to locate articles on your subject, you will find that the reference lists from the first articles you identify will lead you to other pertinent articles. Review articles can be particularly helpful in this way, as they will summarize the findings of several important articles on a given topic. Some journals, such as the APA's *Psychological Bulletin,* publish many such articles.

Also informative are **meta-analyses**, which compile and examine vast numbers of articles pertaining to a given topic. For a description of the meta analysis technique and a concrete example, see Box 11.1.

BOX 11.1   *META-ANALYSIS*

> In conducting a literature review, the major problem is often one of summarizing the literature and tying it together. **Meta-analysis** is the name given to any set of systematic rules for combining and evaluating a collection of independent replications or partial replications of a research question.
>
> Meta-analysis begins with a specification of the independent and dependent variables of interest. Then an exhaustive literature search is undertaken to identify all existing studies that fall within the specified domain. (Modern library com-

puter searchers, based on identifying terms and phrases associated with the phenomena of interest, have led to enormous gains in the speed, efficiency, and thoroughness with which such searches can be conducted.)

Once all the relevant studies have been gathered, meta-analytic statistical techniques are used to convert the outcome of each study to a common format and scale of measurement. There are several different ways to approach this task, but most involve computing a measure of **statistical significance** *and* a measure of **effect size** for each study. The converted data from each of the studies are then weighted and averaged to give a picture of the overall reliability and strength of the relationships of interest. We need not be concerned here with any of the actual statistical procedures involved. The interested reader is referred to Glass et al. (1981) and Rosenthal and Rubin (1982).

As an example of a meta-analysis, let's consider one reported by Findley and Cooper (1983), dealing with the relationship between locus of control and academic achievement. Briefly, *locus of control* refers to the degree to which individuals believe they themselves have control over the events in their lives. Locus of control is a continuous variable, but individuals who for the most part believe they control their own destinies are called "internals," whereas those who believe that what happens to them is mostly determined by fate or luck are called "externals." The question addressed by Findley and Cooper's meta-analysis was whether locus of control is related to academic achievement.

The initial literature search revealed that the question had been posed often. Findley and Cooper found 275 measures of the link between locus of control and academic achievement, reported in 98 different studies. The studies were extremely diverse; they encompassed the whole age range between first graders and adults, and represented both genders and the entire gamut of backgrounds. In addition, 22 different measures of locus of control could be found among the studies, as well as 36 different measures of achievement.

The problem in such situations becomes one of finding a common base on which the studies can be combined and compared. Findley and Cooper converted each study's reported *p* value to a standard or "Z" score. After the Z-scores were calculated, they were combined to compute an overall or meta-analytic Z (Z_{ma}). The meta-analytic Z obtained in this way was highly significant. Indeed, the possibility of getting a Z_{ma} as large as the one obtained by chance in this case is only about one in a million!

There is, however, a potential threat looming over any analysis that reviews and "averages" results reported in the literature. The possibility remains that many other investigators have conducted studies looking for the effect in question, but did not find it. These studies probably would not have been published or reported in any way. Rosenthal (1979) has called this the **file drawer problem**, because null findings are often simply filed away.

The statistical check on this possibility involves calculating the number of unreported studies that would be needed to reduce the obtained Z_{ma} to nonsignificance. In Findley and Cooper's meta-analysis, 3,327 null studies would have tohave been conducted (but unreported) to reduce their Z_{ma} to a nonsignificant level. It is obviously implausible to assume that so many null studies exist. We can therefore conclude with considerable confidence that there is a relationship between locus of control and academic achievement, such that internals tend to achieve more than externals.

Most meta-analyses do not end here, however. Rather they go on to index the strength of the reported relationship, both overall and for various subpopulations. The strength of these relationships, called **effect size**, can be indexed by r (see p. 63), and r can be computed easily from information included in most research reports. This is what Findley and Cooper proceeded to do. The overall r averaging across all the studies was +.18, which is highly significant because of the large sample size involved. However, it also shows that locus of control accounts for barely more than 3% of the variance in academic achievement (.18 × .18 = .032). (Recall we discussed "variance accounting" in Chapter 3.)

The other question that can be answered by meta-analysis is, Across which subpopulations is the relationship strongest and weakest? Table 11-6 presents the average rs found in Findley and Cooper's meta-analysis according to gender, age, race, and socioeconomic status. As can be seen from the table, the relationship between locus of control and academic achievement is stronger for males than for females, stronger for those from the lower class than those from the middle class, and stronger for young adolescents (i.e., those in junior high) than for any other age group.

Meta-analysis has also been used to demonstrate the external validity of the claim that psychotherapy is moderately effective (Smith et al., 1980), that modifying what people say to themselves about themselves ("self-statements") is an effective form of therapy for many psychological problems (Dush et al., 1983), and that males tend to be more aggressive than females (Hyde, 1984).

TABLE 11-6 AVERAGE EFFECT SIZE FOR VARIOUS SUBGROUPS IN FINDLEY AND COOPER'S (1983) META-ANALYSIS OF THE RELATIONSHIP BETWEEN LOCUS OF CONTROL AND ACADEMIC ACHIEVEMENT

Characteristics	Average r
Gender	
Males	0.20
Females	0.11
Age	
College	0.14
High school	0.23
Junior high	0.35
4th–6th grade	0.24
1st–3rd grade	0.04
Race	
Black	0.25
White	0.25
Socioeconomic status	
Middle class	0.26
Lower class	0.35

Source: From data reported in Findley and Cooper (1983).

WRITING AN APA-STYLE RESEARCH REPORT

The limitations of space and the traditions of psychological journals have produced a relatively standard format for research reports. The American Psychological Association (APA, 1990) publishes a manual describing in detail the appropriate presentation for reports.

The format described by APA's *Publication Manual* has been adopted by most psychological journals. These periodicals consider articles for publication only if they conform exactly to the format outlined in the manual. Adherence to these rules and procedures is necessary to ensure standardization of expression, and therefore effective communication of research findings.

General Format

How is the typical journal article organized? A research report suitable for publication should include five essential components: 1) an *abstract* or brief summary of the study; 2) an *introduction*, which provides justification for conducting the study; 3) a *method* section, describing the sample, materials, design, and procedures used; 4) a *results* section or analysis of data; and 5) a *discussion* of the study's results as they relate to previous research and future considerations. These five sections comprise the main body of the report.

Several other components are needed to make a report complete. These include a *title page* naming author and institution (make sure you get credit for your work!), a *reference* section (a list of primary and secondary sources cited) and supplementary elements that provide information not directly presented in the text, such as *appendixes, charts, tables, footnotes,* and *author notes.*

In the following section, each of these components will be discussed in greater detail. An example of an actual research report has been included to clarify several important issues and illustrate how the manuscript looks as a whole.

The Title Page.   The *title page* is the cover sheet used, as its name implies, to convey the title of your study. It also should include the name of the author (or authors, if the study involved collaborative effort), the name of the institution (typically a university) where the study was conducted (this is referred to as one's "affiliation"), and an abbreviated title referred to as the *running head.* (See Figure 11-1.)

Unlike the catchy titles often used by motion pictures and best-selling books, the title of a research report is most effective as a straightforward description. It is best to keep the title brief (APA recommends 12–15 words in length) and to the point. A simple rule of thumb suggests limiting the description to a discussion of the *major* independent and dependent variable(s) used in the study.

Suppose, for example, that you conducted an experiment focusing on how viewing televised violence influences children's subsequent verbalizations. Results indicate that children between the ages of 5 and 10 years are more likely to use expressions such as "#@*%#@!," "*&^%#!" and "*$~&@!" following pro-

Figure 11-1

longed exposure to "shoot 'em up" cops and robbers types of programs. Given this description, which of the following two titles seems to be the most accurate and informative: "Effects of viewing television violence on aggressive verbalizations in children," or "#@*%#@!," "*&^%#!" and "*$~&@!:" What children say when they watch violent TV?" (The latter might be most appropriate as the title of a film documentary or a "pop psych" book.)

The title and the author's name and affiliation should be printed in upper and lower case letters, and centered in the middle of the page. If the author is not affiliated with a particular institution, his/her city and state of residence are used in lieu of an institutional affiliation.

The Running Head and Short Title.   The *running head* is an abbreviated version of the title, used as a quick reference. It is printed entirely in upper case letters, centered at the bottom of the page, and should be limited to 50 characters. Similarly, a *short title* (a condensed version of the running head) is included in the upper right-hand corner of the title page and on each page of the report (printed in lower-case letters).

Page numbering begins with the title page (page 1) and continues throughout the text in consecutive fashion. *All* pages included in the report must be numbered. Appendixes, tables, and other supplementary pages are not exempt from this rule (figures however, *are,* as they should be "camera ready"). The convention is to print the page number at the top right-hand corner of each page.

The Body of the Text

The body of the text begins with the abstract and includes the introduction, methods, results, and discussion sections. The length of the text of an article varies with the complexity of the design employed, and whether the report covers only one, or multiple studies, but generally ranges between 10 and 20 double-spaced, typewritten pages.

The Abstract.   The *abstract* is a brief summary of the study, and generally appears as page 2. It functions as a preview/review of what the reader can expect to find in subsequent sections of the report. Similar to film "trailers" used to promote upcoming movie premieres, the abstract provides a quick glimpse of the study's most salient features. In this way, a potential reader can decide quickly whether he/she wishes to read the full article. If the content of the report seems relevant, the reader can move forward; if not, on to the next available abstract!

The key word here is "brief." An effective abstract should run no longer than 100–150 words, highlighting the most essential aspects of each section, including the purpose of the study, a concise description of subjects, design, and procedure, essential details such as age, number, and sex of subjects, and significant findings/conclusions. (See Figure 11-2.)

Laboratory Induction
2

Abstract

The efficacy of a new procedure for inducing positive mood in the laboratory was evaluated. Results were expected to replicate the findings of McCarrick-Geary (1989). Forty undergraduate volunteers were exposed to either a positive or neutral induction condition using the Music + Imagination Instruction (MII) procedure. Numeric and graphic mood ratings were obtained at pre- and post-induction. Results indicated that on self-report measures, subjects exposed to the positive induction experienced a significant elevation of mood, relative to subjects in the neutral condition. This finding suggests that the MII is an effective method for inducing positive mood states.

Figure 11-2

As you might guess, the abstract is usually written *after* the other sections of the report have been composed. (It's hard to summarize what you have yet to realize!) Wording should be especially concise. Forget about using flowery statements and sophisticated prose; this isn't intended to be a literary tour de force. Avoid using passive expressions such as, "The subjects were asked to complete a personality measure." Instead, use verbs in an active voice (e.g., "Subjects completed a personality measure"). Above all, keep it simple and easy to read!

The Introduction.   The introduction is best thought of as an argument or justification for initiating the study. Its major purpose is to convince the reader that the aims and methods of the research are consistent with previous findings and, in fact, will contribute to the overall understanding in that area of research. Consistent with these goals, an effective introduction 1) states the purpose of the study, 2) reviews relevant studies that have already been conducted by the writer or other researchers, and 3) describes the hypothesis or hypotheses to be investigated.

Related Literature.   Students writing a psychological report for the first time often mistakenly assume that *all* "related" research should be mentioned in the introduction. In fact, an exhaustive review of the literature is unnecessary, potentially misleading, and is itself an "exhausting" enterprise for both the researcher and the reader. Only references directly related to the purpose of the study should be cited.

Perhaps the best way to conceptualize the brief literature review is to consider it a process, not simply an outcome. In this way, a discussion of relevant findings is like a funnel. The initial statement should begin with a more general, broad-based discussion of the topic, gradually becoming more focused and narrow in scope. The reader is thus directed to the specific issue(s) under investigation and the hypotheses of the study within an appropriate contextual framework. (See Figure 11-3.)

Take a look, for example, at the sample manuscript entitled, "Laboratory Induction of Positive Affect: A Replication" (note that the title of the report is always included at the top of the third page, following the abstract). As you can see, the introduction begins by making the claim that mood is an integral part of human experience. Several examples are then provided to support this statement.

Moving from the general topic to a more specific focus, the next paragraph tells the reader that several investigators have attempted to manipulate mood in laboratory settings. Becoming still more narrow in focus, the reader is then provided with a *specific* example of a laboratory-based mood induction procedure, a reference to McCarrick and Liebert's (1989) study. This information leads directly to one of the two purposes of the present investigation, namely to replicate McCarrick and Liebert's findings, and provides a basis for predicting that the newly developed mood induction technique will be effective.

Brief Description of Research Design and Hypotheses.   The introduction thus ends with a specific statement of purpose and a brief description of the study's hypotheses. Although the hypotheses may be stated in concrete or abstract terms,

Laboratory Induction
4
subjects to read statements suggestive of a positive, negative,
or neutral mood, the MII technique exposed subjects to an
audiotape consisting of appropriate mood music in combination
with strong, "hypnoidal" suggestions.

        McCarrick-Geary (1989) reported that on various self-report
measures of current mood, including a numeric rating scale, a
graphic rating scale, and the Multiple Affect Adjective Check
List, both the Velten and the MII positive mood inductions
produced a significant change in subjects relati
control group. However, three other measures,
activity rating scale, an observational measure,
of susceptibility rates, revealed that the MII
more effective as a positive mood induction prod
the Velten.

        The current study's purpose was to replicat
Geary's (1989) central result: that the MII is a
useful technique for inducing positive mood in a
setting, when compared with an appropriate neutr
group. Previous studies involving a music-based
procedure have often failed to include an appro
condition. In this experiment, a neutral mood
to determine whether the positive mood inductio
produce a significant mood elevation.

Laboratory Induction
3
Laboratory Induction of Positive Affect:
A Replication

        Mood, once considered a minor psychological phenomenon
(Diamond, 1957; Wessman & Ricks, 1966), has been shown over the
past 15 years to play a central role in diverse aspects of human
functioning. Research indicates that a person's current mood can
influence cognitive processes such as perception (Forgas, Bower,
& Krantz, 1984; Kitayama, 1991), memory (Bower, 1981), and
creative thinking (Greene & Noice, 1988). Mood states have also
been shown to influence a variety of social behaviors, including
activity preference (Cunningham, 1988), altruism (Batson, 1990),
and aggression (Bell & Baron, 1990).

        Given the possible importance of current mood across
virtually every aspect of human psychological functioning, it is
not surprising that a number of researchers have developed and
attempted to validate laboratory-based mood inductions (e.g.,
Bower & Mayer, 1985; Isen & Gorgoglione, 1983; Teasdale &
Spencer, 1984; Velten, 1968). For example, in one procedure,
music and scripted imagination instructions were highly
successful as a means of inducing positive mood (McCarrick-Geary,
1989). In that study, subjects were randomly assigned to one of
two methods of induction, a traditional, widely used procedure
(Velten, 1968) or the Music + Imagination Instructions Method
(MII) developed by McCarrick and Liebert (1987), and to one of
three types of induction (positive, negative, or neutral). In
contrast to Velten's (1968) procedure, which merely required

Figure 11-3

they are always statements about possible or hypothesized relationships between
(or among) the variables under investigation.

The Method Section

The method section explains the manner in which the variables have been *operationalized*. It provides a clear description of the actual *operations* (instructions or events) involved in both the experimental treatments and in the subsequent measures of behavior. In other words, this portion of the report tells the reader precisely *how* the study was conducted. Accuracy and detail are particularly important here, as this section enables others to replicate your study.

A complete "method" typically includes sections pertaining to 1) *subjects*; 2) *materials, apparatus, and/or measures*; and 3) *design and procedure.* The inclusion/exclusion and arrangement of these subsections may vary, depending on the nature of the investigation. For example, a purely correlational study may involve the use of several paper and pencil *measures*, but no *apparatus* or technical equipment per se. (See Figure 11-4.)

Subjects. The subsection entitled "Subjects" provides the reader with pertinent information about the sample used. This description should include the number of subjects who actually participated in the study, the demographics of the sample (age, gender, and any other relevant personal characteristics), and the setting from which the sample was drawn. The method of subject selection should be discussed, with mention of any subjects who were excluded from participating in the actual study. Finally, if subjects have been assigned to experimental conditions, the manner in which they were assigned (e.g., randomly) should be described.

Materials, Apparatus, and Measures. The subsection that follows "Subjects" can in many ways be thought of as an *operations manual*, the type of instructional guide often included with the purchase of most major appliances, new technologies, and the like. It is, in effect, a list of the equipment needed to conduct the study, with more detailed descriptions of individual components, for example, a personality inventory or a polygraph recording device. As you might expect, this section also tells the reader *how* each of these components was used.

A *materials* section should include description of any tangible stimuli used in the study (e.g., musical selections, excerpted readings, picture cards). An *apparatus* section is generally used to list and describe more technical items, machinery, and equipment (such as stereo components, VCRs, computers, and polygraph devices).

Accurate description of these items facilitates more effective replications. Thus, with the exception of "homemade" equipment, apparatus should always be identified by referring to the make and model number of each item, for example, "A Funn Buzz mechanical joybuzzer (Model number 344-RX) was used to shock and entertain subjects." Written descriptions of such apparatus can be augmented by diagrams or photographs as necessary.

Measures typically refers to assessment instruments, including rating scales, self-report inventories, and checklists. Proper reference sources should be cited for any published and/or established measures used in the study, for example, "All subjects were asked to complete the NEO Personality Inventory (NEO-PI-R, Costa & McCrae, 1992)." Some discussion of each measure's reliability and validity is also of potential use to the reader.

Design and Procedure. The last subsection of *Methods* is usually devoted to *Design and Procedure*, a step-by-step description of how the study was actually conducted. It is convenient to think of this section as a "story" or narrative, including characters (the experimenter and subjects) and a well thought-out

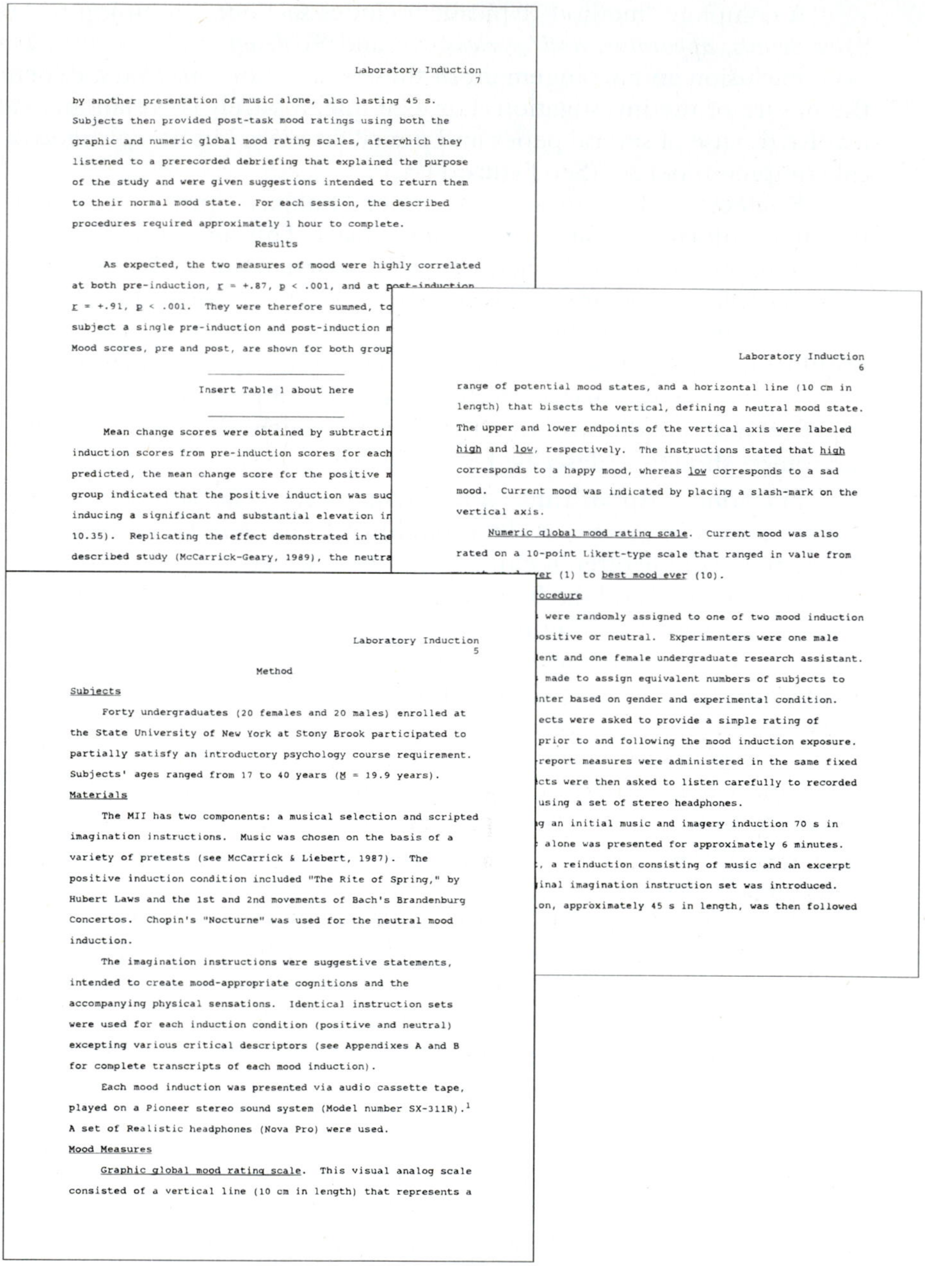

Laboratory Induction
7

by another presentation of music alone, also lasting 45 s.
Subjects then provided post-task mood ratings using both the
graphic and numeric global mood rating scales, afterwhich they
listened to a prerecorded debriefing that explained the purpose
of the study and were given suggestions intended to return them
to their normal mood state. For each session, the described
procedures required approximately 1 hour to complete.

Results

As expected, the two measures of mood were highly correlated
at both pre-induction, r = +.87, p < .001, and at post-induction
r = +.91, p < .001. They were therefore summed, to
subject a single pre-induction and post-induction m
Mood scores, pre and post, are shown for both group

Insert Table 1 about here

Mean change scores were obtained by subtractin
induction scores from pre-induction scores for each
predicted, the mean change score for the positive m
group indicated that the positive induction was suc
inducing a significant and substantial elevation i
10.35). Replicating the effect demonstrated in the
described study (McCarrick-Geary, 1989), the neutra

Laboratory Induction
6

range of potential mood states, and a horizontal line (10 cm in
length) that bisects the vertical, defining a neutral mood state.
The upper and lower endpoints of the vertical axis were labeled
high and low, respectively. The instructions stated that high
corresponds to a happy mood, whereas low corresponds to a sad
mood. Current mood was indicated by placing a slash-mark on the
vertical axis.

Numeric global mood rating scale. Current mood was also
rated on a 10-point Likert-type scale that ranged in value from
___ ___ ___ er (1) to best mood ever (10).

_____ocedure

_____ were randomly assigned to one of two mood induction
_____ositive or neutral. Experimenters were one male
_____ent and one female undergraduate research assistant.
_____ made to assign equivalent numbers of subjects to
_____nter based on gender and experimental condition.
_____ects were asked to provide a simple rating of
_____ prior to and following the mood induction exposure.
_____report measures were administered in the same fixed
_____cts were then asked to listen carefully to recorded
_____ using a set of stereo headphones.
_____g an initial music and imagery induction 70 s in
_____ alone was presented for approximately 6 minutes.
_____, a reinduction consisting of music and an excerpt
_____inal imagination instruction set was introduced.
_____on, approximately 45 s in length, was then followed

Laboratory Induction
5

Method

Subjects

Forty undergraduates (20 females and 20 males) enrolled at
the State University of New York at Stony Brook participated to
partially satisfy an introductory psychology course requirement.
Subjects' ages ranged from 17 to 40 years (M = 19.9 years).

Materials

The MII has two components: a musical selection and scripted
imagination instructions. Music was chosen on the basis of a
variety of pretests (see McCarrick & Liebert, 1987). The
positive induction condition included "The Rite of Spring," by
Hubert Laws and the 1st and 2nd movements of Bach's Brandenburg
Concertos. Chopin's "Nocturne" was used for the neutral mood
induction.

The imagination instructions were suggestive statements,
intended to create mood-appropriate cognitions and the
accompanying physical sensations. Identical instruction sets
were used for each induction condition (positive and neutral)
excepting various critical descriptors (see Appendixes A and B
for complete transcripts of each mood induction).

Each mood induction was presented via audio cassette tape,
played on a Pioneer stereo sound system (Model number SX-311R).[1]
A set of Realistic headphones (Nova Pro) were used.

Mood Measures

Graphic global mood rating scale. This visual analog scale
consisted of a vertical line (10 cm in length) that represents a

Figure 11-4

plot, which might begin with a description of initial instructions and culminate in a subject's post task debriefing. This subsection should read like a recipe: "First we added sugar to the flour mixture. Then we stirred vigorously while adding the milk, poured the mixture into a large pan, and placed it in a preheated oven set at 450 degrees." As in a recipe, descriptions of experimental procedures need to be thorough and detail-oriented.

The design of the study is also mentioned in this subsection. Each condition (treatment and controls) should be described in detail, including any methods used to reduce measurement error (e.g., counterbalancing, random assignment, blind experimenters, etc.).

The Results Section

The actual data, collected by observing subjects during or after the experimental treatment, are presented in the results section. In this section, statistics are used to *describe* the data (*descriptive statistics*) and to test *inferences* from the data (*inferential statistics*). Appendix B is an overview/refresher of some of the most commonly used inferential statistics.

The Discussion Section

In the discussion section, the implications of the results are considered and one or more interpretations offered. If the results are consistent with the hypotheses or theoretical propositions advanced at the outset, these are typically reiterated and elaborated. On the other hand, alternative theoretical concepts or possibilities may be offered at this point if the obtained pattern of results was unexpected. It is this latter type of discussion that often leads to the discovery and exploration of new psychological principles or the modification of old ones. (See Figure 11-5.)

Consider, for example, a hypothetical study that attempted to assess the efficacy of a new antidepressant drug. The medication was expected to alleviate symptoms of depression in a large sample of patients. Results indicated that the drug did not have the predicted effect. Closer inspection of the data, though, revealed that depressed patients who also suffered from anxiety reported that they were less anxious after taking the medication for several weeks. Based on these unexpected findings, subsequent research in this area will most likely take a new direction, focusing on the drug's anxiolytic (anxiety-reducing) properties.

Regardless of the outcome, that is, whether it is expected or unexpected, the results of the study should be discussed as they relate to previous findings in the research literature. Shortcomings of the study should also be addressed, as they may limit the interpretation of findings.

Finally, a concluding statement is often devoted to the implications or potential applications of the findings. This statement may also consider and describe the sort of further research that would be required to clarify or expand upon the obtained results.

```
                                       Laboratory Induction
                                                8
                       Discussion
          One purpose of this experiment was to confirm the reported
   efficacy of a newly developed, laboratory-based procedure for
   inducing positive mood.  McCarrick-Geary (1989) reported the
   Music + Imagination Instructions induction to be superior to the
   traditional Velten technique as a means of effecting mood
   elevation psychologically.  The present study produced results
   supporting the argument that the MII is, in fact, an effective
   and useful method of positive mood induction.
          It may turn out to be of clinical importance that the MII, a
   simple, nondrug procedure, can elevate mood by psychological
   means.  Here, of course, the effect has only been shown to be
   short-term.  Future work is needed to investigate the durability
   of laboratory-induced mood elevation, and to determine whether
   such mood change can be sustained in the face of experiences that
   might otherwise lower one's mood.
```

Figure 11-5

Supplementary Information

All of the supplementary information should follow the main text of a report. Most of these sections will begin on a new page and will be numbered consecutively, following from the end of the text proper.

   References.   Every resource cited in the report must be listed in this section. As the following examples illustrate, different formats are required for each type of reference used. Let us examine the specific elements and their presentation in the first example, that of the journal article with a single author. (From this you should be able to decipher the examples that follow and the ways in which they depart from this format).

Journal article (single author):

Bower, G. H. (1981). Mood and memory. <u>American Psychologist,</u>
   <u>36</u>, 129–148.

   Here, Bower is the last name of the author, followed by the author's initials. The year in parentheses is the year of publication of the work, or copyright year. Mood and memory is the title of the work. (Note that in the case of an article the title is *not* underlined, and only the first word of the title is capitalized.

Exceptions to this rule include proper nouns, which are always capitalized, and the first word of any subtitles, which will be preceded by a colon.) *American Psychologist* is the name of the journal, and it is always underlined, (see also Figure 11-6) along with the volume number (or month) that immediately follows it (in this case the volume number is 36). The last numbers to appear (129–148) indicate the pages of the journal on which the article appears.

The following are examples of other types of resources that might be cited in a report, and the form in which they would appear. While there are some differences in presentation, there are many more similarities.

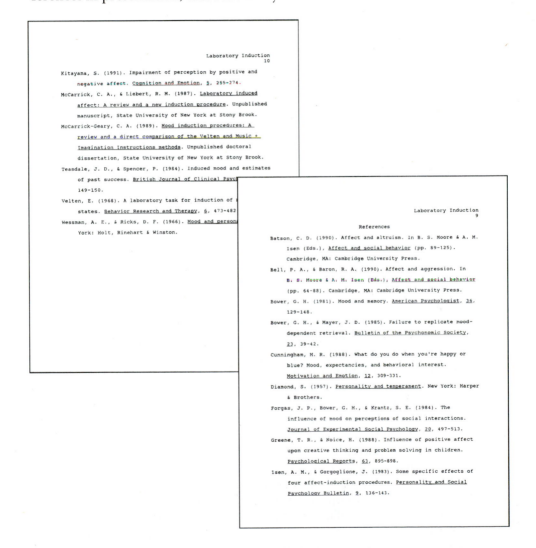

Figure 11-6

Journal article (multiple authors):

Bower, G. H., & Mayer, J. D. (1985). Failure to replicate mood-dependent retrieval. <u>Bulletin of the Psychonomic Society, 23,</u> 39-42.

Book (single author):

Diamond, S. (1957). <u>Personality and temperament.</u> New York: Harper & Brothers.

Book (multiple authors):

Wessman, A. E., & Ricks, D. F. (1966). <u>Mood and personality.</u> New York: Holt, Rinehart, and Winston, Inc.

Chapter in an edited book:

Bell, P. A., & Baron, R. A. (1990). Affect and aggression. In B. S. Moore & A. M. Isen (Eds.), <u>Affect and social behavior</u> (pp. 64-88). Cambridge: Cambridge University Press.

Doctoral dissertation:

McCarrick-Geary, C. A. (1989). <u>Mood induction procedures: A review and a direct comparison of the Velten and Music + Imagination Instructions methods.</u> Unpublished doctoral dissertation, State University of New York at Stony Brook.

Unpublished manuscript:

McCarrick, C. A., & Liebert, R. M. (1987). <u>Laboratory induced affect: A review and a new induction procedure.</u> Unpublished manuscript, State University of New York at Stony Brook.

Citing References in the Text. How are these references cited in the actual text of the report? APA endorses the "author-date" method of citation which, as the name implies, requires that you provide the author's last name and the year of publication wherever reference to a particular article is made: "Mood states have also been shown to influence a variety of social behaviors, including activity preference (Cunningham, 1988), altruism (Batson, 1990), and aggression (Bell & Baron, 1990)."

If the author's name is used in a sentence, only the date of publication is presented in parentheses: "McCarrick (1989) reported that. . . ."

When multiple citations are presented within the same parentheses, the references are listed in alphabetical order: ". . . . a number of researchers have attempted to develop and validate laboratory-based mood inductions (e.g., Bower & Mayer, 1985; Isen & Gorgoglione, 1983; Teasdale & Spencer, 1984; Velten, 1968).

Multiple references by the same author are listed in chronological order in the following way: ". . . . as described in several studies (Liebert, 1986, 1991, 1993)."

The abbreviation "et al." is used 1) when citing a reference that has six or more authors, and 2) for all subsequent citations of a reference (following the initial citation) that has more than two authors: "In that study (Liebert et al., 1987). . . ."

Appendixes.   Appendixes contain detailed supplementary information. Scripted instructions, highly technical descriptions of apparatus, and unpublished measurement instruments are good examples of what is typically included in this section of the report. Appendixes are identified alphabetically and presented in consecutive order, each beginning on a new page, that is, Appendix A, B, C. (See Figure 11-7.)

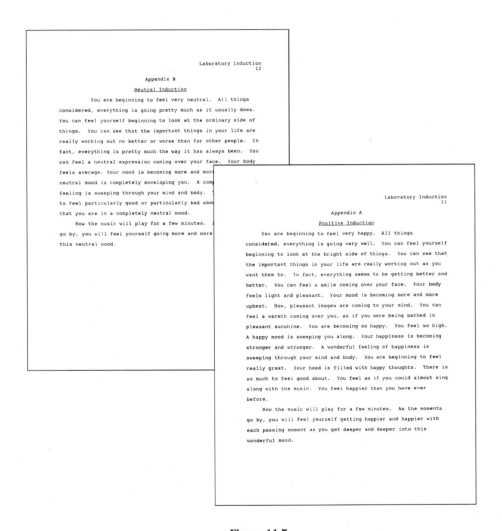

Figure 11-7

Author Notes.   As the name implies, Author identification notes tell the reader something about the person(s) who wrote the report. Typically mentioned are the author's most recent affiliation and address (those included in the title page may differ if there has been a recent change), primary sources of funding (e.g., government agencies), and acknowledgments to those who assisted in preparing the manuscript. Information about requests for article reprints, for example, to whom such correspondence should be directed, is often included as well. (See Figure 11-8.)

Footnotes.   Footnotes can be thought of as appendixes presented on a *much* smaller scale. They provide useful supplementary information that might be considered digressive. Each footnote referred to in the body of the report (by a superscript numeral) is identified by number and listed in consecutive order on a separate sheet. (See Figure 11-9.)

Tables.   Quantitative data and in some cases qualitative data are often best presented in a table, rather than in the text. While it may be difficult to decide which format best suits your needs (and those of the reader), *never* include both. Information presented in tabular form should not be duplicated in the body of the report, and vice versa.

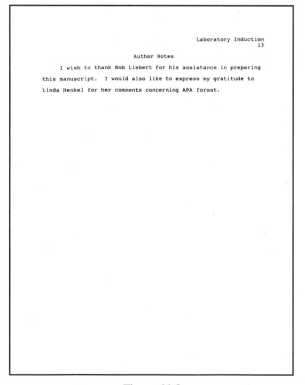

Figure 11-8

Tables are numbered consecutively and placed on separate pages. Each should include a title that describes, in concise terms, the relationship between the variables used. Reference to *all* tables must be made in the body of the report [e.g., ". . . . mean scores listed in Table 4," or "These values were found to be equivalent (see Table 4)"]. All lines within the table should be double spaced. (See Figure 11-10.)

Figures (and Captions).   Figures can include a variety of illustrations, including photographs, technical drawings, charts, and graphs. Deciding which (if any) of these formats you wish to use will depend on the nature of your research and particular aspects of the data you wish to highlight. You may, for example, include a technical drawing of apparatus used in your study if a verbal description seems inadequate.

Because figures are often costly to reproduce, they should be used sparingly, and should not, as a rule, duplicate information presented elsewhere in the report. Hand-drawn figures are in most cases unacceptable for submitted work. If you don't have access to a graphics software program, a plotter, or a laser printer, you may want to consult a professional artist or graphics designer.

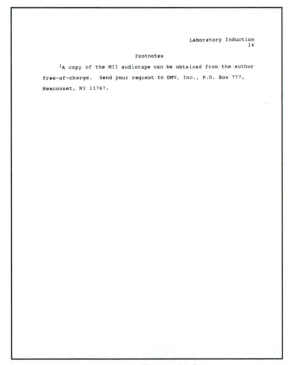

Figure 11-9

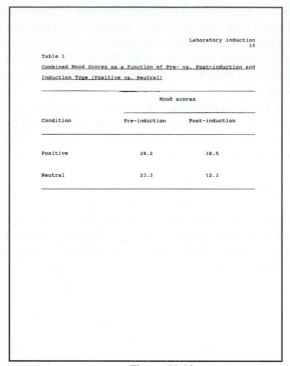

Figure 11-10

  Figure captions are titles that accurately describe the figures used. All captions are listed by corresponding figure number on a separate page, preceding the first figure. Not surprisingly, figure captions should be kept brief. (See Figure 11-11.)

The Order/Arrangement of the Report

  Title page. (numbered page 1)

  Abstract. (numbered page 2)

  Text. (Introduction, Method, Results, and Discussion; numbered page 3 through . . . . .)

  References. (these start on a separate page)

  Appendixes. (new page for each)

  Author notes. (separate page)

  Footnotes. (separate page)

  Tables. (each on a separate page)

  Figure captions. (all included on same page)

  Figures. (pages are not numbered)

Laboratory Induction
16

Figure Caption

Figure 1. Mean composite mood as a function of type of induction
and pre- vs. post-task ratings.

Figure 11-11

A Note on Style

Writing involves the successful integration of many skills. Scientific writing is even more difficult to master, because it requires concise and accurate presentation of material that is technical in nature.

But all hope is not lost. You can begin to acquire and develop these skills by consulting a professional handbook or reference manual that reviews fundamentals of good writing (i.e., grammar, sentence construction, usage). For this purpose, *The Practical Stylist* by S. Baker (1977) is an excellent resource. It is easy to read, highly informative, and relatively brief.

FOR REVIEW AND DISCUSSION

Key Terms
LITERATURE SEARCH
REFEREED JOURNAL
PREPRINTS

PUBLICATION LAG
META-ANALYSIS
STATISTICAL SIGNIFICANCE
EFFECT SIZE
FILE DRAWER PROBLEM

For Discussion

1. Explain why there is such a long lag between the completion of a research project and its publication.
2. Outline the steps involved in conducting a literature search.
3. Explain what is meant by the term "the file drawer problem." What possible threat does this represent to researchers?
4. Many professional journals will not publish reports of research in which the results did not reach at least the .05 level of significance. If you were a journal editor, what defense could you give for this practice? What arguments might be made against it? Consider, for example, a) whether it is possible for data reaching the .10 level to be more meaningful than data reaching .001, and b) the difference between "meaningful" and "significant" findings. If the negative results are correct (that is, there really is no difference between groups) what might be the advantages of publishing them?
5. Authors of journal articles are expected to avoid the use of flowery language. Explain some possible reasons for this policy.
6. Why should the method section of a journal article be *particularly* detailed and specific?

APPENDIX A: DESIGNING QUESTIONNAIRES AND CONDUCTING SURVEYS

A great deal of psychological research involves questioning subjects about their attitudes, behaviors, and experiences. In all these instances we are, in essence, asking subjects for a **self-report**. The aim is to pose the same questions in the same way to all subjects (in other words, to **standardize** the form and administration of the questions). The questionnaire thus becomes a **test** (in the sense defined in Chapter 3), and permits us to combine and compare the responses of different subjects.

The range of circumstances in which research psychologists and other social scientists employ questionnaires is very wide. Sometimes questionnaires are the primary tool of a research project; this is true of **surveys**, about which we will have more to say later. In other instances, questionnaires are used as a secondary tool. For example, many researchers will use **postexperimental questionnaires** to determine subjects' perceptions of the nature and purpose of the experiment in which they have participated, or to insure that the experimental manipulations had the desired effect.

Because all questionnaires rely on self-reports, we are concerned that the questions will be understood clearly and answered honestly. If questions are ambiguous, difficult to answer, or touch on "sensitive" information, the answers subjects give may be distorted. In this appendix we will consider the issues involved in designing effective questionnaires, administering them, and, in the case of surveys, selecting appropriate samples for study.

PREPARING QUESTIONNAIRES

Questionnaires vary enormously in their ability to meet the purposes of the researcher. Preparing an effective questionnaire that fulfills its goals involves making explicit the informational goals of the questionnaire, selecting or producing specific questions, and then structuring and formatting the questionnaire in a way that will make it clear and inviting to your subjects.

Clarifying the Purpose of Your Questionnaire

The first step in preparing a questionnaire is to clarify for yourself what exactly you wish to learn from your questionnaire data. General questions, such as "How do people feel about health care reform?" must be broken down into specific issues such as "How satisfied are you with the quality of the health care now available?" "What would you like to see retained in any new health care plan?" (e.g., ability to choose your own physician) "Do you think health care reform will increase, decrease, or leave unchanged your own health care costs?"

Some questionnaires may have more than one purpose. For instance, in a post-experimental questionnaire we may wish both to assess subjects' perception of the purpose of an experiment *and* to learn how these perceptions may have influenced their performance.

Most survey researchers will wish to collect at least some **demographic data** about the respondents, such as their gender, age, socioeconomic status, and political party affiliation (if any). This information will allow the researcher to do "break-outs" of the data along demographic lines; for example, recent surveys in the United States have indicated that older and poorer people are more likely to favor health care reform than younger or wealthier ones. Without clarifying *all* the information you might want from respondents in advance, you may overlook some important points that will make interpretation of your data difficult or impossible after it is collected.

The Importance of Wording

Precisely how questions are worded can have a tremendous impact on the outcome of survey research. For example, most people may be very reluctant to provide a total stranger with detailed information about their personal finances. However, a question phrased such that the respondent need only identify a range within which his or her family income falls may help the respondent to be much more cooperative. Thus, instead of asking "What was your family income last year?" one might ask

Was your income last year:

_____   Less than $20,000
_____ $20,000–$39,999
_____ $40,000–$59,999
_____ $60,000–$79,999
_____ $80,000 or above

Topics other than finance may also be experienced as sensitive or objectionable by responders. It is extremely important that the writer of the questionnaire avoid potentially offensive language. In approaching items that most people might be inclined to deny, **legitimization** can be a helpful strategy. For instance, most people may be reluctant to admit to negative feelings. An item aimed at determining the frequency with which people become angered with others might open with the phrase "Everyone becomes angry with friends and family members from time to time," before going on to ask how often and in which circumstances this happens to respondents.

Another important strategy in eliciting cooperation and ensuring accurate responding is to keep items brief, and to make responding as simple and easy as possible. One way to facilitate responding is to print out the available choices in such a way that the respondent need only circle answers or place a check mark, rather than having to write out complete answers to each item.

All of these issues need to be considered as a researcher begins to approach the task of selecting items for a questionnaire.

Selecting Items.   Items for use in questionnaires may come from a variety of sources. Sometimes items are borrowed from item pools used previously by other researchers. Many of today's widely used personality inventories are based in part on items taken from earlier inventories; the same is true of many surveys.

One of the advantages of using items that have been used before is that you can compare your questionnaire data with those obtained from other samples or given at earlier times. People's political attitudes often change markedly in the months before an election, a fact that can only be established by re-using the same questionnaire items periodically as the election approaches.

Another advantage of using existing items is the speed and efficiency with which a new questionnaire can be assembled. Moreover, the potential existence of reliability and validity data about these items gives some assurance that they will, indeed, serve their intended purpose.

Often, though, suitable items may not be found among available alternatives. In these instances a researcher may need to supplement existing items, or construct an entire questionnaire from scratch.

Writing Original Items.   Writing original items offers some advantages over making use of existing ones. Questions can be tailored very specifically to the purpose of the new questionnaire. But writing good items is a demanding task. A good item is brief, clear, and worded in a way that all respondents can be expected to understand. Once you have written a set of prospective items, it is always desirable to pretest them with people who are as similar (e.g., in educational level) as possible to those whom you will use as your final subjects.

Structuring Your Questionnaire

A set of items, even very clear and specific ones, does not by itself mean you have a questionnaire that is ready to go. The questionnaire itself must be structured in a way that will invite complete and accurate responding.

Length.   If you give or send a person a 15-page questionnaire, their immediate reaction may well be that it is long and complicated. This impression will lead many respondents to fail to answer, or to answer in a quick and careless way. Thus, in general, a good questionnaire should be as short and simple as you can make it, while still achieving your purpose.

Formatting Items.   Almost any given question you wish to pose can be presented (or *formatted*) in a number of different ways. Your choice of question format will depend on a number of factors. Here we will describe briefly some of the most commonly used formats.

Checklists.   Some questions are best suited to a checklist format. Rather than offering the choice of making a check versus leaving an item blank, you should require the respondent to make an overt response to every item. For example, instead of:

CHECK EACH OF THE EMOTIONS YOU EXPERIENCED IN THE PAST WEEK:

_____   Happy

_____   Sad

_____   Angry

_____   Pleased

_____   Frustrated

It is better to ask:

FOR EACH OF THE EMOTIONS BELOW, CHECK WHETHER YOU DID OR DID NOT EXPERIENCE IT DURING THE PAST WEEK:

YES	NO	
_____	_____	Happy
_____	_____	Sad
_____	_____	Angry
_____	_____	Pleased
_____	_____	Frustrated

Open-ended Items.   An **open-ended item** is one in which the respondent is asked a question and invited to answer in his or her own words. For example, an open-ended item about health care might be:

DESCRIBE THE ISSUE YOU CONSIDER MOST IMPORTANT IN HEALTH CARE REFORM:_____

_____

_____

_____

The most important feature of the open-ended format is that it is unstructured. Some respondents may answer in one or two words. Others may write an extensive statement and even use the back of the questionnaire to continue answers for which there was, in their view, insufficient room to express their thoughts.

In order to summarize and combine answers to open-ended items, you will need to develop some sort of scoring system *and* demonstrate that your scoring system will produce the same results when used by different raters who attempt to apply it. (This is an example of **inter-rater reliability**; see Chapters 3 and 4).

The open-ended format can be most useful as a tool in exploring and clarifying the issues surrounding a question, but it is rarely used as the final form of a professional questionnaire or survey.

Yes/No Questions.   The simplest type of **closed-ended items** are of the form, Yes/No. Such items are easily understood and scored, and allow you to obtain answers to many specific questions in a format that seems easy and brief. This format is made even easier by providing both alternatives on the printed form and asking the subject to circle his/her answer or darken it on a form that can be scanned electronically. For example:

Y   **N**   I am satisfied with my current health care coverage.

Y   **N**   Everyone has a right to health care.

Y   **N**   I don't care if I can choose my own doctor, as long as he/she is competent.

Multiple-Choice Formats.   Multiple-choice formats are familiar to all college students. They provide a statement, followed by three or more alternatives, from which the respondent must choose one. For example:

IF THE ELECTION FOR PRESIDENT WERE HELD TODAY, I WOULD VOTE FOR:
   a) George Bush
   b) Bill Clinton
   c) Ross Perot

Multiple-choice questions can be written to be **partially open-ended**, so that respondents can choose one of the listed alternatives or name their own. For example:

IF THE ELECTION FOR PRESIDENT WERE HELD TODAY, I WOULD VOTE FOR:
   a) George Bush
   b) Bill Clinton
   c) Ross Perot
   d) Other _____

Likert Scales.   One limitation of the True/False and Multiple-Choice formats is that they fail to distinguish among opinions or preferences of different intensities. To deal with this problem, you can use the so-called **Likert Scale Format** (named after the survey researcher who devised it in the 1930s). A Likert Scale offers the respondent five choices for each statement:

Strongly Agree	Agree	Undecided	Disagree	Strongly Disagree
(5)	(4)	(3)	(2)	(1)

A typical item might be:

_____   I am satisfied with the quality and extent of my present health care coverage.

_____   I believe everyone has a right to health care, regardless of income.

Visual Analog Scales.   In a Likert type scale, subjects have a fixed number of alternatives (usually five) from which to choose. In a **visual analog scale**, subjects are asked to make a mark anywhere on a line or other visual representation of the extent, intensity, or certainty of their feelings about a particular question or statement. Such scales are always *anchored* at the end points, indicating the most extreme possible answers. An example of a visual analog scale is:

I see myself as:

Extremely   Extremely
Introverted   Extraverted

Visual analog scales can be scored by using a ruler, measuring the distance from the left (or right) anchor point to the line or mark made by the subject. Subjects find visual analog scales easy to understand and use, and feel they have been given a fuller range of choices than with other forms of scaling.

ADMINISTERING YOUR QUESTIONNAIRE

Once you have clarified your purposes, and written and formatted your questionnaire, you will still have to decide how to administer it. As with the issues we have already discussed, there are several considerations to keep in mind when administering a questionnaire.

Researcher Responsibilities

Administering a questionnaire is a form of research, and thus all the ethical responsibilities we discussed in Chapter 2 apply. The most important of these is **confidentiality**. You must guarantee and assure questionnaire respondents that the information they provide will be held in strict confidence, and prepare your questionnaire so that the names and other identifying information about respondents will not fall into the hands of others.

Responding to a questionnaire must be presented as a voluntary activity, and no coercion or pressure should be used to induce or force subjects to complete a questionnaire.

Self- Versus Interviewer Administration

Questionnaires may be either self-administered or administered by an interviewer who reads the questions to subjects and records their answers. One issue in making this decision is cost; it is obviously less expensive to have subjects self-administer a questionnaire than to employ an interviewer.

The advantages of using an interviewer include assuring that each question will be understood and that no questions will be omitted through the subject's oversight. Often it is necessary to use an interviewer when questioning children, elderly persons, or others who might have difficulty with written material.

Eliciting Cooperation and Minimizing Bias

It is advisable to tell subjects in advance *why* you wish to question them, and to explain the importance of obtaining the information you seek (e.g., making it possible to achieve certain scientific or social goals). Your initial statement should include the promise of confidentiality and, where feasible, offer subjects an opportunity to receive feedback on the overall outcome of your research. A word of thanks and appreciation is always helpful—and always in order.

RESPONSE SETS

One important assumption often made by research psychologists who use questionnaires in gathering data is that an individual's response to any particular question reflects his or her attitude toward the *content* of that item. To the extent that this assumption is not correct, questionnaire data may be misleading.

Suppose a man is presented with the statement: "I attend a party at least once a week." If he answers "Yes" or "True," or otherwise indicates that the statement applies to him, can we assume that he *does* attend social gatherings frequently? Often the answer appears to be "no." It has been found that people with certain test-taking "sets" may not respond to this type of item on its manifest content. Several types of **response sets**, as these orientations are called, have been identified.

Response acquiescence, or "yea-saying," is the tendency to agree with statements regardless of their content. **Response dissension** ("nay-saying"), on the other hand, is the tendency to *dis*agree with items regardless of their content. One way to limit the effect of these biases is to vary the direction of items, so that equal numbers of items reflecting a particular attitude or trait require affirmative and negative replies. Below are four questionnaire items designed to measure the trait Extraversion. Items 2) and 4) have "(R)" after them to indicate that the scoring is to be reversed. Thus, a person answering "5" on item 1) would get a score of "5" for that item; however, a person answering "5" on item 2) would get a score of "1" for the item.

How true is this of you?	*Not at All*				*Very*	
1) I make friends easily.	1	2	3	4	5	
2) I tend to be shy.	1	2	3	4	5	(R)
3) I like to be with others.	1	2	3	4	5	
4) I often do things alone.	1	2	3	4	5	(R)

Response deviation is the tendency to answer items in an uncommon or extreme way regardless of their content. Persons answering many items in a deviant way usually have their questionnaires disregarded as invalid.

Social desirability is a response set characterized by answering questions in the direction that is most socially accepted, regardless of whether such an answer is actually correct for the respondent. For instance, in the example above, a man who dislikes (and avoids) parties might say he attends them frequently because he feels that such a response is likely to be considered "right" or appropriate.

To illustrate the problem of social desirability and some possible solutions, let us describe the pioneering work of Edwards (1953, 1957). Edwards began with an investigation designed to assess the relationship between the likelihood that an item would be endorsed and the social desirability of the item as measured independently.

First, a large number of subjects were asked to judge 140 different self-descriptions on a 9-point scale, in terms of the degree of desirability or undesirability of these traits. Some of these items are listed below:

1. To like to punish your enemies.
2. To like to read psychological novels.
3. To like to make excuses for your friends.
4. To like to go out with your friends.

In the next phase of the study, Edwards presented the same 140 items to a different sample of subjects. These new subjects were asked to respond *yes* if the particular item was characteristic of their own behavior and *no* if it was not. The percentage of subjects responding *yes* to each of the items was computed and then correlated with the previously rated social desirability of the response.

An impressively high correlation was obtained, leading Edwards to conclude that if we know where a statement lies on the social desirability-undesirability dimension, ". . . we can then predict, with a high degree of accuracy, the proportion of individuals who will say, in self-description, that the statement does describe them" (1957, p. 3). The effect does not appear to be reduced when respondents are led to believe that they will remain anonymous. Thus, several methods have been devised for controlling the influence of social desirability.

One method is to measure the respondent's tendency to give socially desirable answers and then to adjust his or her other responses to take this tendency into account. Unfortunately, some very complicated assumptions would have to be met to make such a technique legitimate. For example, one would have to show that the tendency to give socially desirable responses is highly general across different content items.

Alternatively, a **forced-choice inventory** may be used, in which items of differing content are equated in terms of their (independently determined) social desirability. Edwards himself used this latter technique in constructing his *Personal Preferences Schedule*. The manner in which it forces respondents to choose between equally desirable (or undesirable) alternatives and thus to make a content-related response can be seen from the two examples below:

Choose A or B
I. A: I like to tell amusing stories and jokes at parties.
    B: I would like to write a great novel or play.

II. A: I feel like blaming others when things go wrong for me.
     B: I feel that I am inferior to others in most respects.

Another attempt to reduce the problem of response sets in self-reports involves the use of so-called **behavioroid measures** (Aronson & Carlsmith, 1968). Such measures require subjects to *commit themselves to a particular action* (though they are never actually required to perform it later). For example, a person who is willing to sign up for a specific appointment to donate blood is more committed to action than someone who has simply checked "yes" to the general question, "Would you be willing to donate blood?"

SURVEYING A POPULATION

Research psychologists and other social scientists are often interested in the frequency of an attitude in a general population (e.g., all potential voters in the U.S.). Research directed at characterizing a population's attitudes is usually referred to as **survey research**. Manufacturers conduct surveys to determine the percentage of people who may buy a new product; television networks survey people to determine the popularity of shows so they can fix the price of advertising time; and people's attitudes toward political figures and significant social or political issues are under continual scrutiny by the survey researcher.

Defining the Population of Interest

Regardless of the actual sampling procedure undertaken, the first step in any type of research is to define the population of interest. This definition will typically involve some exclusions. In surveys that are pertinent to national elections, one would systematically exclude all individuals who are not yet of voting age. Or, in the case of certain market surveys, individuals below (or above) a certain economic level might well be excluded.

Choosing a Sample

A key issue in survey research is that it would be uneconomical and impractical to survey everyone. In predicting whether a particular political candidate will win next November's election, one might wish to determine the percentage of voters who favor his or her candidacy. This question could be answered by surveying the preferences of the entire voter population. A comprehensive survey such as this is called a **census**. In a census every member of the target population *is* included in the survey. However, such a strategy is not usually feasible; the full population is simply too large to be studied economically.

So, to determine the frequency of an attitude or disposition in the population, social scientists will typically draw a sample to represent the population of interest. After questioning the sample, the researcher will wish to generalize back to the parent population. As explained in Chapter 3, such generalizations must be made with considerable caution. They involve an *inference* and can only be made according to a series of assumptions and rules that tend to assure that we have employed a **representative sample**.

The **population validity** of any survey hinges on the method of sampling that was used in gathering the data. Population validity is always uncertain when the method of sampling is unspecified, as in many TV commercials. Consider a TV ad depicting a series of taste comparisons between Coke and Pepsi. Four people appear in the ad, and each claims to be a one-time Coke drinker who has switched to Pepsi. But how many people were sampled to find these four? Perhaps the company had to question 1,000 Coke drinkers to find four who had switched!

A somewhat better but still inadequate ad claims that "Four out of five dentists surveyed recommend Brand X gum for their patients who chew gum." Here we know that four of five made the recommendation, but we do not know how many dentists actually participated in the survey, or how they were selected.

The first sampling decision facing the serious survey researcher is between *probability* and *nonprobability sampling*. **Probability sampling** refers to any procedure in which each population element has a specifiable likelihood, or probability, of being included in the sample. Within this category falls a number of specific procedures, including random probability sampling that parallels random selection procedures discussed in Chapter 3. **Nonprobability sampling** refers to any selection procedure into which the foregoing restriction is not built.

Recall that in experimental research **random selection** is often overlooked, on the assumption that **random assignment** and **internal validity** are more critical considerations for demonstrating cause and effect relationships.

In the case of survey research, the researcher's primary goal is to ascertain and describe the attitudes or behaviors of a population of interest. In this case **external validity** and the ability to draw legitimate inferences about the population at large are central concerns. It is therefore much more imperative that the survey researcher make every possible effort to ensure that the sampling procedures employed yield an adequately representative sample of the population of interest. Often cost considerations or availability limit a researcher's sampling options. In this case researchers may choose to use a nonprobability sampling method; however, they must be mindful of the resulting limitations of their data and any conclusions based on them.

Nonprobability Sampling

Nonprobability sampling can take a variety of forms. We might select the first 100 people we meet on the street (as is typically done in many TV news surveys) or the first 50, 100, or 500 people whose names appear in the telephone book. A second, and more sophisticated, form of nonprobability sampling is **quota sampling**.

In quota sampling, the sample is selected so that it is a "replica" of the population along certain dimensions. If the population at large contains approximately 20% people of color, the sample would be selected in such a fashion that it, too, contains 20% nonwhite subjects. Samples are sometimes drawn so that they replicate the population with respect to race, ethnic background, age, geographic location, and so on.

It is easy to see why nonprobability sampling may yield nonrepresentative samples. Consider the case of accidental sampling where the first 100 people one met on the street are surveyed. The resulting sample might very well differ from the population at large, simply because of their presence on a particular street corner at a particular time of day. For instance, a greater percentage of those questioned between the hours of 9:00 AM and 11:00 AM might be unemployed than would be expected in the general population based on current unemployment rates. Due to the sampling procedure used, the vast majority of people working in 9 to 5 office jobs has been systematically *excluded*!

Selecting individuals from the phone book also presents difficulties. The very wealthy and the very poor are somewhat less likely to appear than middle-class persons. Single women may be somewhat less likely than families to have listed phone numbers. Sampling errors caused by using the phone book or similar directories as a source of potential respondents can be quite serious and extremely embarrassing, as the publishers of a once-famous magazine learned more than 50 years ago.

The *Literary Digest* Debacle.   In 1936 pollsters for the *Literary Digest* (which was then a widely known and highly respected periodical) predicted that Republican Alf Landon would defeat Democrat incumbent Franklin Delano Roosevelt by a landslide, based on a survey of more than two million people. The outcome was indeed a landslide, but favoring Roosevelt rather than Landon! The mistake the pollsters made was to use telephone directories and automobile registration lists as a source for identifying respondents. In 1936 only 35% of all households had telephones (and these tended to be the more affluent families, who have always disproportionately favored the Republicans). The same problem obviously plagued the automobile registration sample, thus yielding the misleading results obtained.

The Problem with Quota Sampling.   Potential biases in the quota sampling procedure are somewhat more difficult to see intuitively, but they are present. The problem lies in the relationship between the *sampled* subpopulation and its parent subpopulation in the overall population at large.

For example, including Asian Americans as 5% of our sample (when the population at large is 5% Asian American) will not ensure that the characteristics of Asian Americans in our sample will correspond to characteristics of Asian Americans in the population. By merely using a quota sample, we might end up surveying a group of Asian Americans who are substantially wealthier (or poorer) than would be true of the overall Asian American population. Thus, although quota sampling procedures may appear reasonable, they are not recommended for drawing inferences to the population at large. To do so confidently, the investigator is advised to turn to a probability sampling procedure.

Probability Sampling

The critical aspect of any probability sampling procedure is that each element in the population has some *specifiable* probability of inclusion in the sample. This is not to say, however, that the probability of each element being represented must be equal to that of other elements. (Although in some cases this will be true.)

Random Probability Sampling.   The major advantage of **random probability sampling** (or simply random sampling) is that the investigator can draw explicit inferences regarding the frequency of certain characteristics in the population in which he or she is interested. This is because in this procedure, every member of the target population has an equal chance of inclusion in the sample drawn for study. Thus, the resulting sample (depending of course on size—see Chapter 3) should be highly representative of the population of interest.

For example, with a random probability sample of about 800 homes, in which it is found that 98% have television sets, the investigator can specify with a particular certainty level (for example, 19 chances in 20) that somewhere between 97% and 99% of all American homes are equipped with televisions.

Stratified Probability Sampling.   **Stratified probability sampling** refers to any procedure in which the population of interest is first divided into segments (or strata) on some characteristic presumed to be pertinent to the purpose of the study. Subjects for study are then drawn randomly from each of the strata, so as to produce a sample that adequately reflects all of the groups that may be expected to respond differently to the survey.

A stratified sampling procedure has several related advantages over a simple random one. Two are particularly important. When the investigator is employing a small sample, a simple random procedure is fairly likely to exclude characteristics of the population that have a low frequency of occurrence. A stratified random sampling procedure will ensure that they have some representation, and thus it will increase the accuracy of the population estimate.

Stratified sampling is especially valuable when the basis for stratification does, in fact, relate to the characteristics being measured. Gender of the respondent may matter little and economic status a lot on certain political issues (such as taxation). In the latter case, estimates to the population will be markedly more accurate if stratified random sampling according to economic status is employed.

Because few investigators will be able to stratify on all the conceivable dimensions, some sort of *a priori* judgment of which characteristics are likely to matter will be required. Typically the outcome of earlier research will serve the investigator in good stead when making such decisions.

Choosing a Sample Size

Whenever sampling is employed, the question arises: How large a sample should be drawn? Clearly, a variety of economic considerations must be brought to bear on this question. *As a general rule, the larger the sample the more precise will be the estimate of the characteristic in the population.* This is especially true in the smaller range of sample size, say below 100.

Techniques of Surveying

There are three major techniques in survey research: the distributed questionnaire, the phone survey, and the systematic interview. The first two are typically chosen for the sake of economy. Whether the economic gain outweighs the cost introduced by other problems is often doubtful, however, as we shall see.

The Distributed Questionnaire. The distributed questionnaire is employed whenever individuals are mailed written materials to be completed, or invited to respond to a series of items about some product in movie theaters, restaurants, and the like. The major disadvantage of this approach is that even if a stratified random sampling procedure is employed in the distribution of the materials, there is a fairly high likelihood of **self-selection bias** among the respondents.

Consider the situation in which audience ratings of a particular film are gathered. All members of the audience might be distributed a questionnaire to complete, with a return rate of 50%. Suppose that *among the returned questionnaires,* the response to the film is overwhelmingly favorable. What can be concluded about the population? In this circumstance it is very likely that the investigator will obtain an inflated estimate of the potential popularity of the film. Individuals who liked the film may have been more likely to complete and return the questionnaire than those who did not.

The same problem should also be apparent in those restaurants that invite their customers to fill out a response card evaluating food and service, or in mailed political surveys. A disproportionately large number of extremely *negative* views can also be picked up through mail research. Clearly, in this situation, a "silent majority" of neutral persons is left out.

Similarly, advertisements indicating that "four out of five doctors" have recommended a particular product are particularly susceptible to an overwhelming positive bias about physicians' approval of the product. Those who did not like it may not have responded at all.

Phone Surveys. Fewer persons will fail to reply to a phone questionnaire than to a distributed questionnaire, but the telephone survey still involves systematic bias regarding a failure to answer particular questions. It is likewise very difficult to make an immediate distinction between accurate and inaccurate replies on the telephone. It has been found, for example, that individuals will provide evaluations (sometimes quite strong ones) of nonexistent television programs when asked to do so over the telephone (Greenberg, 1971, personal communication).

Again, telephone interviews are limited by the biased nature of the available sample. Very poor people may not have telephones at all. These days, more and more people have unlisted numbers. And the proliferation of "junk phone calls" (some of them sales pitches delivered by recorded messages) make many people quite hostile toward calls from persons they do not know.

The Total Design Method. Dillman (1978) has developed an approach to mail and telephone surveys referred to as "the total design method." The basic idea behind the method is that the survey researcher must give close attention to every detail of a proposed survey that might affect responses. For example, among the factors that might increase response to a mail survey are:

1. Advance notification by letter or phone that a questionnaire is being sent.
2. Use of certified mail for delivery.
3. Personalization of correspondence.
4. Offering or enclosing incentives for completing the questionnaire.
5. Emphasis in the cover letter on the social importance of the survey.
6. Inclusion of self-addressed stamped envelope for response return.
7. Well-timed, repeated follow-ups to nonresponders.

Dillman also urges a close analysis of the type of information being sought. This is especially important because people may be particularly sensitive to any preferences implicit in the wording of the questions. Suggesting that the status quo is "about right," for example, may bias respondents in the direction of approval. For example, Schuman and Duncan (1974) reported markedly different outcomes of an attempt to measure U.S. attitudes toward the Vietnam War in 1969, depending on the way the survey question was worded. Here are the two versions and the results:

I. President Nixon has ordered the withdrawal of 25,000 troops from Vietnam in the next 3 months. How do you feel about this—do you think troops should be withdrawn at a faster rate or slower rate?
    42% faster
    20% same as now (not mentioned as an alternative, but accepted if offered)
    16% slower
    13% no opinion

II. In general do you feel the pace at which the President is withdrawing troops is too fast, too slow, or about right?
    28% too slow
    49% about right
    6%   too fast
    18% no opinion
         (as quoted in Dillman, 1978, p. 85)

Systematic Interviews.   Surveying by systematic personal interview is an effective technique for reducing some of the biases we have mentioned. The major advantage of this approach is that respondents' comprehension of and attitude toward the questions can be assessed by the interviewer. Nonetheless, the investigator must still be wary of a variety of potential problems.

Face-to-face interviews are the most expensive way of obtaining questionnaire information. In addition, respondents may respond to the characteristics of the interviewer, such as his/her age, style of dress, and manners, rather than the content of questions alone.

Generally, interviews that follow a systematic sampling plan are likely to provide adequate data, but a large number of checks will be necessary to assure that the plan is carried out. If not constrained formally, interviewers will tend to meet their own quotas by sampling friends, concentrating on areas where there are large numbers of people, and favoring home visits when some potential respondents are more likely to be available than others. Finally, interviewers will tend to avoid upper stories and dilapidated buildings (Selltiz, Jahoda, Deutsch, & Cook, 1959). These problems are all compounded by the fact that interviewers are usually paid by the unit, that is, for each interview secured.

But these disadvantages can be largely overcome, and the personal interview is the preferred technique for gathering survey data. It is possible to arrange systematic "call-backs" to obtain information from potential respondents who are not available for a first interview. It is also possible to obtain a reliability estimate of the information gathered by systematically reinterviewing a subsample of persons. In this event the investigator will get at least some feel for the degree to which the information obtained is reliable from one interview to the next.

In addition to securing reliability data, personal interviews that involve the cooperation of the respondents may also permit obtaining data on the *validity* of the information gathered. Bechtel, Achelpohl, and Akers (1972) were able to compare information obtained from interview and diary data with actual monitoring of the television-watching behavior of a number of respondents. (Interestingly, although Bechtel found rather good agreement between direct observations and interview data, he did find a tendency for persons to overestimate the amount of time they spent watching television.) As LoSciuto (1972) has noted, the quality of interview data may also be improved by following these recommendations:

1. Provide detailed training and explicit instructions concerning the way in which respondents are recruited and the way in which the interview is to be conducted.
2. Ensure means of checking samples of the interviewers' work.
3. Provide incentives for respondents if a good deal of work is required of them, for example, keeping a weekly diary of TV viewing.

APPENDIX B:
STATISTICS REFRESHER

Throughout the text we have had several occasions to mention statistical tests. In this Appendix we briefly review the statistical tests most commonly used by research psychologists. Statistical tests are used for two broad purposes: to describe data (**descriptive statistics**) and to draw inferences from **samples** to **populations** (**inferential statistics**).

DESCRIPTIVE STATISTICS

Although the raw data for each subject in a psychological investigation could be reported individually, it is customary to provide an arithmetical summary of psychological data by statistical presentation. *Descriptive statistics* condense and summarize raw data (e.g., numerical or categorical scores resulting from individual observations of subjects' behavior), so that they can be reviewed easily.

The three most commonly used descriptive statistics in psychological research are the **mean** (commonly abbreviated X or M), the **standard deviation** (abbreviated SD), and the **correlation coefficient** (abbreviated as r). As you may recall from Chapter 3, the mean is simply the arithmetic average of a group of numbers, whereas the standard deviation is an index of the dispersion or "spread" of individual scores around the mean. The square of the standard deviation (abbreviated S^2) is called the **variance**.

The correlation coefficient is a statistic that deals with association; it provides a measure of the direction and magnitude of the relationship between two variables, and ranges from +1.00 to −1.00. Recall that raw correlations cannot be compared directly. Percentage comparisons (e.g., to determine the degree of **shared variance** between two variables) are given by r^2 (the **coefficient of determination**).

INFERENTIAL STATISTICS

A sample, even when randomly selected, is not the same as its parent population. Thus descriptive statistics, such as the mean and standard deviation, might not have the same value (or even differ in the same direction) as they would if they were based on *all* members of the population. Therefore *inferential statistics*, a set of rules and procedures that allow the investigator to determine the likelihood that an observed association or difference in sample data is due to chance, must be employed.

More specifically, after calculating an appropriate inferential statistic, the investigator can state the probability that his/her results were a mere chance occurrence. Such a statement is referred to as a "p" value. The expression "$p < .05$," for example, is a frequently encountered shorthand way of saying that the probability (p) is less than .05 (5 chances in 100) that the mean difference between groups or association between variables occurred by chance. Thus the smaller the p value, the greater is the confidence that can be placed in generalizing from your sample results to the population at large.

Traditionally, psychologists consider results that might occur more often than 5 times in 100 by chance to be nonsignificant (sometimes abbreviated *ns*).

Note that a result described as *non*significant (i.e., with an associated p value *greater* than .05) is not necessarily *insignificant,* but rather one from which we cannot generalize to the population with the traditional level of confidence. Likewise, a result in which we can have very high statistical confidence (e.g., $p <$ .0001) is not necessarily of any theoretical or practical importance.

In order to obtain a p value of the sort described above, the investigator must perform one or more statistical tests. The actual test used depends, in part, upon both the purpose of the investigation and certain mathematical characteristics (or **statistical parameters**) of the variables involved. Below we describe some of the most commonly used inferential statistics.

The *t*-test

The **t-test** (also called Student's t, after its anonymous inventor) is the most commonly used test to evaluate the difference between two sample means. The value of t is calculated using computational procedures that can be found in any standard statistics book. Your computed t value is looked up in a table of critical values for t, arranged according to p values (e.g., .05, .01., .001) for the number of subjects involved.

Analysis of Variance (ANOVA) and the *F*-test

When three or more groups of subjects are to be compared, the **F-test** is used in conjunction with a statistical technique called **analysis of variance (ANOVA)**. Beyond providing a means of simultaneous comparison among several groups, analysis of variance also allows the researcher to assess separately the effects of several different variables that are under investigation simultaneously in a complex design (such as those discussed in Chapter 8).

Consider a hypothetical experiment in which a 2×2 factorial design is used. The purpose of the experiment is to determine the effects of the age and clothing of door-to-door male solicitors on the size of the contributions they are given toward a charitable cause.

The age variable is manipulated by using solicitors who are either 15 or 30, and who "look their age." The clothing variable is manipulated by having the solicitors wear either sweatshirts and jeans or a neat business suit with white shirt and tie. A condominium complex of 48 units in a middle-class neighborhood is selected, and the units are randomly distributed among the solicitors so that 12 units are visited by each of the four solicitor groups. The dependent measure is the amount of contributions collected for a local charity. (All the contributions are actually given to the charity at the end of the study.)

An analysis of variance of the contributions by treatment group is then performed. The analysis produces three F-tests (or F-ratios, as they are sometimes called.) These are tests for the overall effects of the age and clothing variables (usually termed "main effects") and for the **interaction** between these two variables. Recall from Chapter 8 that an interaction is said to occur when the effects of one variable differ at different levels of one or more other variables.

TABLE B-1   ANALYSIS OF VARIANCE SUMMARY TABLE (HYPOTHETICAL DATA)

Source	df	MS	F
Age of solicitor (A)	1	38.76	$38.76/8.80 = 4.41*$
Clothing of solicitor (B)	1	33.84	$33.84/8.80 = 3.85$
A × B Interaction	1	110.51	$110.51/8.80 = 12.56**$
Error	44	8.80	

df = degrees of freedom.

$*p < .05;$ $**p < .01.$

Table B-1 displays the ANOVA summary table for this hypothetical study. The righthand column of the table lists *F* values corresponding to the three effects described above. Note that these values are actually ratios. Specifically, the numerator of each of these *F* values is a function of the difference between (or among) group means on the corresponding variable, and is reflected in the terms appearing under the "mean square" (abbreviated MS) column. The denominator of each ratio is the MS for the error term and primarily reflects the degree of dispersion among all the scores involved in the analysis that was *not* accounted for by the treatments.

The larger the *F*-ratio, the smaller is the probability that the observed differences occurred by chance. As signified by the asterisks, two of the three *F*-ratios in Table B-1 are significant. The main effect for age of solicitor was significant at the .05 level, and the interaction between age and clothing of solicitor was significant at the .01 level. Finally, note that Table B-1 shows the "degrees of freedom" (df) for each *F*-ratio. Degrees of freedom is a complex concept, and we will not attempt a complete explanation here. Briefly, however, the number of degrees of freedom associated with any statistical test is derived, in part, from the number of scores in the sample upon which the test was performed and/or the number of experimental treatments involved.

As is often the case in complex factorial designs, interpretation of ANOVA results involves inspection of the actual cell means and further statistical clarification. The cell means in our hypothetical study are shown in Table B-2. As you can see, the interaction occurred because 30-year-olds in business suits received

TABLE B-2   MEAN CONTRIBUTIONS ACCORDING TO AGE
AND CLOTHING OF SOLICITOR (HYPOTHETICAL DATA)

Age of Solicitor	Clothing	
	Business Suit	Sweats and Jeans
15 years old	$3.05	$2.84
30 years old	$5.20	$2.97

substantially higher donations than 30-year-olds in sweats and jeans; in contrast, clothing made little difference in the contributions received by 15-year-olds. This impression is confirmed by the use of appropriate follow-up statistical tests among the group means (e.g., the Newman-Keuls test), but the specific nature of these tests need not concern us here.

Chi-Square (χ^2)

Technically, statistics such as t and F are not appropriate unless certain assumptions about the population from which your sample was drawn can be met. Moreover, when raw data appear in the form of **categorical ratings** such as "agreement vs. disagreement" or "sharing vs. not sharing," t and F are inapplicable. The chi-square (χ^2) test is often used when working with categorical ratings.

Consider a hypothetical experiment in which the investigators wished to determine the effects on expressed attitudes of having another subject (in fact, a confederate of the investigators) 1) agree with them, 2) mildly disagree with them, or 3) strongly disagree with them on the question of whether marijuana possession should be de-criminalized (on which they had already expressed an opinion). After being exposed to the confederate's views, the subjects were asked to state their opinion on the marijuana de-criminalization question again.

The investigators then compared the frequency with which subjects changed their minds as a result of being exposed to the confederate. The outcome of this hypothetical experiment is shown in Table B-3. If the confederate had no affect on subjects' subsequently expressed attitudes, the percentage of subjects holding to their original opinions would be roughly the same in all three groups. However, as you can see from the table, this was not the case.

Although all of the subjects who heard a confederate agree with them "stuck to their guns," 15% of the subjects exposed to mild disagreement changed their minds, and 96% of those who were exposed to strong disagreement reversed their stated views. A chi-square test revealed that in this instance $\chi^2 = 118.53$, which is significant at the .01 level. From this result it can be concluded that the agreement/disagreement of another person can have a powerful ef-

TABLE B-3 PERCENT OF SUBJECTS CHANGING THEIR STATED VIEWS ON MARIJUANA DECRIMINALIZATION AS A FUNCTION OF BEING EXPOSED TO ANOTHER PERSON'S VIEWS (HYPOTHETICAL DATA)

Confederate's View	N	Percent of Subjects Who Changed Their Stated View
Agreed with subject	53	0%
Mildly disagreed	55	15%
Strongly disagreed	49	96%

N = Number of subjects in each condition.

fect on subjects' stated opinions. (Note, though, that we do not know whether the subjects "really" changed their minds, or whether they were just succumbing to the **demand characteristics of the situation;** see Chapter 10).

COMPUTATION

All statistical procedures involve using computational formulas, many of them rather complex. These procedures, the **mathematical assumptions** underlying each test, and tables for determining p values, can be found in virtually all elementary statistics books. Before using any test, it is important to review the assumptions underlying it and the effects of violating these assumptions. Some statistical tests are **robust**, meaning that the p values they yield are valid even when the assumptions have not been fully met. Other tests are not robust; if you use them inappropriately you will threaten the **statistical conclusion validity** of your findings (see Chapter 6).

Statistical Software

Early psychologists were forced to do their computations by hand, aided (at best) with crude mechanical adding machines and sometimes an abacus. Today most computations are done with the aid of statistical packages tailored for computer use. Among the most popular packages used by psychologists today are Statistical Package for the Social Sciences (SPSS), Statistical Analysis System (SAS), BioMeDical Computer Programs (BMDP), and Minitab.

New packages and new versions of older packages appear several times a year; they are becoming more and more "user friendly", and many offer "hotlines" you can call for assistance. In addition to their ability to perform a wide variety of statistical tests, many of these programs can also produce tables and graphs of your data. Programs for personal computers are advertised monthly in the American Psychological Association's newspaper, the *APA Monitor*, and are also available through many computer stores and magazines.

Key Terms
    DESCRIPTIVE STATISTICS
    SAMPLES
    POPULATIONS
    INFERENTIAL STATISTICS
    MEAN
    STANDARD DEVIATION
    CORRELATION COEFFICIENT
    VARIANCE
    SHARED VARIANCE

COEFFICIENT OF DETERMINATION
STATISTICAL PARAMETERS
t-TEST
F-TEST
ANALYSIS OF VARIANCE (ANOVA)
INTERACTION
CATEGORICAL RATINGS
DEMAND CHARACTERISTICS OF THE SITUATION
MATHEMATICAL ASSUMPTIONS
ROBUST
STATISTICAL CONCLUSION VALIDITY

GLOSSARY

A Priori Matching. Matching of subjects on some variable before exposure to an experimental manipulation.

A-B Design. A design in which subjects are observed before and then after an experimental treatment.

A-B-A Design. A design in which subjects are observed before and after a treatment and then again after a return to baseline (no treatment) conditions.

A-B-A-B Design. A design like the A-B-A design with the addition of a second administration of treatment and subsequent observation.

A-B-C-B Design. A design in which two different treatments are used (B and C) after an initial observation period, with a return to the first treatment after introduction of treatment number two.

Accepting the Null Hypothesis. Concluding that no difference exists (in the population of interest) based on finding no differences between two groups or treatment conditions. In most circumstances this conclusion is *not* logically justifiable.

Accessible Population. The population to which the researcher has access; the available population.

Active Placebo. In an experiment, a substance or procedure not expected to have any effect on the dependent variable of interest, but which has irrelevant side effects that make it seem to be a real drug or legitimate treatment.

Analysis of Variance (ANOVA). A statistical procedure that divides the total variance of a set of scores into its component parts.

Antagonistic Interaction. A situation in which the *direction* of the effect of one treatment depends on the level of one or more other treatments.

Archives. The ongoing and continuing records of an institution or society.

Associations. Observed relationships between variables.

Automation. The use of mechanical, computerized, or other devices in research to minimize (error) variability (or bias) introduced by human experimenters.

Baseline. Data from an untreated group or condition used as a reference point for assessing treatment effects.

Behavioroid Measures. Measures which re-

258

quire subjects to commit to a particular action (which they in fact will not ultimately be called on to perform).

Best Possible Comparisons. An alternative to the use of placebo controls, in which a new treatment is compared with the "best possible" alternative treatment to demonstrate its effectiveness.

Between-Subjects Comparisons. Designs in which separate groups of subjects are compared after one or more groups receives an experimental treatment.

Biased Sample. A sample that does not adequately reflect the characteristics of the population of interest.

Blind. As in blind experimenters; kept ignorant of.

Blind Experimenter. An experimenter who is kept ignorant of the treatment group assignment of particular subjects. This procedure minimizes the risk of experimenter bias.

Blind to Group Assignment. Same as blind experimenter.

Block Designs. Designs in which subjects are first grouped on some presumably relevant variable, and then randomly assigned to treatment groups.

Carryover Effects. Persisting consequences, resulting from a treatment, that affect subjects' responses to one or more subsequent treatments; practice and fatigue are common carryover effects.

Case Study. Intensive study of a single individual; also called a case history.

Categorical Ratings. Data that are composed of subjects' assignments to categories predetermined by the investigator.

Catalytic Interaction. A situation in which two or more treatments are effective only when they occur together.

Causal Analysis. An analysis of cause and effect, usually based on analysis of several possible causal chains.

Causal Chain. An analysis of causal links among three or more variables, e.g., A > B > C.

Causal Relationships. Relationships in which changes in one or more variables result in changes in another variable.

Census. A survey in which the entire population of interest is included.

Central Tendency. A number calculated to represent the most "typical" score in a set of scores.

Changing Criterion Design. A design in which the criterion required for reinforcement (or punishment) changes progressively to become increasingly stringent over trials.

Classificatory Variable. A variable beyond the control of the experimenter on which subjects are grouped (such as age or gender).

Closed-ended Item. An item that forces respondents to choose between or among alternatives provided by the researcher.

Clinical Trial. A test of the effectiveness of a treatment, usually with one or a few subjects, using a simple A-B design.

Coefficient of Determination. r^2; a statistic reflecting the variance overlap (shared variance) between two variables.

Cohort. Any group that passes through a set of experiences or institutions at the same time.

Cohort Differences. Differences observed between two or more cohort groups.

Compensatory Equalization. A situation in which untreated individuals or groups obtain something "equally good" for themselves.

Compensatory Rivalry. The situation in which an untreated group works extra hard to see to it that the expected superiority of the treatment is not demonstrated.

Component Control Comparisons. A technique in which a treatment is broken down into its component parts, and the components are then experimentally compared with one another and with the full treatment.

Confidentiality. A researcher's responsibility to protect subjects from sharing of information gathered about them without their knowledge or consent.

Construct Validity. Validation of the meaning or interpretation placed on a theoretical construct, usually after observing a network of relationships.

Constructive Replication. Replicating an experiment so as to preserve the theoretically essential features while varying features presumed to be irrelevant.

Content Validity. The extent to which a test or measurement instrument samples from the population of items of interest.

Contiguous Cohorts. Cohorts that pass through an institution or experience in immediately adjacent time periods.

Contributory Causal Relationship. A relationship in which one variable increases the likelihood of occurrence of another variable.

Control Group. A group employed for comparison in experiments that is *not* subjected to the experimental manipulation.

Controlled Accretion. The collection of traces or remains left by some activity of interest *after* the environment has been specifically prepared to collect them.

Controlled Erosion. A measure of wear used to assess activity level *after* the environment has been specifically prepared to measure it.

Controlled Experimental Situation. A situation in which all extraneous variables have been maintained at a constant level so as to isolate the effects of the independent variable.

CORIHS Committees. *C*ommittee *O*n *R*esearch *I*nvolving *H*uman *S*ubjects; committees made up of local people who evaluate the safety and importance of research on human subjects before it is approved to be conducted.

Correlation. The co- or joint relationship between (or among) two or more variables.

Correlation Coefficient. A numerical index of the magnitude and direction of a correlation; it can range from +1.00 to -1.00.

Correlation Matrix. A table of correlations in which the rows and columns list the variables and the entries display the correlations between each possible pair of variables.

Cost-Restricted Sampling. Sampling that is conducted on a limited subset of the population of interest because of practical constraints.

Counter Demand. Information provided to subjects to help minimize the threat of demand on the outcome of research. Counter demand often involves telling subjects to expect something other than the actual antici-

pated results, or not to expect any effects for a period of time exceeding that delay actually expected by the researcher.

Counterbalancing. The practice of running subjects in a repeated measures design so as to balance the order in which treatments are experienced, e.g., order A-B and order B-A.

Covert Assessment. Assessment or measurement carried out without the knowledge of the subjects involved.

Criterion Validity. Validation of a measure based on its association with another (presumably related) measure.

Criterion Variable. In regression, the variable to be predicted.

Cross-Sectional Studies. Studies that look at individuals of several different ages at approximately the same point in calendar time.

Curvilinear. A shape that is not straight and linear, but appears curved.

Curvilinear Relationship. A relationship that when plotted resembles a curved rather than a straight line.

Debriefing. The explanation provided to subjects at the conclusion of their participation as to the purpose and outcome of the research.

Deception. The practice of providing false or misleading information to subjects in the course of their participation in research.

Deduction. Reasoning from general principles to specific conclusions; *cf* induction.

Deductive Reasoning. Reasoning that follows a deductive path.

Dehoaxing. Information provided to subjects in the course of debriefing that reveals to them the nature of any deception to which they were exposed in the course of participation.

Demand Characteristics. Hints and cues in a research situation that influence subjects' perceptions of what is expected of them.

Demographic Data. Information describing the personal characteristics of individuals or groups (e.g., gender, age, socio-economic status, etc.)

Dependent Measure. The measure employed to assess changes on the dependent variable.

Dependent Variable. The variable assessed by the researcher after (and assumed to be dependent on) manipulation of the independent variable.

Desensitization.   An aspect of the debriefing process in which subjects are encouraged to express any negative feelings or concerns that may have been generated as a result of their research participation, especially in situations where subjects may have been encouraged to behave in ways of which they themselves disapprove or find distressing.

Developmental Trends.   Consistent, age-related changes in behavior.

Differential Attrition.   Differences in the number or characteristics of subjects who drop out of a study that are related to the treatment they received.

Differential Incidence.   A difference in the rate of occurrence of some phenomenon in groups that have or have not had a particular experience or treatment.

Diffusion.   The spread of treatment effects from treated to untreated groups.

Directionality Problem.   The inability to determine with confidence which of two related variables causes the other.

Double Blind Experiment.   In medicine, an experiment in which neither the physician nor the patients know who is getting the "real medication" and who is getting the placebo.

Ecological Validity.   The degree to which research results can be generalized to all the environmental contexts of interest.

Effect Size.   An index of the magnitude (as opposed to the statistical significance) of any given effect.

Empirically Blind.   The situation in which the experimenters are kept ignorant of the working hypotheses of the researchers. This practice helps to minimize the risk of experimenter bias influencing results.

Empiricism.   The practice of acquiring knowledge through direct observation.

Erosion Measures.   Measures that rely on naturally occurring wear to estimate use or activity level.

Error Variance.   Variability generated by unknown or uncontrolled factors.

Ex Post Facto Matching.   Matching of subjects undertaken *after* completion of research or data collection.

Experimental Hypothesis.   The hypothesis being tested; in null hypothesis testing, it is often referred to as H_1.

Experimenter Bias Effect.   Research outcomes influenced by the experimenter's belief about the probable outcome of the investigation.

Experimenter Characteristics.   Aspects of the experimenter's appearance or behavior that influence the data collected in research.

Experimenter Role.   Behavior of the experimenter that is influenced by the fact that he or she is in the role of experimenter.

External Validity.   The degree to which conclusions can be generalized.

Extreme Groups Technique.   The practice of blocking subjects into groups by employing only those subjects with the most extreme scores (in either direction) on the blocking variable (for example the highest and lowest 10% on a given measure).

Factorial Experiment.   An experiment in which two or more independent variables are manipulated; it permits looking at the effects of each experimental variable and the interaction(s) among them.

Falsification.   The practice of attempting to *dis*prove, rather than prove phenomena experimentally.

Fatigue Effect.   Any deterioration in performance due merely to becoming tired, bored, or the like.

Feedback Loop.   A causal chain in which one variable influences another variable, which in turn then affects the first variable.

Field Setting.   Any naturally occurring setting or environment in which research is undertaken.

File Drawer Problem.   The possibility that null results are simply filed away, thereby biasing the published literature toward Type I errors.

Forced-choice Inventory.   Questionnaires in which respondents must choose between alternatives provided by the researcher.

Free Random Assignment.   Assignment of subjects to groups based on some randomization procedure and not constrained by the need for matching.

Fully Randomized Designs. Designs in which subjects are assigned randomly to each cell; often contrasted with block and repeated measures designs.

Haphazard Sampling. Sampling done in such a way that every possible opportunity to sample the population is exploited.

Hierarchical Regression Model. A model in which the researcher first ranks the variables (based on theoretical considerations) to be entered into a regression equation.

History. Any environmental event other than the treatment of interest that occurs between successive measurements or tests.

Homogeneous Groups. Groups of subjects which are highly similar on some or all variables.

Hypotheses. Propositions to be tested through research.

Hypothesis Testing. The logical and empirical process through which hypotheses are tested.

Impressionistic Modal Sampling. Selecting several different samples judged to be typical of the various population subgroups of interest.

Independent Variable. The condition or stimulus manipulated in an experiment.

Individual Differences. Pre-existing differences observed between subjects on a variable of interest.

Induction. Reasoning from particular facts to a general conclusion.

Inductive Reasoning. Reasoning based on an inductive approach, and moving from specific facts to a general conclusion.

Inferences. Conclusions about the existence of relationships based on indirect observation.

Informed Consent. The ethical requirement that subjects have sufficient information about a research project to make an informed decision as to whether they choose to participate.

Instrument Change. Any change in the characteristics of a measurement instrument over time.

Inter-Item Reliability. A measure of the degree to which items on a test are correlated or measure the same thing.

Inter-Rater Reliability. A measure of the level of agreement of observations between two or more independent observers.

Interaction. An outcome in a factorial design in which the effect of one factor is not the same at every level of one or more other factors.

Internal Validity. Validity of empirical statements dealing with the question of whether X (as manipulated) causes a change in Y (as measured).

Interrupted Time Series Designs. Designs in which observations are made, a treatment is introduced, and observations are made again.

Interval Scale. A scale of measurement in which the numbers represent equal intervals, e.g., on such a scale going from 2 to 3 has the same meaning as going from 9 to 10.

Investigator Role. The role of designing, analyzing, interpreting, and reporting research results.

IRB. (Institutional Review Board) A committee of local people who review proposed research for safety and value before it is approved to be conducted (see also CORIHS committee).

"John Henry Effect." See compensatory rivalry.

Laboratory Setting. Any environment that is devoted exclusively to the conduct of research and can be discriminated by subjects from the natural environment.

Legitimization. Any efforts aimed at making a socially undesirable attitude or behavior more acceptable.

Likert Scale Format. A scale that allows for intensity ratings.

Literature Search. A process of sifting through the body of published material in an effort to identify all that is relevant to a given topic.

Local History. Any environmental event other than the treatment of interest that has occurred for only some groups.

Logical Positivism. A philosophy of science in which theoretical variables are defined by the operations employed to represent them.

Longitudinal Studies. Studies that follow a group of individuals over time to observe age-related changes.

Low Statistical Power. Limited ability to detect "real" effects in research. Low statistical power often results from inadequate samples, or a high degree of error variance in the measures of interest.

Manipulated Variable. That variable which is under the control of the experimenter, and manipulated in an attempt to detect an effect on the dependent measure.

Matched Random Assignment. Assignment of subjects to groups using randomization procedures *after* subjects are matched (in pairs or groups) on some variable presumed to be related to the variable of interest in the research.

Matching. Pairing of subjects on a variable presumed to be related to the variable of interest in such a way that subjects with very similar scores are paired and then members of each pair can be assigned to groups. (This procedure helps to ensure that groups will begin roughly equated on the matched variable, thus reducing its influence on outcome measures.)

Mathematical Assumptions (of Statistical Tests). Mathematical characteristics attributed to a population in order to test samples. Statistical tests differ in the mathematical assumptions that underlie them. Violation of these assumptions constitutes a threat to statistical conclusion validity.

Maturation. Any changes in behavior over time due to the subject's simply becoming older, wiser, stronger, or the like.

Mean. The arithmetic average of a set of numbers, the mean is a common measure of central tendency.

Measurement Error. That portion of any score due to random or irrelevant factors.

Median. That score above which and below which lay fifty percent of a distribution of scores. The median is a measure of central tendency, and is less affected by extreme scores than the mean.

Median Split. Dividing a set of scores at the median to create a classificatory variable for a mixed design.

Meta-Analysis. Name given to any set of systematic rules for combining and evaluating a collection of independent replications or partial replications.

Method of Agreement. One of Mill's criteria for determining causality, in which two variables are compared so that if (all else being equal) one occurs, then so does the other.

Method of Differences. One of Mill's criteria for determining causality, in which two variables are compared so that if one does not occur, neither does the other.

Mixed Design. A research design that combines both between and within subjects comparisons.

Mode. A measure of central tendency, the mode is the most frequently occurring score in a set of data.

Moderate-Sized Sample. Samples which are selected so as to be large enough to ensure representativeness, but not so large as to yield statistically significant findings based on trivial real effects.

Multiple Baseline. Measurement of a number of target variables over a period of time in which treatments are introduced sequentially, while effects on all variables (some presumably unrelated) continue to be assessed.

Multiple Discrete Leveling. Dividing a set of scores into three or more levels to create a classificatory variable for a mixed design.

Multiple Pretests. The use of two or more pretests before the introduction of a treatment.

Multiple Regression. A technique for weighting, combining, and ordering two or more predictor variables nonredundantly into a mathematical equation.

Natural Accretion. The depositing of traces or remains after some activity of interest.

Naturalistic Observation. Observations made in a natural or field setting, without any intrusion by the researcher.

Necessary and Sufficient Causal Relationship. A relationship in which one variable occurs if and only if another variable occurs.

Necessary But Not Sufficient Causal Relationship. A relationship in which one condition must be present for the other to occur, but the first condition is not in itself causal.

Nominal Scale. A scale of measurement with no underlying quantitative metric; numbers in such scales merely serve as labels rather than as quantities which can be compared.

Nomological Net. A network of empirical relationships used to validate or support a theoretical construct.

Nonequivalent Control Group Designs. A class of quasi-experiments in which assignment to groups was not done randomly; the possibility always remains that the treated and control groups were not equivalent on some variable other than the treatment of interest.

Nonprobability Sampling. Any sampling procedure that does not include an explicit statement of the likelihood of inclusion of various population elements.

Null Hypothesis. The hypothesis of "no difference," created as a means of logically testing actual research hypotheses.

Null Hypothesis Testing. The practice in research of testing the assumption of no differences (rather than attempting to test for actual differences).

Open-ended Item. Any question or statement that allows respondents to answer in their own words.

Operational Definition. A unique specification of the meaning of a term as equivalent to a single set of operations.

Operationalism. The practice of defining theoretical variables by the operations used to represent them.

Ordinal Scale. A scale of measurement in which the numbers represent a rank ordering.

Overt Assessment. Assessment conducted openly, with the knowledge of the subject.

Pact of Ignorance. The tendency of both subject and researcher to behave as if the experimental deception was effective, due to the investment of time and effort of each party in the research enterprise.

Paradigms. The "world views" and implicit assumptions underlying a theory or theoretical outlook.

Partial Correlation. The correlation between X and Y after the effects of Z have been removed statistically.

Partial Regression Coefficients. Regression coefficients in which the effects of one or more prior variables have been removed statistically.

Pecking Orders. Power hierarchies that evolve in groups (named for the observed ritual in chickens of pecking at one another to achieve dominance).

Physical Traces. Evidence of a behavior left behind that can be detected later.

Placebo. Any pharmaceutical or treatment assumed by the researcher to be inert.

Placebo Effect. Real or apparent changes produced by the administration of a placebo.

Plausible Rival Hypotheses. Any explanation of an effect that might possibly account for it other than that one favored by the researcher.

Population. Any well defined collection of objects, events, or organisms.

Population of Ultimate Interest. That population to which a researcher wishes to generalize conclusions drawn from research.

Population Validity. The degree to which research results can be generalized to the populations of ultimate interest.

Post-experimental Questionnaire. A questionnaire administered at the close of participation in a study to determine subjects' perceptions of the research and/or the effectiveness of experimental manipulations.

Posttest-Only Control Group Design. A research design in which no pretest is used; comparison between the control and experimental group is based on only one observation occurring *after* the administration of the experimental treatment.

Potential for Falsifiability. The degree to which a prediction is "risky," and thus likely to be disproved under close examination.

Power. Sensitivity of a statistical procedure or research design for detecting differences or effects when they are in fact present.

Practice Effect. Any improvement resulting merely from experience with a task or procedure.

Predictor Variable. In regression, the variable used to predict the criterion variable.

Preprints. Copies of a manuscript that are distributed to interested parties in advance of its actual publication.

Pretest-Posttest Control Group Design. A research design in which both the control and experimental groups are observed twice: once before and once after the administration of the experimental treatment.

Pretest-Posttest Nonequivalent Peer Control Group Design. A design in which two groups not generated by random assignment are observed both before and after one of them has received the treatment of interest.

Prediction. Accurate anticipation of future or as yet unobserved events.

Principle of Aggregation. The principle which states that the sum or average of a set of multiple measurements has less random error than a single measurement.

Privileged Frame of Reference. The underlying assumption by some researchers that their perspective on reality is universal, and shared by all other observers. Einstein concluded that there is no privileged frame of reference, and that all observation is relative.

Prospective Accounts. Ongoing reports of behavior that are collected over time as events occur.

Publication Lag. The time elapsing between the submission of a completed manuscript and its actual publication (often as much as a year or more depending on the length and type of manuscript).

Quasi-Experiment. Any study that employs experimental units of analysis and manipulated treatments but without comparing groups formed by random assignment.

Quota Sampling. Sampling that attempts to mirror the existing ratio of various population elements.

Random Assignment. Assigning subjects to treatments or groups such that each subject has an equal likelihood of being assigned to any treatment or group and the assignment of any one individual does not influence the assignment of any other individual.

Random Error Variance. Variability in a set of data that cannot be accounted for by the researcher.

Random Measurement Error. Measurement error resulting from chance factors that vary from one observation to the next.

Random Sample. A sample drawn in such a way that (1) every member of the population has an equal chance of being selected for the sample, and (2) the selection of any one member of the population does not influence the chances of any other member being selected.

Random Selection. The practice of choosing subjects from the population of interest in such a way that all members have an equal chance of being chosen.

Random Time Series Single-Subject Design. A design in which observations are made, a treatment is introduced at some randomly chosen point in time, and further observations are made.

Range. One measure of spread or variability of a set of scores, the range is equal to the largest score minus the smallest score in the set, plus one.

Ratio Scale. A scale of measurement in which the numbers represent equal intervals and the scale has a meaningful zero point. In such scales ratios can be compared, e.g., a ratio of 2 to 1 has the same meaning as a ratio of 16 to 8.

Rationalism. An approach to acquiring knowledge that depends solely on reason.

Reactive Measures. Measures that are influenced by the act of measurement itself.

Reduction Sentence. A statement defining a theoretical variable in terms of a specific operationalization.

Refereed Journal. Any publication in which peers are called upon to evaluate the worth of a manuscript before its acceptance for publication.

Regression. (1) A numerical measure of association between (or among) variables in which predictor and criterion variables are specified. (2) A tendency for individuals with unusually high or low scores to go back toward the mean on subsequent testing; also called statistical regression.

Regression Analysis. A procedure used to predict one variable, the criterion, from one or more other variables, the predictor(s).

Regression Coefficient. An element in the regression equation.

Regression Constant. An element in the regression equation.

Regression Discontinuity Design. A quasi-experimental design in which a discontinuity ("break") in the regression line is used to assess a possible treatment effect.

Regression Equation. The equation used in linear regression analysis.

Regression Line.. The line on a graph showing predicted values of Y, based on observed values of X.

Reliability. Repeatability or consistency.

Reliability of Measurement. The degree to which measurements are stable (e.g., free of measurement error) over repeated measurements.

Repeated Measurement. The use of multiple observations on the same subjects (usually for comparison against their own scores) in a within-subjects design. Observations are often made before and after the introduction of an experimental treatment.

Repeated Measures Designs. A research design that includes some repeated measurement of the same subjects for within-subjects comparisons.

Repeated Testing. A threat to internal validity, in which a person's scores on a test change simply as a result of having been tested before.

Representative Sample. A sample that adequately reflects the characteristics of the population of interest.

Representativeness. The degree to which a sample reflects the population of ultimate interest.

Resentful Demoralization. The situation in which individuals in an untreated or control group become less efficient, productive, or motivated because of feelings of resentment toward those in the treated group(s) or toward the experimenters.

Response Acquiescence. The response set in which respondents tend to agree with items regardless of their content.

Response Deviation. The response set in which subjects tend to give unusual responses to items.

Response Dissension. The response set in which respondents tend to disagree with items regardless of their contents.

Response Sets. Any tendency for respondents to respond to the form rather than the content of an item.

Retest Reliability. The degree of association between scores on the first and second administrations of a test.

Retrospective Accounts. Reports of *past* behavior provided by a subject.

Rival Hypothesis. Any explanation that competes with the account put forth by a researcher.

Robust. Somewhat insensitive to minor deviations—used specially in terms of statistical tests relatively unaffected by violations of their underlying mathematical assumptions.

Role Behavior. Specific behavior dictated by the current circumstances of a person.

Rules of Membership. Those specifications used to define a population of interest.

Sample. A subset of a population, usually selected with the aim of generalizing to one or more populations.

Sample of Convenience. A sample chosen because it was easily accessible.

Scales of Measurement. A term for the scheme in which the scores used in research are described in terms of their correspondence to the real number system. The four scales of measurement are nominal, ordinal, interval, and ratio.

Scatter Plot. A graphic depiction of a set of data in which points are plotted against two perpendicular axes representing variables of interest.

Science. A body of knowledge, or a specific method of acquiring knowledge.

Scores. Numbers assigned to observations.

Selection Bias. Any systematic difference between comparison groups other than experiencing the treatment of interest.

Selection-Maturation. Any changes in the amount of difference between groups over time due to the groups developing at different rates.

Self-Fulfilling Prophecy. A type of bias in which observers or experimenters act so as to bring about the outcome or results they expect to obtain.

Self-Identified Clinical Populations. Subjects voluntarily presenting for treatment in a clinical setting.

Self-report. Subjects' statements, oral or written, about their attitudes, behaviors, or experiences.

Self-selection Bias. Distortion introduced through the study of volunteer subjects only. (See also Volunteer Bias.)

Shared Variance. Variance within a data set that can be accounted for by more than one variable.

Simulated Control Group Design. Quasi-experimental design in which two groups drawn randomly from the same population are compared at the point when one has already been exposed to the treatment, but the other has not yet been exposed to it.

Single Blind. A research strategy in which subjects do not know to which treatment group they have been assigned.

Single-Subject Designs. Research designs that employ only one subject, but attempt to demonstrate causal relationships through careful observation under controlled circumstances.

Social Desirability. The response set in which subjects tend to give the most socially acceptable responses to items.

Split-Half Reliability. Association between the scores on two halves of a test.

Spontaneous Remission. Improvement due simply to the passage of time.

Standard Deviation. A measure of the variability in a set of scores; the square root of the variance.

Standardization. The practice of assuring that all subjects within a group receive exactly the same treatment, by holding every aspect of their treatment constant.

Statistical Conclusion Validity. The validity of a conclusion about whether two or more numerical values (e. g., group means) are statistically different; see statistical significance.

Statistical Power. The ability of statistical tests to detect actual effects within a given research design.

Statistical Regression. The tendency for extreme scores in a distribution to move (i.e., regress) toward the mean on subsequent testing due to shifts in the distribution of measurement error.

Statistical Significance. A numerical index of the probability that a particular difference occurred by chance; sometimes expressed as or called a "p value."

Statistical Tests. Tests employed by researchers to aid in making inferences about the population of interest based on observations made on samples.

Statistically Significant Difference. A difference between observed groups that would be extremely unlikely in the absence of a "true" existing difference.

Stratified Probability Sampling. Sampling procedures that randomly select subjects from within specified segments (strata) of the population of ultimate interest.

Subject Role. A subject's understanding of the expectations placed on her/him as a research participant.

Sufficient But Not Necessary Causal Relationship. A relationship in which one variable is sufficient to cause a change in another variable, but need not be present for the effect (other variables might also be sufficient).

Sufficient Cause. An event that is sufficient, by itself, to produce a particular effect or outcome.

Survey. A research strategy aimed at sampling broadly in an effort to characterize the attitudes, opinions, or preferences of a sample through the use of questionnaires.

Syllogism. A logical tool, consisting of a major premise, a minor premise, and a conclusion based on the combination of the two.

Synergistic Interaction. A situation in which the effects of one variable are altered or exaggerated by the presence of another variable.

Systematic Variance. Extent to which the presence or absence of an experimental manipulation causes the scores in the groups to depart from the overall mean of the distribution of the combined scores; a measure of treatment effect.

Systematically Unmatching. Reducing the similarity of subjects on one variable by attempting to match (or increase similarity) on another.

Temporal Precedence. Preceding in time; in causal relationships a cause must logically precede an effect to be plausible.

Temporal Validity. The degree to which research results can be generalized across time.

Terminative Interaction. A situation in which two or more treatments are each effective, but their effectiveness is not increased or enhanced when they are combined.

Test. Any systematic procedure for making and scoring observations.

Test Score. The numerical reading of a measurement instrument.

Test Validity. The degree to which a test measures what it purports to measure.

Theoretical Model. An explicit model of the relationships expected among a set of variables.

Theoretical Modeling. The process of generating an explicit model of the relationships among a set of variables.

Theoretical Construct. Any entity posited to be meaningful by a theory; often simply called a construct (CON-struct).

Theoretical (Construct) Validity. The degree to which a research result is correctly interpreted or the degree to which the formulation of a construct is "true."

Third Variable. Any variable that might serve to explain an observed association between X and Y.

Third Variable Problem. The problem in correlational research of the possibility of any observed relationship between two variables being caused by yet another (unobserved) variable.

Time Series. Any procedure that examines behavior over time.

Treatment. Any manipulation employed in research.

True Experiment. A research design in which a control group is employed and groups are formed through random assignment.

True Score. That portion of any score due to the real characteristics of the thing being measured (as opposed to measurement error).

True Zero Point. On a ratio scale of measurement, the absolute absence of the property in question.

Truncated Range. A range of scores that does not represent the full range of the population of scores, but only a restricted segment of it.

Type I Error. Rejecting the null hypothesis when it is in fact true.

Type II Error. Failing to reject the null hypothesis when it is in fact false.

Unobtrusive Measures. Measures that can be taken without interfering with natural ongoing behavior.

Validity. Correctness or truth; measuring what one wants to or purports to measure.

Validity of Scientific Inferences. The degree to which an inference drawn from research is justified by logic and data.

Variability. The degree of spread in a set of scores.

Variance. A numerical index of the variability or "scatter" in a set of scores.

Variance Statistic. A measure of variability within a set of data, specifically, a measure of the average deviation of scores from the overall mean of scores.

Verification. Concluding that a particular hypothesis has been confirmed by research.

Verification Principle. The principle that the purpose of research is the confirmation of hypotheses.

Visual Analog Scale. A scale that allows respondents to mark a line or other visual representation to indicate the extent, intensity, or certainty of their feelings about an item.

Volunteer Bias. The tendency of volunteers to be different from the general population of ultimate interest.

Within-Subjects Comparison. Comparisons made using repeated measurement of the same subjects over time, or before and after the administration of treatments.

REFERENCES

ALLEN, V. L., & LEVINE, J. M. (1969). Consensus and conformity. *Journal of Experimental Social Psychology, 55,* 389–399.

American Psychological Association Ethics Committee. (1992). APA's code of ethics and conduct and principles of psychologists. *American Psychologist, 47,* 1597–1611.

ANASTASI, A. (1968). *Psychological testing* (3d ed.). New York: Macmillan.

ASCH, S. (1951). Effects of group pressure upon the modification and distortion of judgment. In H. Guetzkow (Ed.), *Groups, leadership and men* (pp. 177–190). Pittsburgh: Carnegie Press.

ATKINSON, J. W., & FEATHER, N. T. (1966). *A theory of achievement motivation.* New York: Wiley.

ATKINSON, J. W., & LITWIN, G. H. (1960). Achievement motive and test anxiety conceived as motive to approach success and avoid failure. *Journal of Abnormal and Social Psychology, 60,* 52–63.

BAKER, S. (1977). *The practical stylist.* New York: Harper & Row.

BANDURA, A. (1963). What TV violence can do to your child. *Look,* October 22, 1963, 46–52.

BARLOW, D. H., & HERSEN, M. (1984). *Single case experimental designs.* Elmsford, NY: Pergamon Press.

BAUMRIND, D. (1964). Some thoughts on ethics of research: After reading Milgram's "Behavioral study of obedience." *American Psychologist, 19,* 421–423.

BECHTEL, R. B., ACHELPOHL, C., & AKERS, R. (1972). Correlates between observed behavior and questionnaire responses on television viewing. In E. A. Rubinstein, G. A. Comstock & J. P. Murray (Eds.), *Television and social behavior,* (Vol. IV: *Television in day-to-day life: Patterns of use.*) Washington, D.C.: United States Government Printing Office.

BEECHER, H. K. (1966). Ethics and clinical research, *New England Journal of Medicine, 274,* 1354–1360.

BOFFEY, P. M. (1985, January 8). Study reported to tighten link of aspirin and Reyés Syndrome, *New York Times.*

BOGATZ, G. A., & BALL, S. (1972). *The second year of Sesame Street: A continuing evaluation.* Princeton, N.J.: Educational Testing Service.

CAMPBELL, D. T., & ROSS, H. L. (1968). The Connecticut crackdown on speeding: Time-series data in quasi-experimental analysis. *Law and Society Review, 3*, 33–53.

CAMPBELL, D. T., & STANLEY, J. C. (1966). *Experimental and quasi-experimental designs for research.* Chicago: Rand McNally.

CHAFFEE, S. H., & MCLEOD, J. M. (1971). Adolescents, parents, and television violence. Paper presented at symposium "The early window: The role of television in childhood," American Psychological Association Convention, Washington, D.C.

CHAPIN, F. S. (1955). *Experimental designs in sociological research.* New York: Harper & Row.

CHRISTENSEN, L. (1988). Deception in psychological research: When is its use justified? *Personality and Social Psychology Bulletin, 14,* 664–675.

CLARK, K. E. et al. (1967). Privacy and behavioral research: Preliminary summary of the report of the panel on privacy and behavioral research. *Science, 155*, 535–538.

COLLINS, F. L., KUHN, F., & KING, G. D. (1979). Variables affecting subjects' ethical ratings of proposed experiments. *Psychological Reports, 44,* 155–164.

COOK, T. D., APPLETON, H., CONNER, R. F., SHAFFER, A., TOMKIN, G., & WEBER, S. J. (1975). *Sesame Street Revisited.* New York: Russell Sage Foundation.

COOK, T. D., & CAMPBELL, D. T. (1979). *Quasi-experimentation.* Chicago: Rand McNally.

COOK, T. D., GRUDER, C. L., HENNIGAN, K. M., & FLAY, B. R. (1978). *The history of the sleeper effect: Some logical pitfalls in accepting the null hypothesis.* Unpublished manuscript, North-western University, Evanston, IL.

COSTA, P. T., & MCCRAE, R. R. (1992). *NEO-PI-R professional manual.* Odessa, FL: Psychological Assessment Resources.

DILLMAN, D. A. (1978). *Mail and telephone surveys: The total design method.* New York: John Wiley.

DUSH, D. M., HIRT, M. L., & SCHROEDER, H. (1983). Self-statement modification with adults: a meta-analysis. *Psychological Bulletin, 94,* 408–422.

EDWARDS, A. L. (1953). *Manual for Edwards Personal Preference Schedule.* New York: Psychological Corporation.

EDWARDS, A. L. (1957). *The social desirability variable in personality research.* New York: Dryden.

EIBL-EIBESFELDT, I. (1989). *Human ethology.* New York: Aldine de Gruyter.

FANCHER, R. E. (1990). *Pioneers of psychology, 2nd ed.* New York: Norton.

FINDLEY, M. J., & COOPER, H. M. (1983). Locus of control and academic achievement: A literature review. *Journal of Personality and Social Psychology, 44,* 419–427.

FRANK, J. D. (1961). *Persuasion and healing.* New York: Schocken Books.

FREEDMAN, J. L., WALLINGTON, S. A., & BLESS, E. (1967). Compliance without pressure: The effect of guilt. *Journal of Personality and Social Psychology, 7,* 117–124.

GALTON, F. (1872). Statistical inquiries into the efficacy of prayer. *Fortnightly Review, 12,* 125–135.

GERGEN, K. J. (1973). The codification of research ethics: Views of a Doubting Thomas. *American Psychologist, Oct,* 907–912.

GLASS, G. V., MCGAW, B., & SMITH, R. (1981). *Meta-analysis in social research.* Beverly Hills, CA: Sage Publications, Inc.

GORSUCH, R. L. (1966). The general factor in the test anxiety questionnaire. *Psychological Reports, 19,* 308.

GREENWALD, A. (1975). Consequences of prejudice against the null hypothesis. *Psychological Bulletin, 82,* 1–20.

HALL, R. V., & FOX, R. G. (1977). Changing criterion designs: An alternate applied behavior analysis procedure. In C. C. Etzel, G. M. LeBlanc, & D. M. Baer (Eds.), *New developments in behavior research.* Hillsdale, NJ: Erlbaum.

HEELAN, P. A. (1983). *Space-perception and the philosophy of science.* Berkeley, CA: University of California Press.

HEISENBERG, W. (1958). *Physics and philosophy.* New York: Harper & Row.

HOLD, B. (1977). Rank and behaviour: An ethological study of pre-school children. *Homo, 28,* 158–188.

HOLMES, D. S. (1976a). Debriefing after psychological experiments: I. Effectiveness of post deception dehoaxing. *American Psychologist, Dec,* 858–867.

HOLMES, D. S. (1976b). Debriefing after psychological experiments: II. Effectiveness of postexperimental desensitizing. *American Psychologist, Dec*, 868–875.

HOUTS, A. C., & LIEBERT, R. M. (1984). *Bedwetting: A Guide for Parents and Children.* Springfield, IL: Charles C Thomas.

HOUTS, A. C., & PETERSON, J. K. (1985). *Prevention of relapse in full-spectrum home training for primary enuresis: A components analysis.* Unpublished manuscript. Memphis State University, Memphis, TN.

HUNSICKER, J. O., & MELLGREN, R. L. (1977). Multiple deficits in the retention of an appetitively motivated behavior across a 24-hr period in rats. *Animal Learning and Behavior, 5,* 14–16.

HYDE, J. S. (1984). How large are gender differences in aggression? A developmental meta-analysis. *Developmental Psychology, 20,* 722–736.

JOHNSON, M. K., & LIEBERT, R. M. (1977). *Statistics: Tool of the behavioral sciences.* Englewood Cliffs, N.J.: Prentice-Hall.

KAIL, R. V., & WICKS-NELSON, R. (1993). *Developmental psychology.* Englewood Cliffs, NJ: Prentice Hall.

KRATOCHWILL, T. R. (1978). *Single subject research: Strategies for evaluating change.* New York: Academic Press.

KUHN, T. S. (1957). *The Copernican revolution.* Cambridge, Mass: Harvard University Press.

KUHN, T. S. (1970). *The structure of scientific revolutions.* Chicago: Univ. of Chicago Press.

LEAK, G. K. (1981). Student perception of coercion and value from participation in psychological research. *Teaching of Psychology, 8,* 147–149.

LENNEBERG, E. H. (1962). Understanding language without the ability to speak: A case report. *Journal of Abnormal and Social Psychology, 65,* 419–425.

LIEBERT, R. M. (1976). Sesame Street around the world: Evaluating the evaluators. *Journal of Communication, 26,* 165–171.

LIEBERT, R. M., & MORRIS, L. W. (1967). Cognitive and emotional components of test anxiety: A distinction and some initial data. *Psychological Reports, 20,* 975–978.

LIEBERT, R. M., & SPRAFKIN, J. (1988). *The early window.* New York: Simon & Schuster.

LOFTUS, E. F., & FRIES, J. F. (1979). Informed consent may be hazardous to your health. *Science, 204,* 6.

LOSCIUTO, L. A. (1972). A national inventory of television viewing behavior. In E. A. Rubinstein, G. A. Comstock, & J. P. Murray (Eds.), *Television and social behavior* (Vol. IV: *Television in day-to-day life: Patterns of use*). Washington, D.C.: United States Government Printing Office.

MANICAS, P. T., & SECORD, P. F. (1983). Implications for psychology of the new philosophy of science. *American Psychologist,* April, 399–413.

MEIER, P. (1978). The biggest public health experiment ever: The 1954 field study of the Salk poliomyelitis vaccine. In J. M. Tanur, et al. *Statistics: A guide to the unknown.* San Francisco: Holden-Day.

MILGRAM, S. (1963). Behavioral study of obedience. *Journal of Abnormal and Social Psychology, 67,* 371–378.

MILGRAM, S. (1977). Ethical issues in the study of obedience. In S. Milgram (Ed.) *The individual in a social world* (pp. 188–199). Reading, MA: Addison-Wesley.

MILLER, P. M., HERSEN, M., EISLER, R. M., & WATTS, J. G. (1974). Contingent reinforcement of lowered blood/alcohol levels in an outpatient chronic alcoholic. *Behavior Research and Therapy, 12,* 261–263.

MOOK, D. G. (1983). In defense of external invalidity. *American Psychologist,* April, 379–387.

MORRIS, L. W., & LIEBERT, R. M. (1969). Effects of anxiety on timed and untimed intelligence tests: Another look. *Journal of Consulting and Clinical Psychology, 33,* 240–244.

MORRIS, L. W., & LIEBERT, R. M. (1970). Relationship of cognitive and emotional components of text anxiety to physiological arousal and academic performance. *Journal of Consulting and Clinical Psychology, 35,* 332–337.

OLDROYD, D. (1986). *The arch of knowledge.* New York: Methuen.

O'LEARY, K. D., & BORKOVEC, T. D. (1978).

Conceptual, methodological, and ethical problems of placebo groups in psychotherapy research. *American Psychologist, 33*, 821–830.

ORNE, M. T. (1962). On the social psychology of the psychological experiment: With particular reference to demand characteristics and their implications. *American Psychologist, 17*, 776–783.

ORNE, M. T. (1969). Demand characteristics and the concept of quasi-controls. In R. Rosenthal & R. Rosnow (Eds.), *Artifact in behavioral research.* New York: Academic Press.

ORNE, M. T., & SCHEIBE, K. E. (1964). The contribution of nondeprivation factors in the production of sensory deprivation effects: The psychology of the panic-button. *Journal of Abnormal and Social Psychology, 68*, 3–12.

PAUL, G. L. (1966). *Insight vs. desensitization in psychotherapy.* Stanford: Stanford University Press.

POULOS, R. W., & DAVIDSON, E. S. (1971). Effects of a short modeling film on fearful children's attitudes toward the dental situation. Unpublished manuscript, State University of New York at Stony Brook.

POULOS, R. W., & Liebert, R. M. (1972). The influence of modeling, exhortative verbalization, and surveillance on children's sharing. *Developmental Psychology, 6*, 402–408.

REID, J. B. (1970). Reliability assessment of observation data: A possible methodological problem. *Child Development, 41*, 1143–1150.

RESNICK, J. H., & SCHWARTZ, T. (1973). Ethical standards as an independent variable in psychological research. *American Psychologist, February*, 134–139.

ROCK, I. (1983). *The logic of perception.* Cambridge: MIT Press.

ROMANCZYK, R., KENT, R. N., DIAMENT, C., & O'LEARY, K. D. (1973). Measuring the reliability of observational data: A reactive process. *Journal of Applied Behavior Analysis, 6*, 175–184.

ROSÉN, L. A., O'LEARY, S. G., JOYCE, S. A., CONWAY, G., & PFIFFNER, L. J. (1984). The importance of prudent negative consequences for maintaining the appropriate behavior of hyperactive students. *Journal of Abnormal Child Psychology, 12*, 581–604.

ROSENHAN, D., & SELIGMAN, M. E. P. (1984).

Abnormal psychology. New York: W. W. Norton & Co., Inc.

ROSENTHAL, D., & FRANK, J. D. (1956). Psychotherapy and the placebo effect. *Psychological Bulletin, 53*, 294–302.

ROSENTHAL, R. (1978). How often are our numbers wrong? *American Psychologist*, November, 1005–1008.

ROSENTHAL, R. (1979). The "file drawer problem" and tolerance for null results. *Psychological Bulletin, 86*, 638–641.

ROSENTHAL, R., & FODE, K. L. (1963). The effect of experimenter bias on the performance of the albino rat. *Behavioral Science, 8*, 183–189.

ROSENTHAL, R., & ROSNOW, R. L. (1969). The volunteer subject. In R. Rosenthal & R. Rosnow (Eds.), *Artifact in behavioral research.* New York: Academic Press.

ROSENTHAL, R., & ROSNOW, R. L. (1984). *Essentials of behavioral research.* New York: McGraw-Hill.

ROSENTHAL, R., & RUBIN, D. B. (1982). Comparing effect sizes of independent studies. *Psychological Bulletin, 92*, 500–504.

RUSHTON, J. P., BRAINERD, C. J., & PRESSLEY, M. (1983). Behavioral development and construct validity: The principle of aggregation. *Psychological Bulletin, 94*, 18–38.

SAVIN-WILLIAMS, R. C. (1979). Dominance hierarchies in groups of early adolescents. *Child Development, 50*, 923–935.

SAWYER, H. G. (1961). The meaning of numbers. Speech before the American Association of Advertising Agencies.

SCHACHTER, S. (1982, April). Recidivism and self-cure of smoking and obesity. *American Psychologist*, pp. 436–444.

SCHUMAN, H., & DUNCAN, O. D. (1974). Questions about attitude survey questions. In H. L. Costner (Ed.). *Sociological methodology, 1973–1974.* San Francisco: Jossey-Bass.

SELLTIZ, C., JAHODA, M., DEUTSCH, M., & COOK, S. W. (1959). *Research methods in social relations* (rev. ed.). New York: Holt, Rinehart & Winston.

SIDMAN, M. (1960). *Tactics of scientific research.* New York: Basic Books.

SIEBER, J. E., & STANLEY, B. (1988). Ethical and professional dimensions of socially sensitive research. *American Psychologist, 43*, 49–55.

SIEGMAN, A. W. (1956). The effect of manifest anxiety on a concept formation task, and on timed and untimed intelligence tests. *Journal of Consulting Psychology, 20,* 176–178.

SIZEMORE, C. C., & PITTILLO, E. S. (1977). *I'm Eve.* Garden City, N.Y.: Doubleday.

SMITH, M. L., GLASS, G. V., & MILLER, T. I. (1980). *The benefits of psychotherapy.* Baltimore: Johns Hopkins University Press.

SMITH, S. S., & RICHARDSON, D. (1983). Amelioration of deception and harm in psychological research: The important role of debriefing. *Journal of Personality and Social Psychology, 44,* 1075–1082.

SPIEGLER, M. D., MORRIS, L. W., & LIEBERT, R. M. (1968). Cognitive and emotional components of test anxiety: Temporal factors. *Psychological Reports, 22,* 451–456.

STEVENS, S. S. (1968). Measurement, statistics and the schemapiric view. *Science, 161,* 849–856.

SULZER-AZAROFF, B., & CONSUELO DE SANTAMARIA, M. (1980). Industrial safety hazards reduction through performance feedback. *Journal of Applied Behavior Analysis, 13,* 287–295.

TATE, B. G., & BAROFF, G. S. (1966). Aversive control of self-injurious behavior in a psychotic boy. *Behavior Research and Therapy, 4,* 281–287.

THIGPEN, C. H., & CLECKLEY, H. (1954). *The three faces of Eve.* Kingsport, TN: Kingsport Press.

WEBB, E. J., CAMPBELL, D. T., SCHWARTZ, R. D., & SECHREST, L. (1966). *Unobtrusive measures: Nonreactive research in the social sciences.* Chicago: Rand McNally.

WEIZMANN, F. (1971, February 12). Correlational statistics and the nature-nurture problem. *Science,* p. 589.

WELKOWITZ, J., EWEN, R. B., & COHEN, J. (1971). *Introductory statistics for the behavioral sciences.* New York: Academic Press.

WILLIAMS, B. (1972). Rene Descartes. In *The encyclopedia of philosophy, Vols I & II, A-E,* pp. 344–354. New York: Macmillan.

INDEX